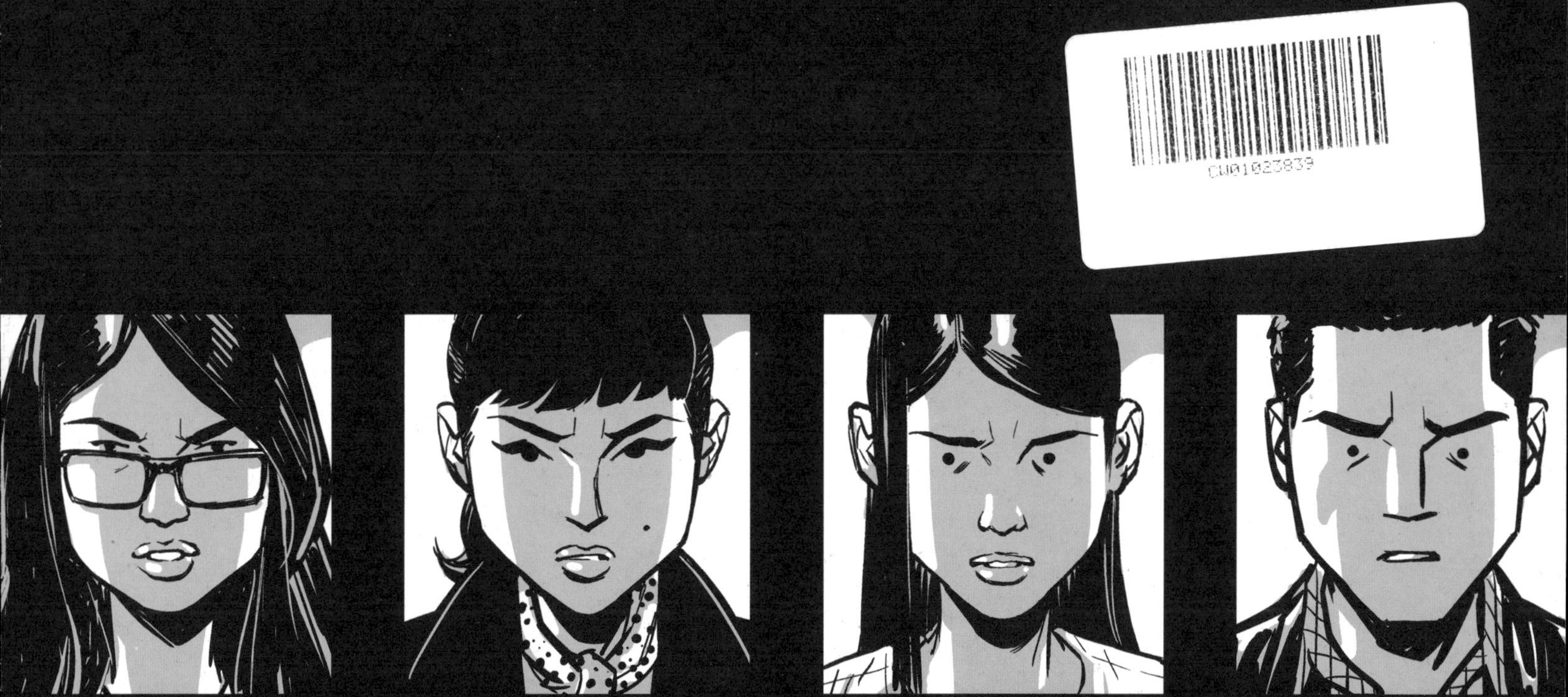

Sin Titulo

CAMERON STEWART

DARK HORSE BOOKS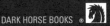

President & Publisher **MIKE RICHARDSON**

Editor **SIERRA HAHN**

Associate Editor **JIM GIBBONS**

Assistant Editor **AARON WALKER**

Digital Production **ALLYSON HALLER**

Design **AMY ARENDTS**

Special thanks to Karl Kerschl, Brenden Fletcher, Michael Cho, Claudia Dávila, Andy Belanger, Scott Hepburn, Ramón Pérez, Brian McLachlan, Audrey Bonnemaison, David Aja, Esther Whang, Sierra Hahn, Scott Allie, Mario Freitas, Michele Foschini, and Amanda Marie Wolf. Thanks also to everyone who read *Sin Titulo* as it was serialized online, helped spread the word, and gave their support and donations. This book would not exist without you.

Neil Hankerson *Executive Vice President* • Tom Weddle *Chief Financial Officer* • Randy Stradley *Vice President of Publishing* • Michael Martens *Vice President of Book Trade Sales* • Anita Nelson *Vice President of Business Affairs* • Scott Allie *Editor in Chief* • Matt Parkinson *Vice President of Marketing* • David Scroggy *Vice President of Product Development* • Dale LaFountain *Vice President of Information Technology* • Darlene Vogel *Senior Director of Print, Design, and Production* • Ken Lizzi *General Counsel* • Davey Estrada *Editorial Director* • Chris Warner *Senior Books Editor* • Diana Schutz *Executive Editor* • Cary Grazzini *Director of Print and Development* • Lia Ribacchi *Art Director* • Cara Niece *Director of Scheduling* • Tim Wiesch *Director of International Licensing* • Mark Bernardi *Director of Digital Publishing*

Published by Dark Horse Books
A division of Dark Horse Comics, Inc.
10956 SE Main Street
Milwaukie, OR 97222

DarkHorse.com
Cameron-Stewart.Tumblr.com
SinTituloComic.com

International Licensing: (503) 905-2377
Comic Shop Locator Service: (888) 266-4226

First edition: September 2013
ISBN 978-1-61655-248-0

10 9 8 7 6 5 4 3 2 1
Printed in China

This volume collects *Sin Titulo*, previously published online at SinTitulo.com.

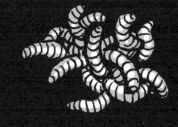

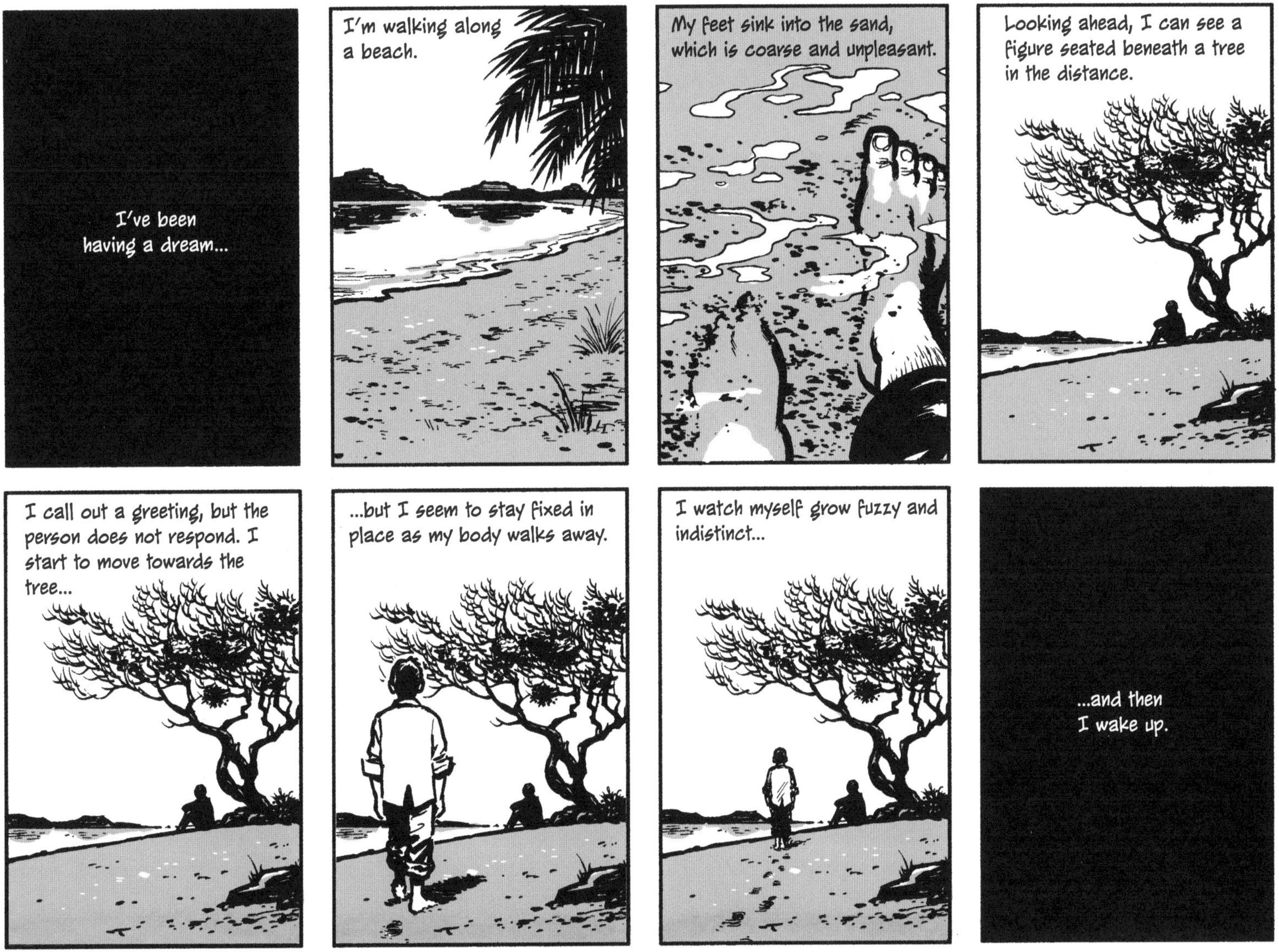
I've been having a dream...
I'm walking along a beach.
My feet sink into the sand, which is coarse and unpleasant.
Looking ahead, I can see a figure seated beneath a tree in the distance.
I call out a greeting, but the person does not respond. I start to move towards the tree...
...but I seem to stay fixed in place as my body walks away.
I watch myself grow fuzzy and indistinct...
...and then I wake up.

SIN TITULO

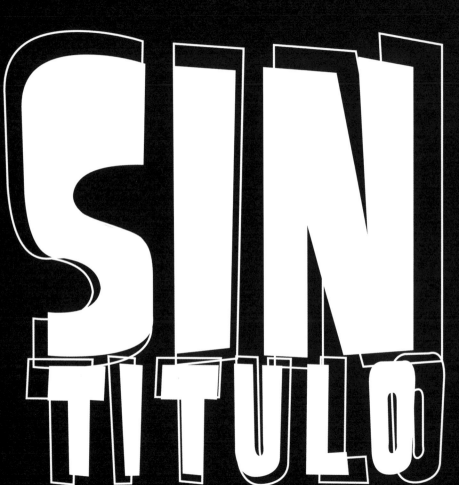

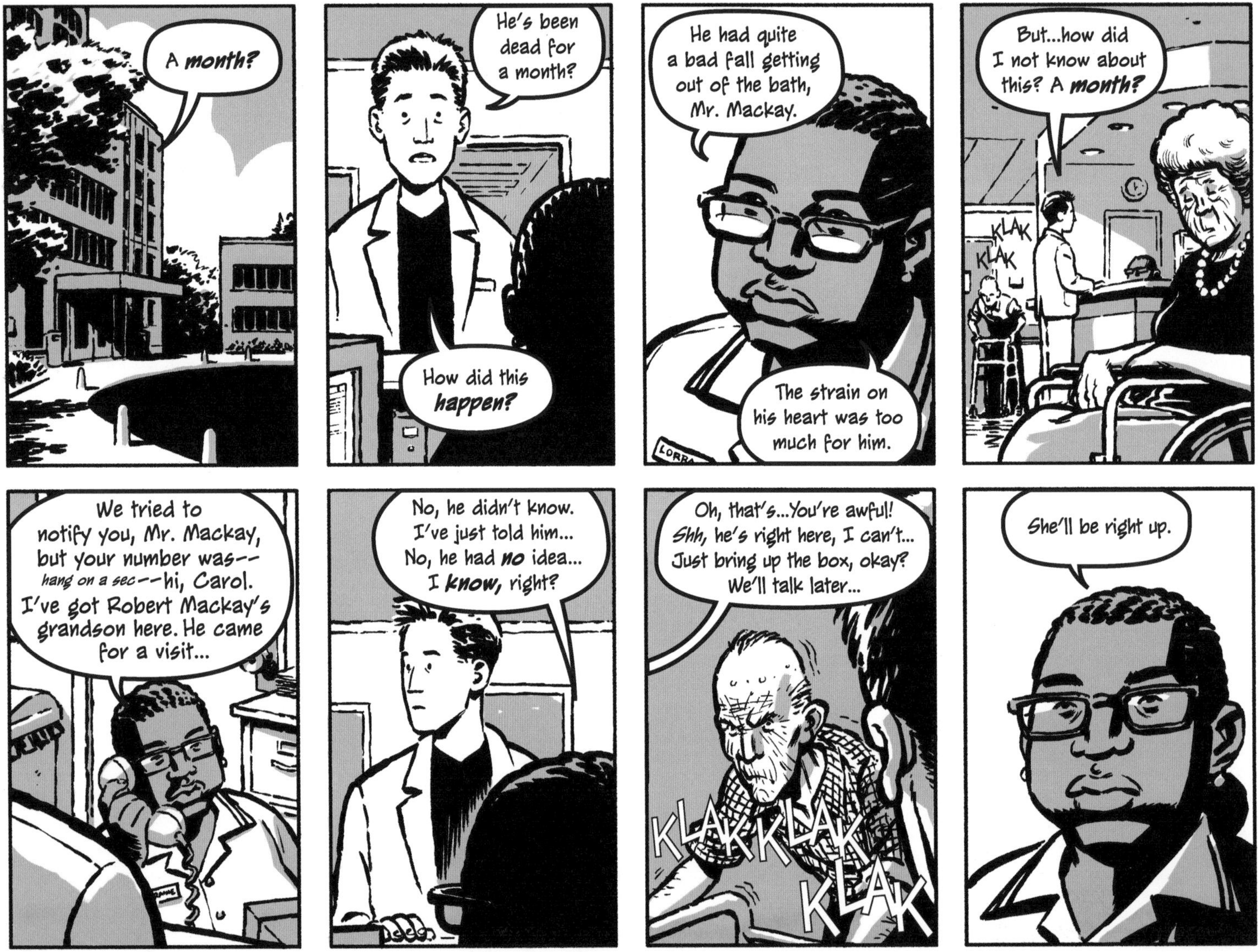
A *month?*
He's been dead for a month?
How did this *happen?*
He had quite a bad fall getting out of the bath, Mr. Mackay.
The strain on his heart was too much for him.
But...how did I not know about this? A *month?*
KLAK
KLAK
We tried to notify you, Mr. Mackay, but your number was-- *hang on a sec*--hi, Carol. I've got Robert Mackay's grandson here. He came for a visit...
No, he didn't know. I've just told him... No, he had *no* idea... I *know,* right?
Oh, that's...You're awful! *Shh,* he's right here, I can't... Just bring up the box, okay? We'll talk later...
KLAK KLAK KLAK
KLAK
She'll be right up.

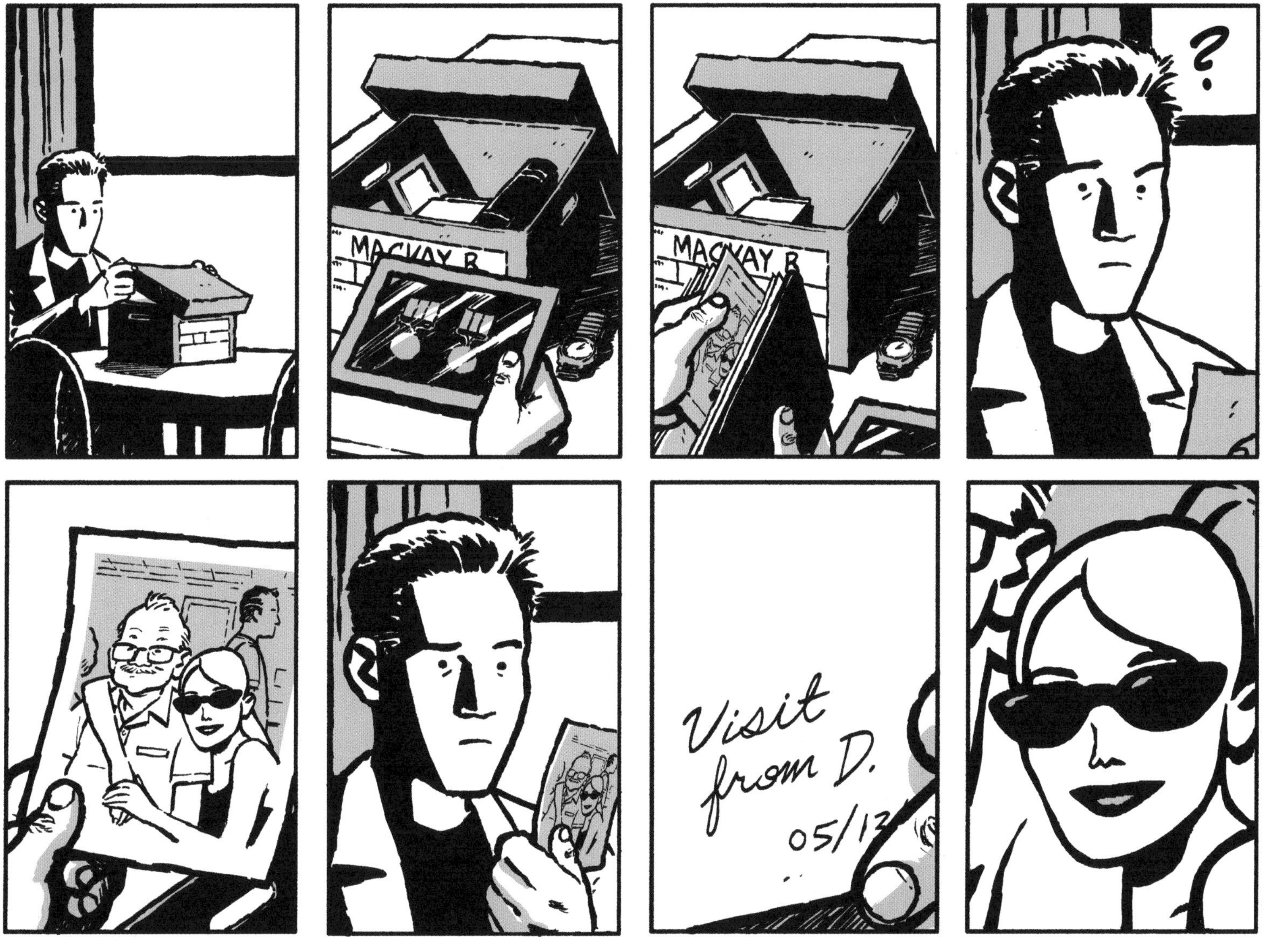
MACKAY B
MACKAY B
?
Visit from D.
05/13

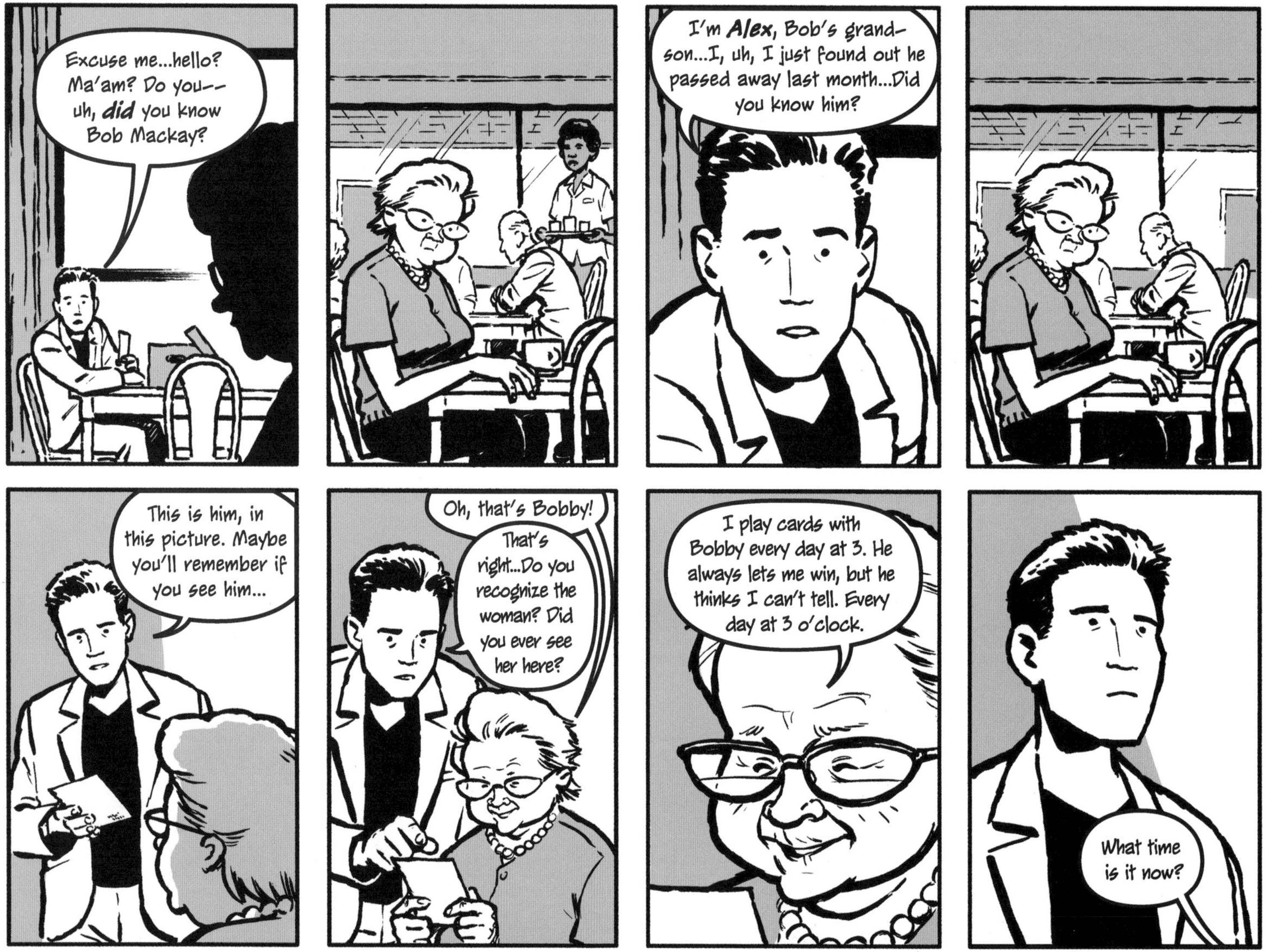
Excuse me...hello? Ma'am? Do you-- uh, did you know Bob Mackay?
I'm Alex, Bob's grand-son...I, uh, I just found out he passed away last month...Did you know him?
This is him, in this picture. Maybe you'll remember if you see him...
Oh, that's Bobby!
That's right...Do you recognize the woman? Did you ever see her here?
I play cards with Bobby every day at 3. He always lets me win, but he thinks I can't tell. Every day at 3 o'clock.
What time is it now?

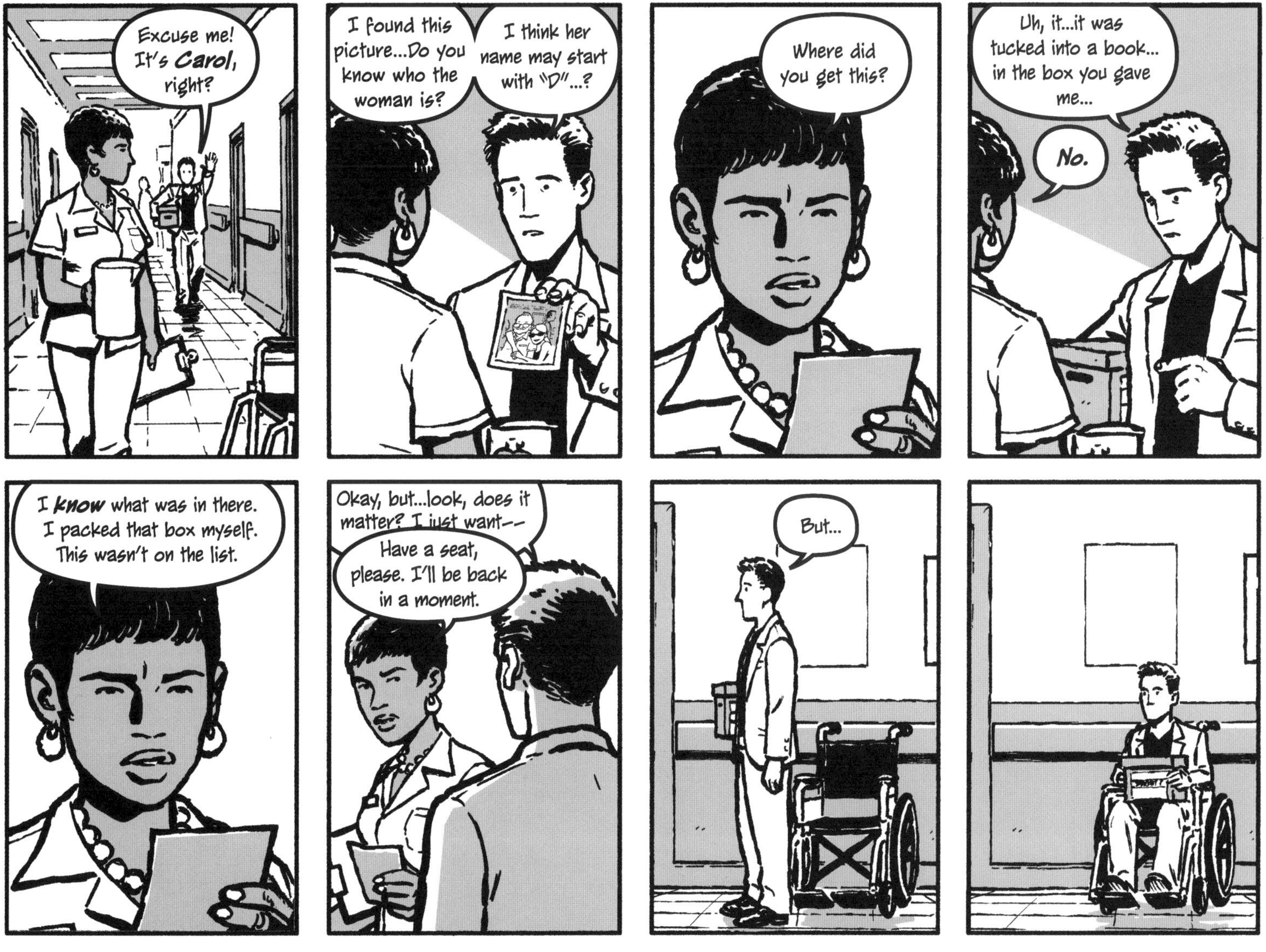

Excuse me! It's **Carol**, right?
I found this picture...Do you know who the woman is?
I think her name may start with "D"...?
Where did you get this?
Uh, it...it was tucked into a book... in the box you gave me...
No.
I **know** what was in there. I packed that box myself. This wasn't on the list.
Okay, but...look, does it matter? I just want--
Have a seat, please. I'll be back in a moment.
But...

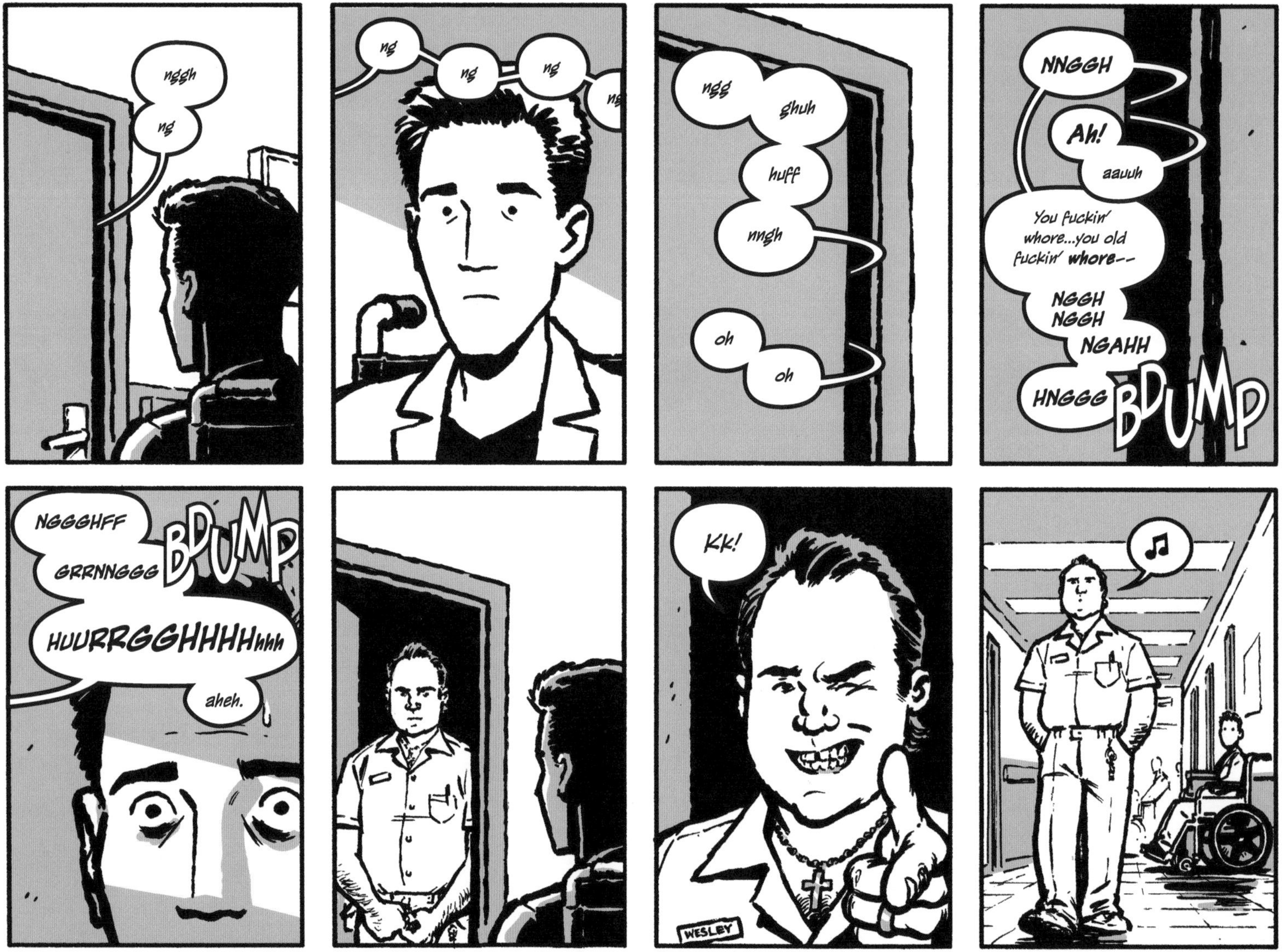

nggh
ng
ng
ng
ng
ngg
ghuh
huff
nngh
oh
oh
NNGGH
Ah!
aauuh
You fuckin' whore...you old fuckin' whore--
NGGH NGGH
NGAHH
HNGGG
BDUMP
NGGGHFF
GRRNNGGG
BDUMP
HUURRGGHHHHhhh
aheh.
Kk!
WESLEY

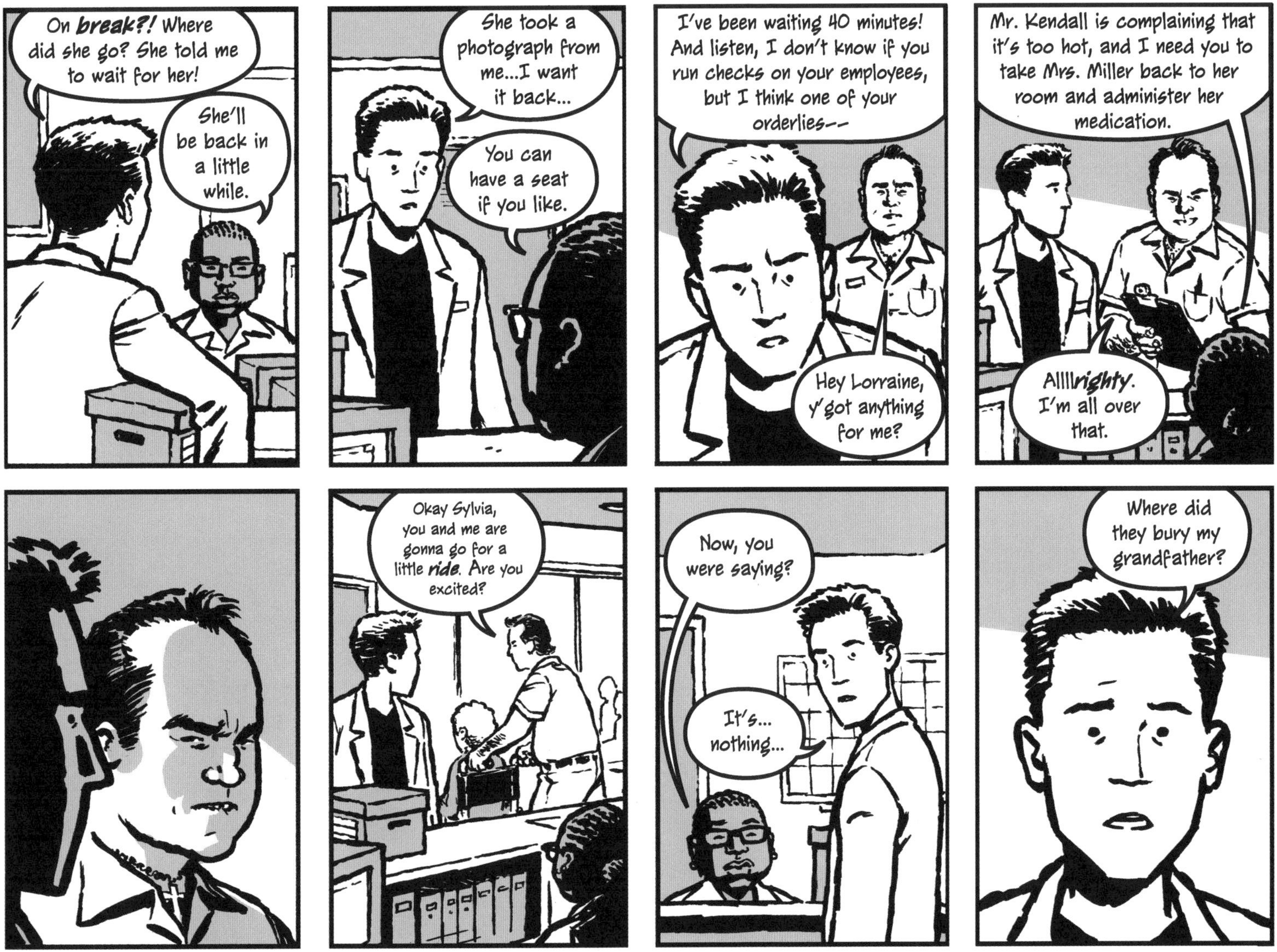
On **break?!** Where did she go? She told me to wait for her!
She'll be back in a little while.
She took a photograph from me...I want it back...
You can have a seat if you like.
I've been waiting 40 minutes! And listen, I don't know if you run checks on your employees, but I think one of your orderlies--
Hey Lorraine, y'got anything for me?
Mr. Kendall is complaining that it's too hot, and I need you to take Mrs. Miller back to her room and administer her medication.
Allll*righty*. I'm all over that.
Okay Sylvia, you and me are gonna go for a little *ride*. Are you excited?
Now, you were saying?
It's... nothing...
Where did they bury my grandfather?

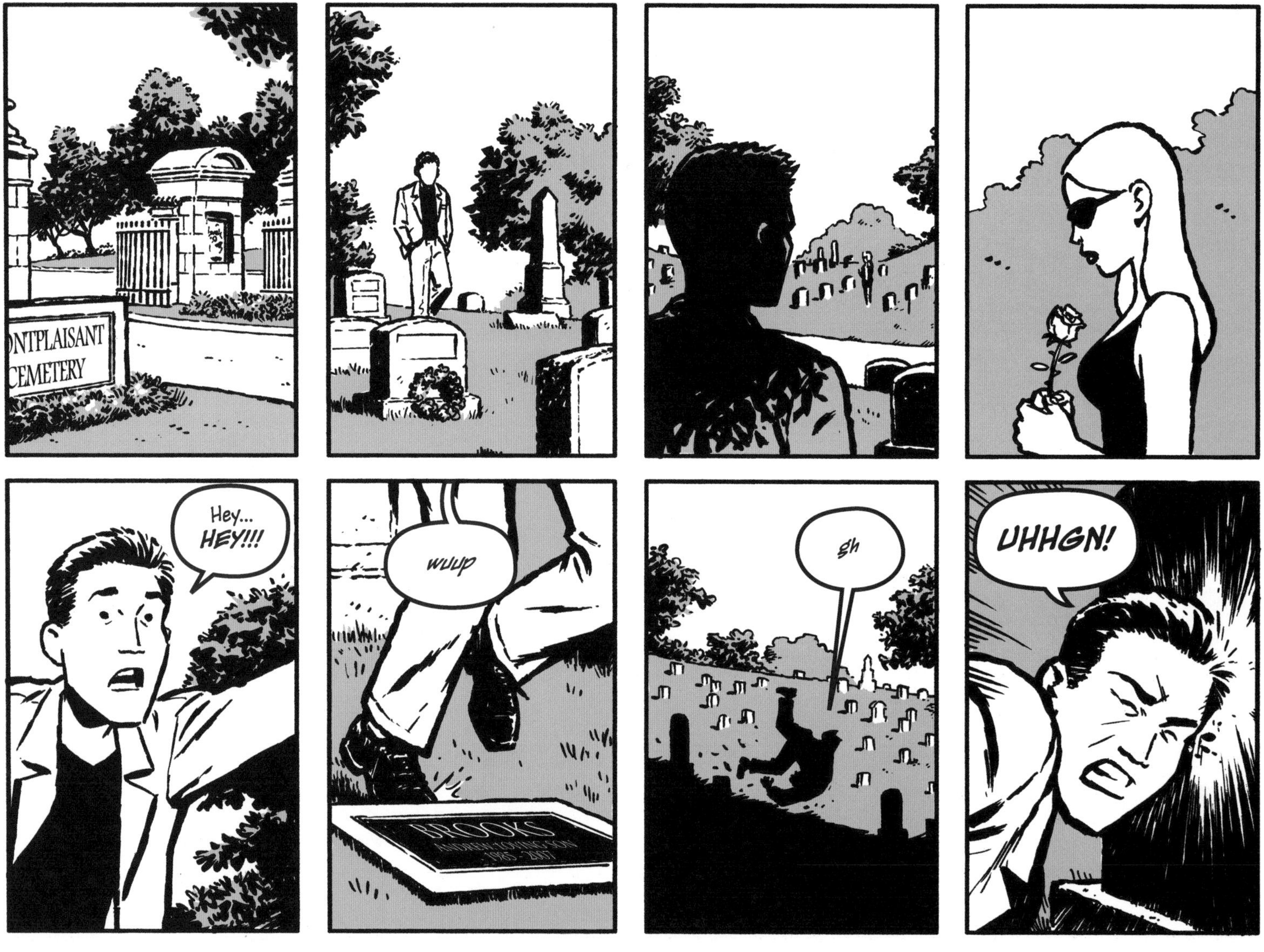
ONTPLAISANT
CEMETERY
Hey... HEY!!!
wuup
BROOKS
ANDREW LOVING SON
1985 - 2007
gh
UHHGN!

16

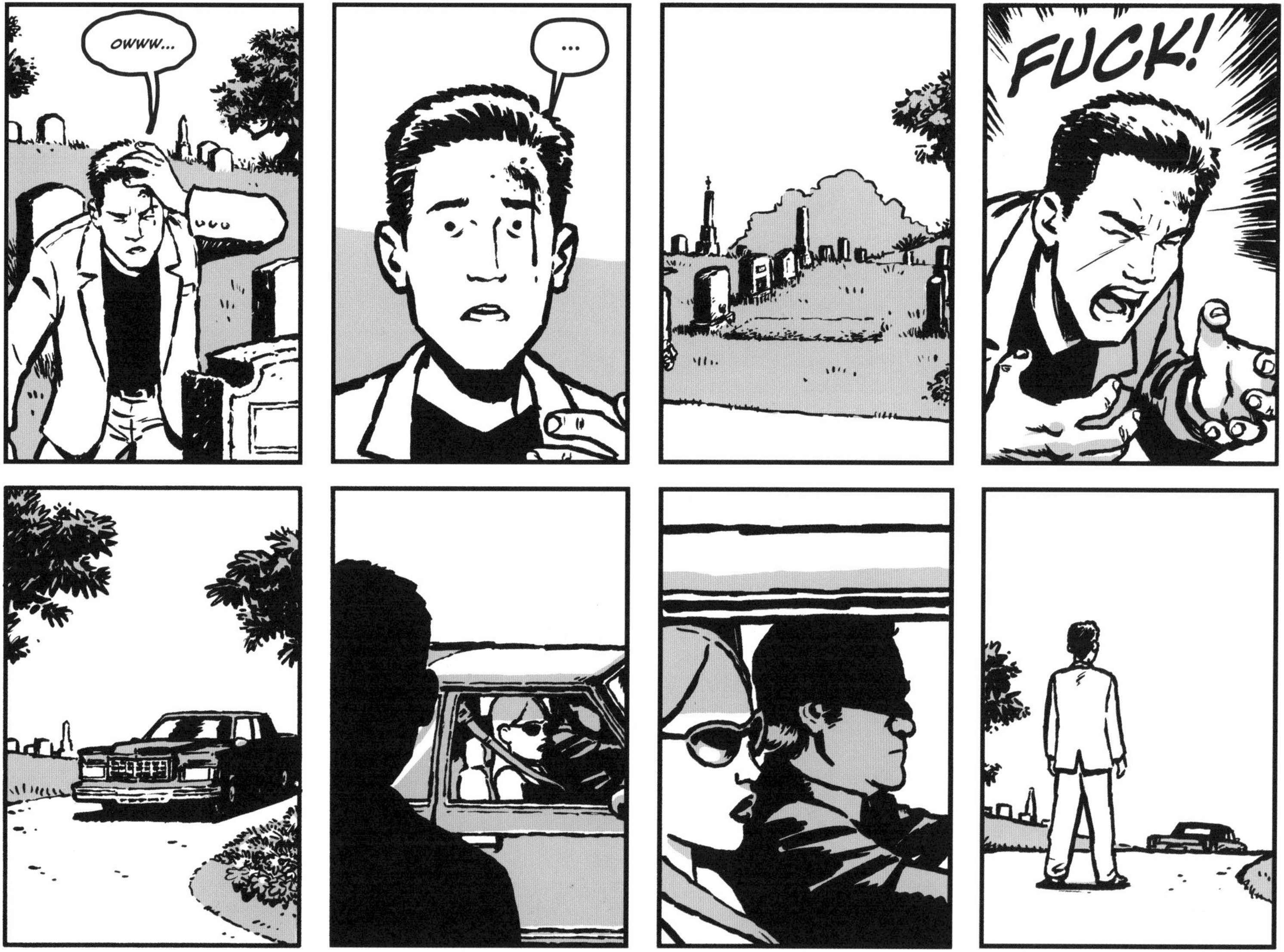
OWWW...
...
FUCK!

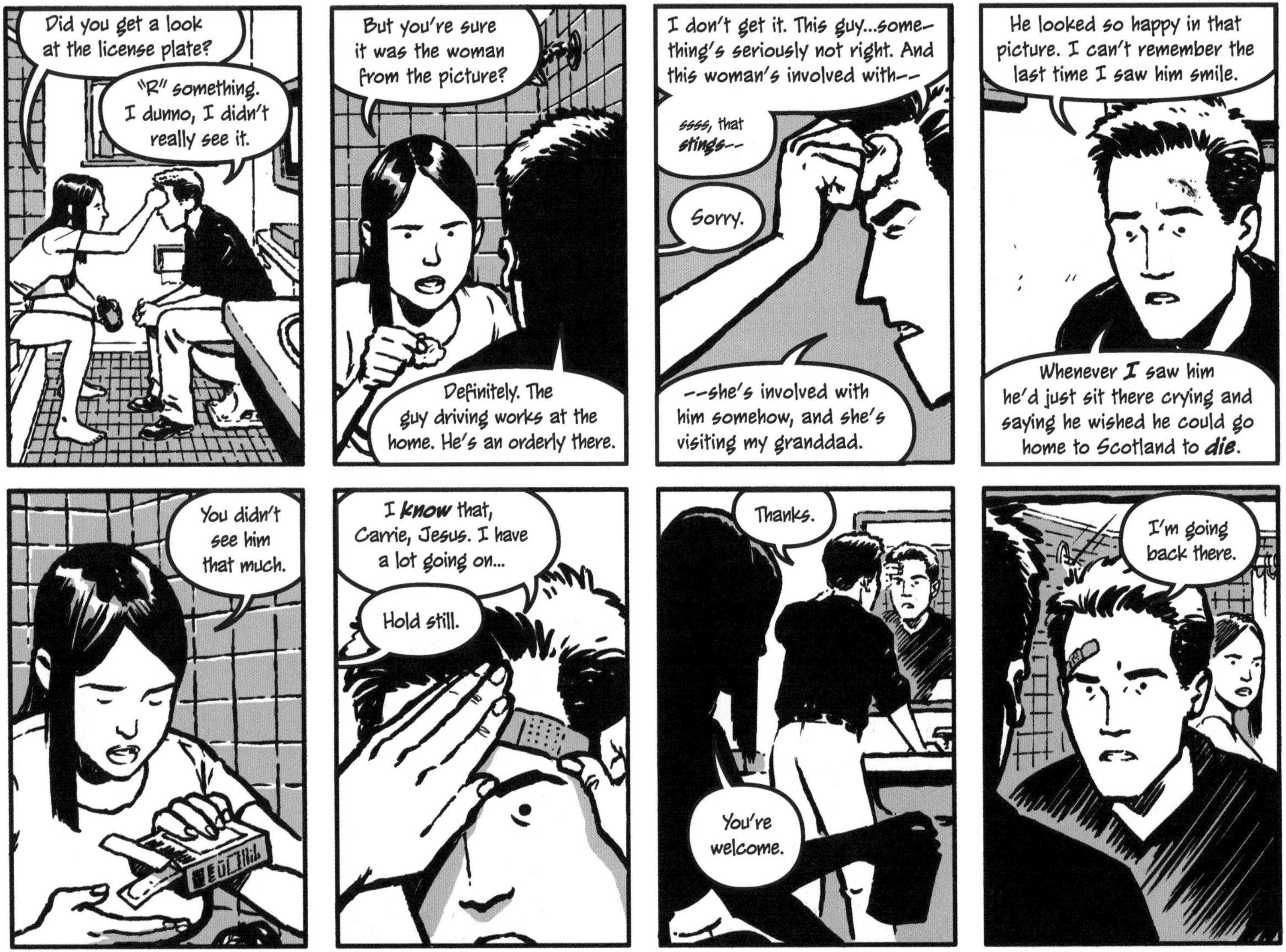
Did you get a look at the license plate?
"R" something. I dunno, I didn't really see it.
But you're sure it was the woman from the picture?
Definitely. The guy driving works at the home. He's an orderly there.
I don't get it. This guy...something's seriously not right. And this woman's involved with--
ssss, that stings--
Sorry.
--she's involved with him somehow, and she's visiting my granddad.
He looked so happy in that picture. I can't remember the last time I saw him smile.
Whenever I saw him he'd just sit there crying and saying he wished he could go home to Scotland to die.
You didn't see him that much.
I know that, Carrie, Jesus. I have a lot going on...
Hold still.
Thanks.
You're welcome.
I'm going back there.

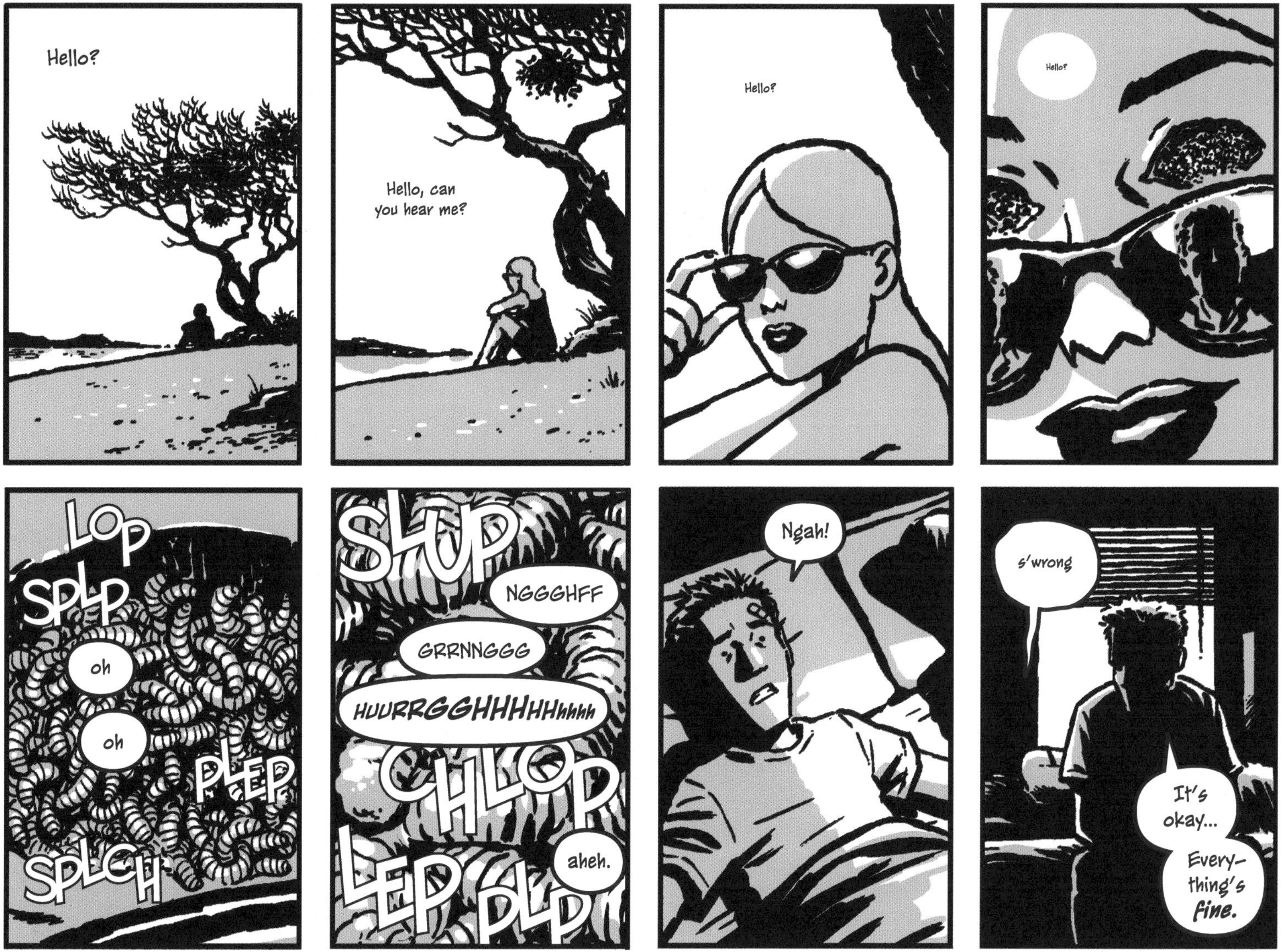
Hello?
Hello, can you hear me?
Hello?
Hello?
LOP
SPLP
oh
oh
PLEP
SPLCH
SLUP
NGGGHFF
GRRNNGGG
HUURRGGHHHHhhhh
CHLLOP
LEP
PLP
aheh.
Ngah!
s'wrong
It's okay...
Every-thing's *fine.*

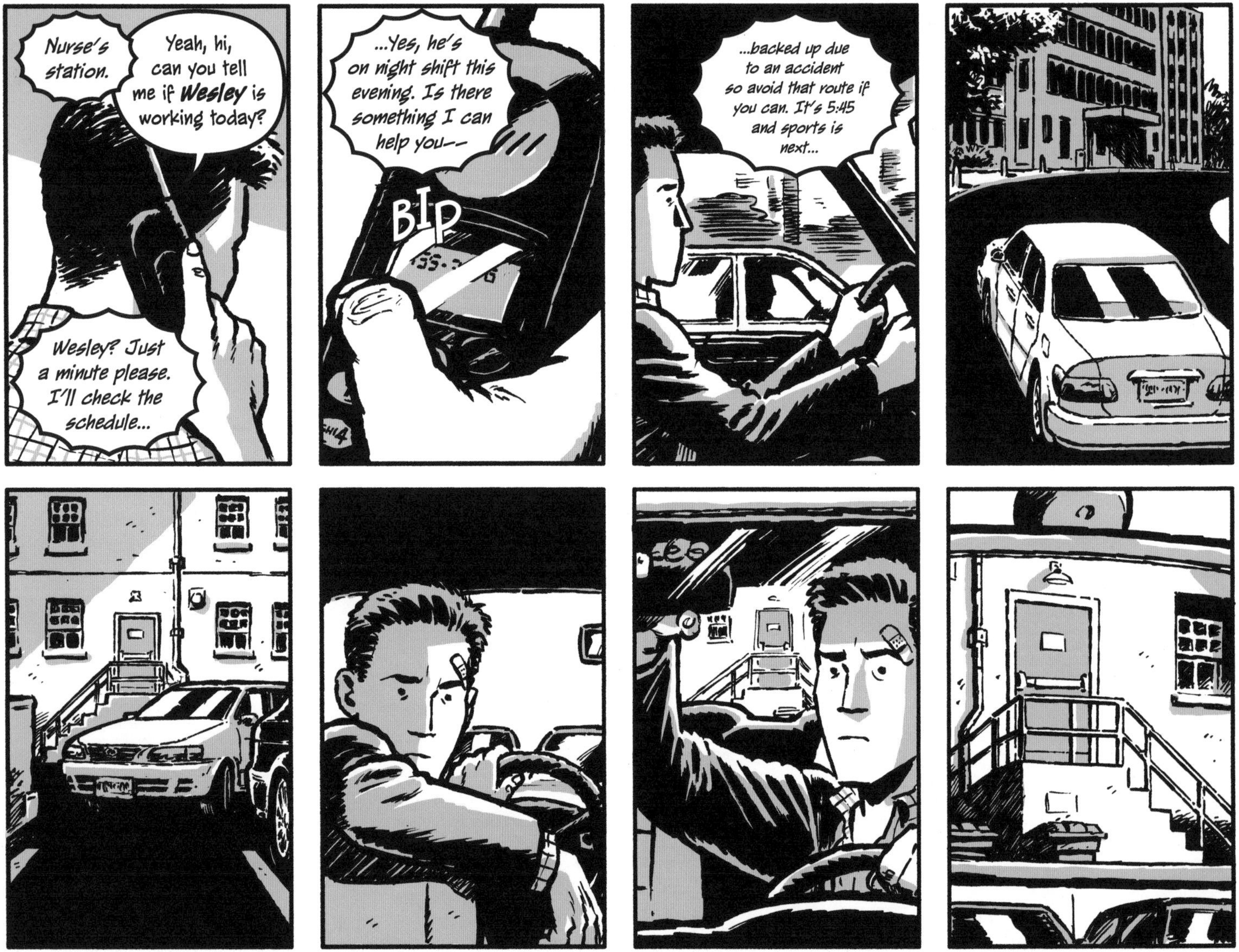
Nurse's station.
Yeah, hi, can you tell me if Wesley is working today?
Wesley? Just a minute please. I'll check the schedule...
...Yes, he's on night shift this evening. Is there something I can help you--
BIP
...backed up due to an accident so avoid that route if you can. It's 5:45 and sports is next...

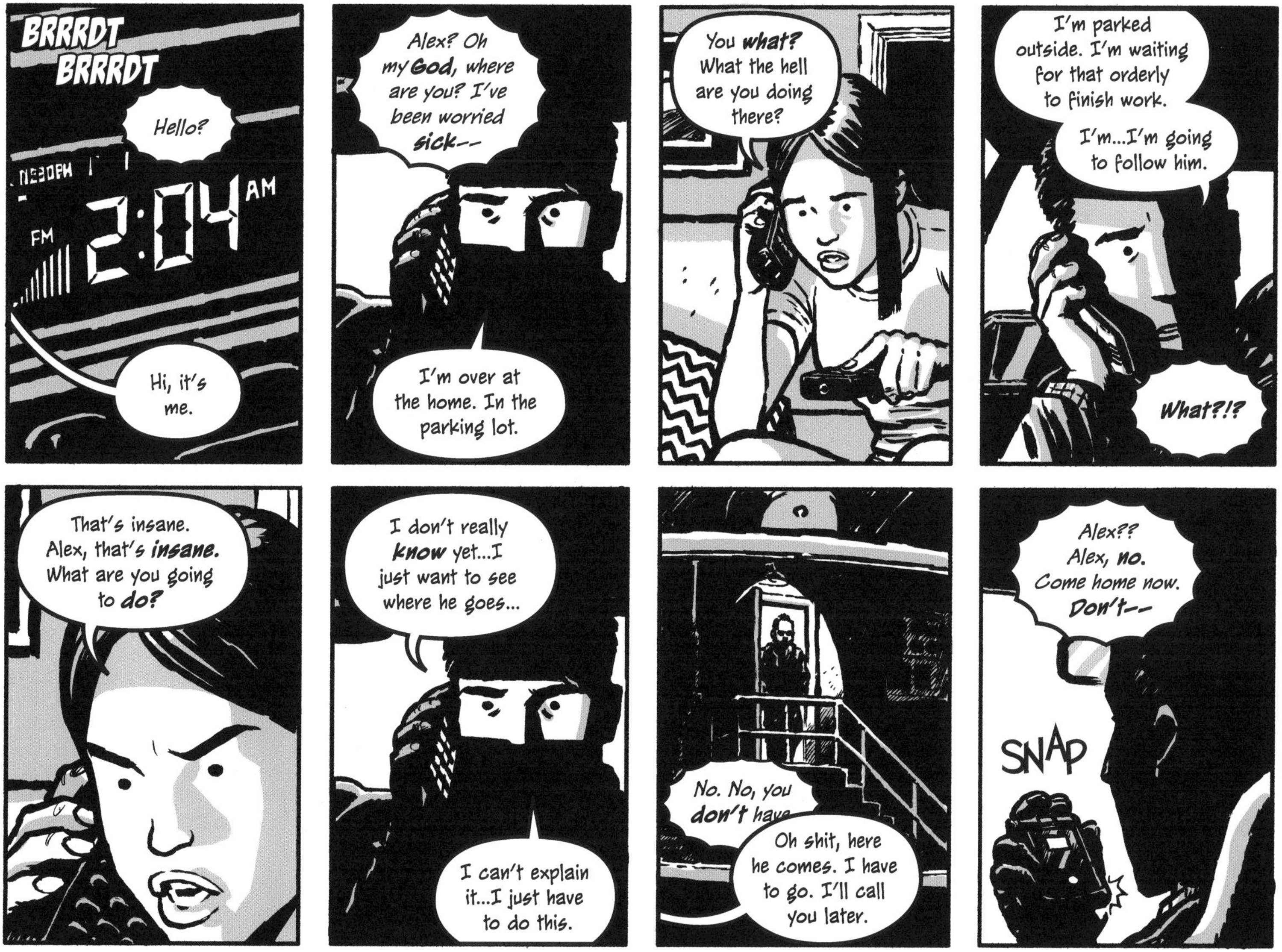
BRRRDT
BRRRDT
Hello?
2:04 AM
Hi, it's me.
Alex? Oh my God, where are you? I've been worried sick--
I'm over at the home. In the parking lot.
You what? What the hell are you doing there?
I'm parked outside. I'm waiting for that orderly to finish work.
I'm...I'm going to follow him.
What?!?
That's insane. Alex, that's insane. What are you going to do?
I don't really know yet...I just want to see where he goes...
I can't explain it...I just have to do this.
No. No, you don't have
Oh shit, here he comes. I have to go. I'll call you later.
Alex?? Alex, no. Come home now. Don't--
SNAP

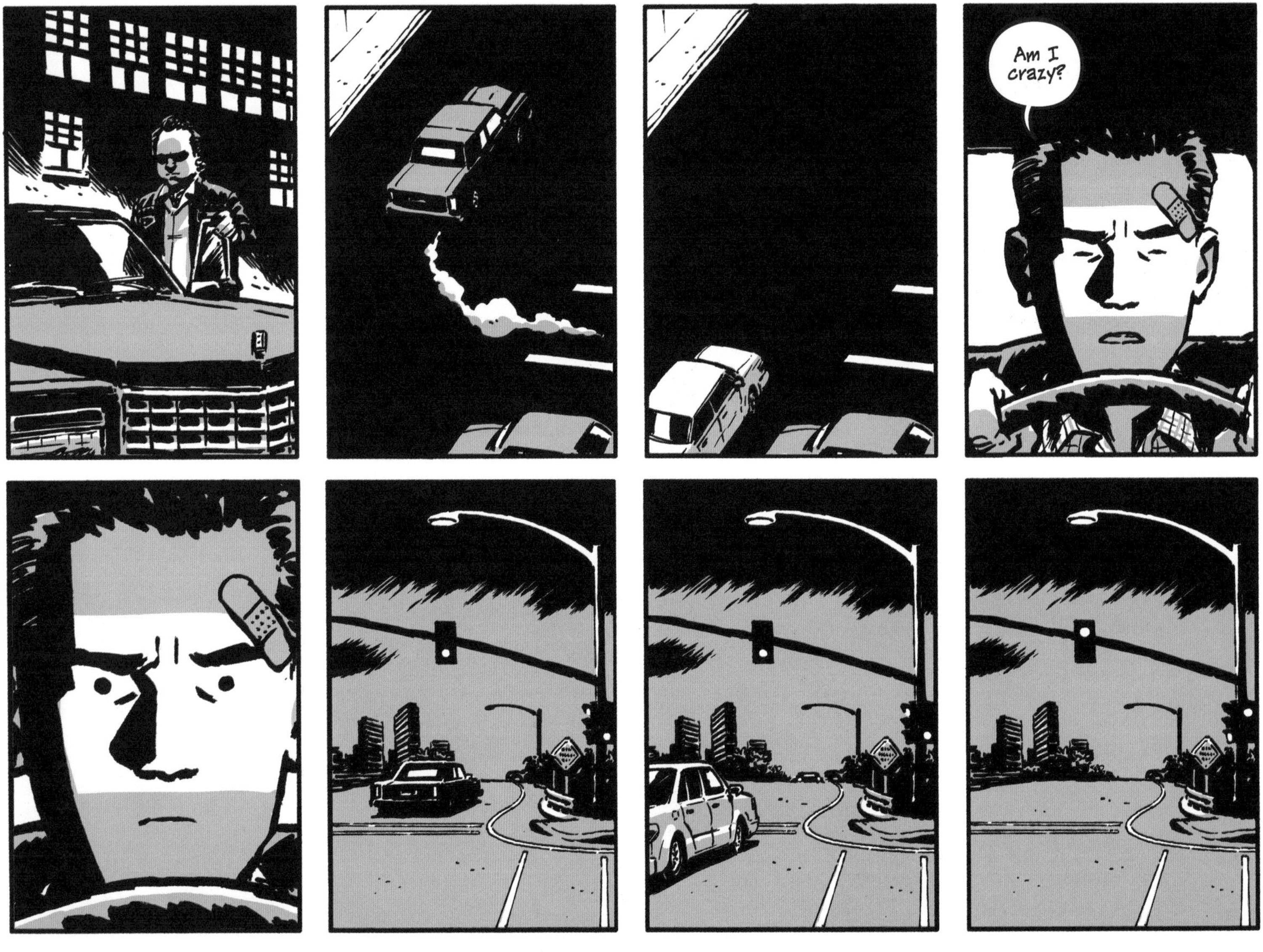
Am I crazy?

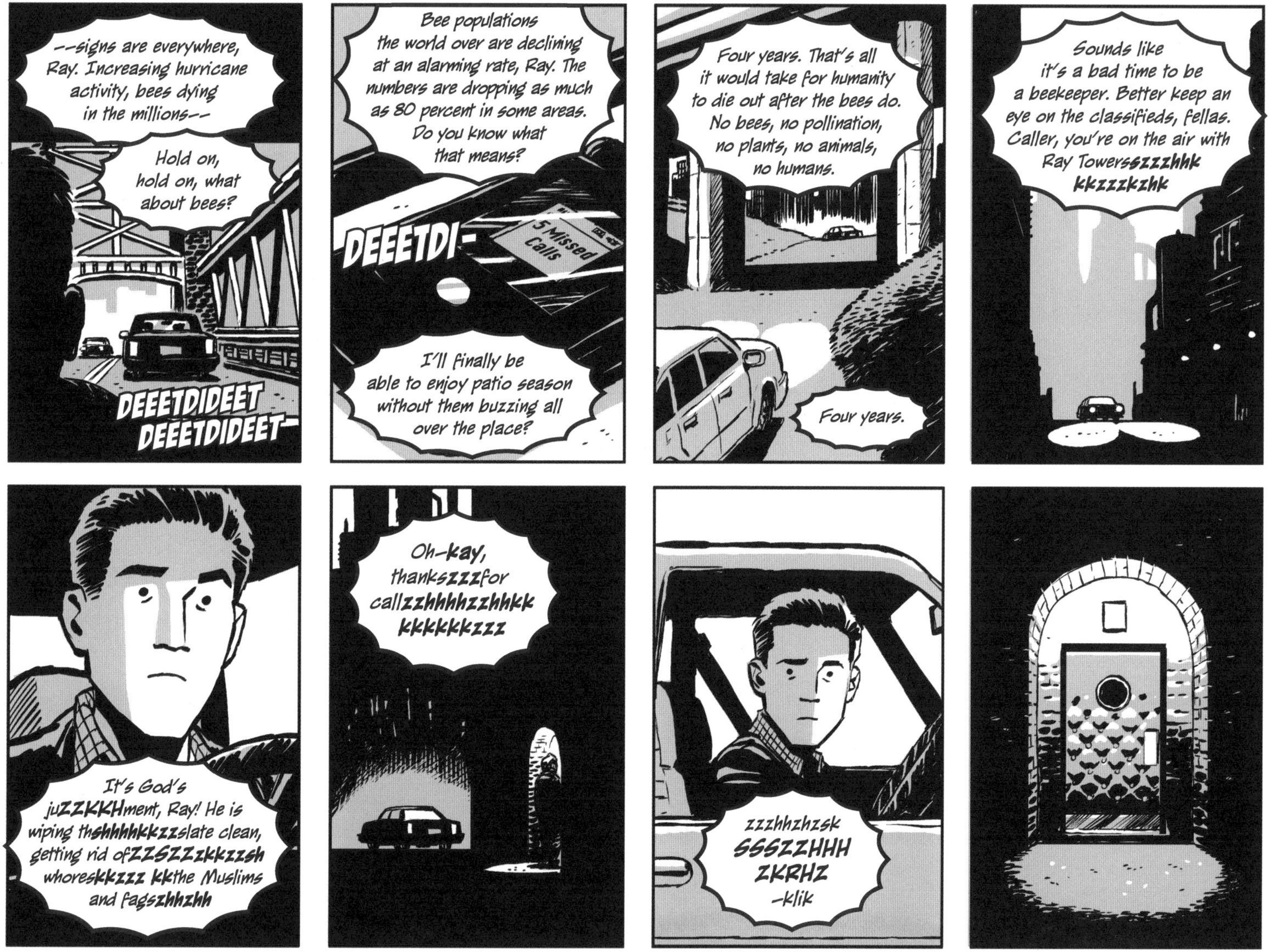
--signs are everywhere, Ray. Increasing hurricane activity, bees dying in the millions--
Hold on, hold on, what about bees?
DEEETDIDEET
DEEETDIDEET-
Bee populations the world over are declining at an alarming rate, Ray. The numbers are dropping as much as 80 percent in some areas. Do you know what that means?
DEEETDI-
5 Missed Calls
I'll finally be able to enjoy patio season without them buzzing all over the place?
Four years. That's all it would take for humanity to die out after the bees do. No bees, no pollination, no plants, no animals, no humans.
Four years.
Sounds like it's a bad time to be a beekeeper. Better keep an eye on the classifieds, fellas. Caller, you're on the air with Ray Towerszzzhhk kkzzzkzhk
It's God's juZZKKHment, Ray! He is wiping thshhhhkkzzslate clean, getting rid ofZZSZZzkkzzsh whoreskkzzz kkthe Muslims and fagszhhzhh
Oh-kay, thankszzzfor callzzhhhhzzhhkk kkkkkkzzz
zzzhhzhzsk SSSZZHHH ZKRHZ -klik

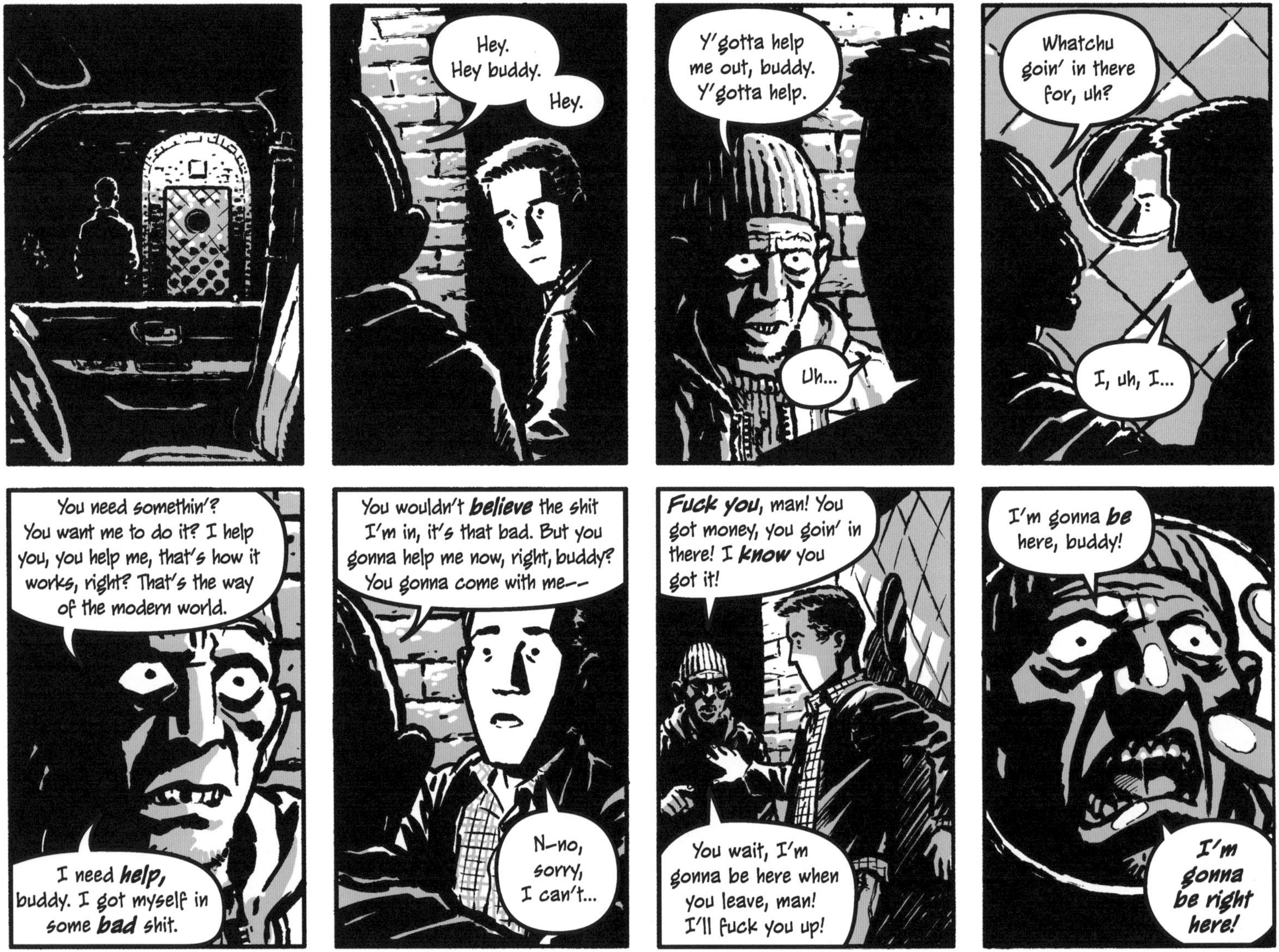

Hey.
Hey buddy.
Hey.
Y'gotta help me out, buddy. Y'gotta help.
Uh...
Whatchu goin' in there for, uh?
I, uh, I...
You need somethin'? You want me to do it? I help you, you help me, that's how it works, right? That's the way of the modern world.
I need **help,** buddy. I got myself in some **bad** shit.
You wouldn't **believe** the shit I'm in, it's that bad. But you gonna help me now, right, buddy? You gonna come with me--
N-no, sorry, I can't...
Fuck you, man! You got money, you goin' in there! I **know** you got it!
You wait, I'm gonna be here when you leave, man! I'll fuck you up!
I'm gonna **be** here, buddy!
I'm gonna be right here!

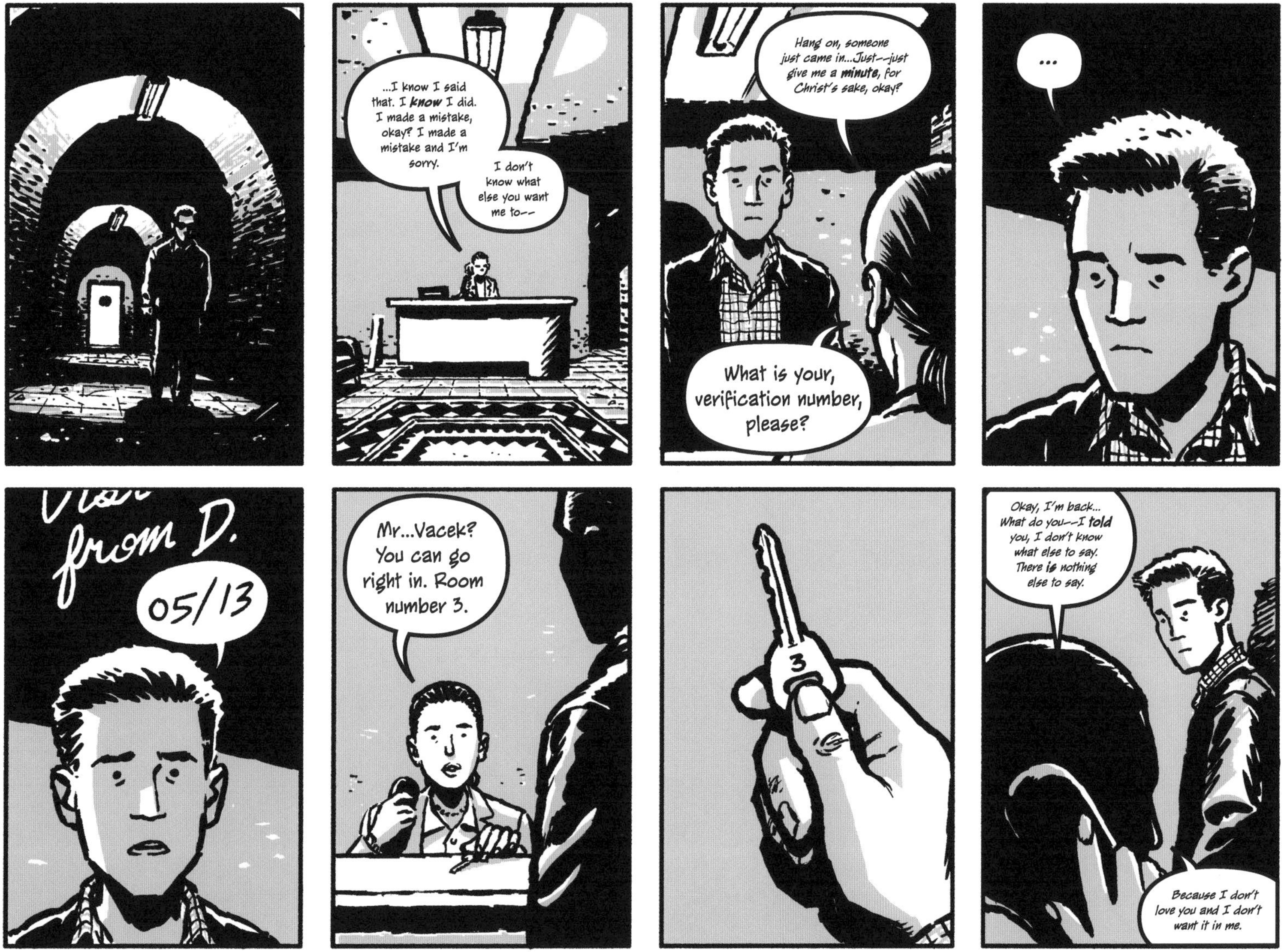
...I know I said that. I *know* I did. I made a mistake, okay? I made a mistake and I'm sorry.
I don't know what else you want me to--
Hang on, someone just came in...Just--just give me a **minute**, for Christ's sake, okay?
What is your, verification number, please?
...
from D.
05/13
Mr...Vacek? You can go right in. Room number 3.
3
Okay, I'm back... What do you--I **told** you, I don't know what else to say. There **is** nothing else to say.
Because I don't love you and I don't want it in me.

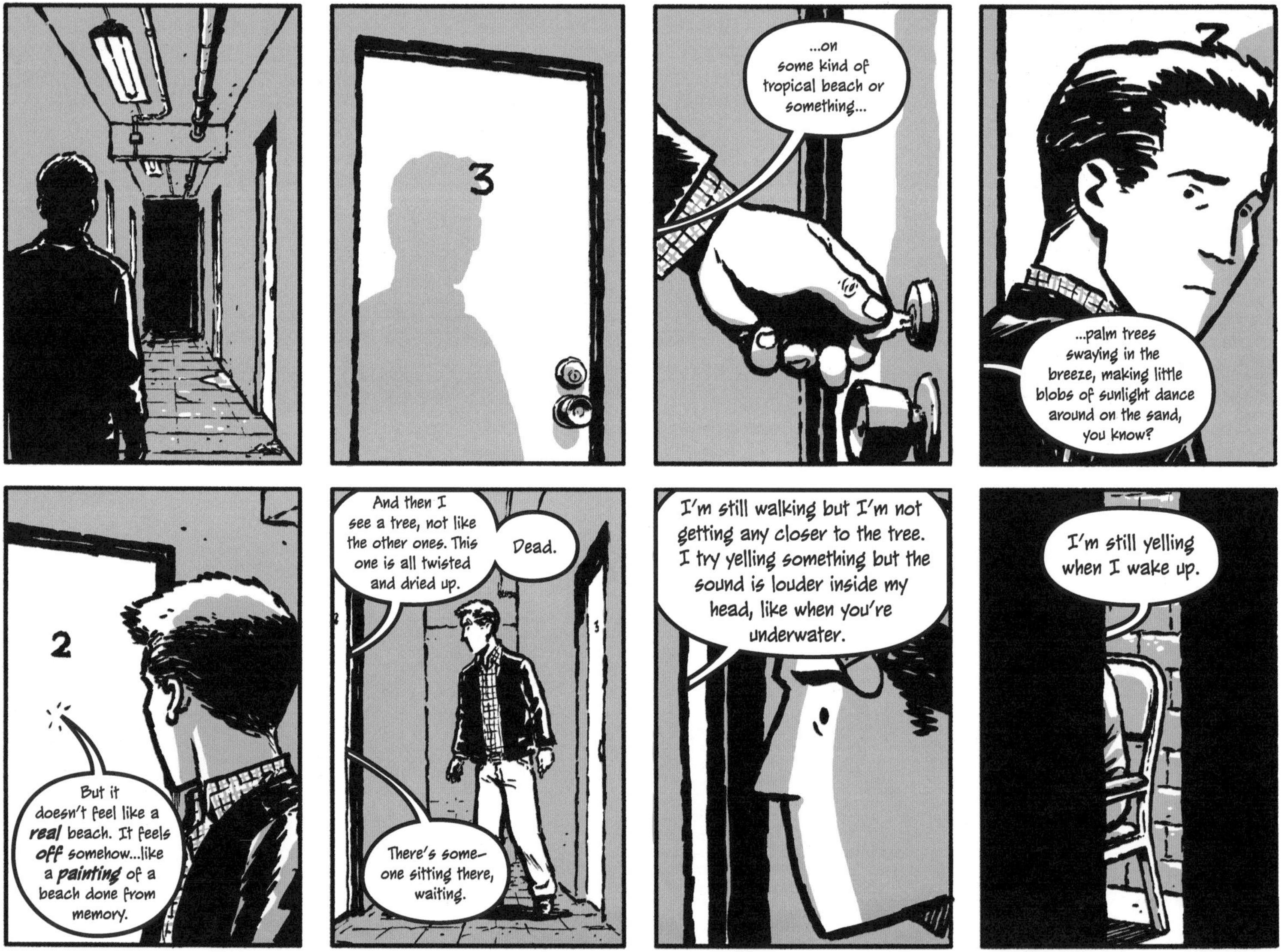
3
...on some kind of tropical beach or something...
...palm trees swaying in the breeze, making little blobs of sunlight dance around on the sand, you know?
2
But it doesn't feel like a *real* beach. It feels *off* somehow...like a *painting* of a beach done from memory.
And then I see a tree, not like the other ones. This one is all twisted and dried up.
Dead.
There's some-one sitting there, waiting.
I'm still walking but I'm not getting any closer to the tree. I try yelling something but the sound is louder inside my head, like when you're underwater.
I'm still yelling when I wake up.

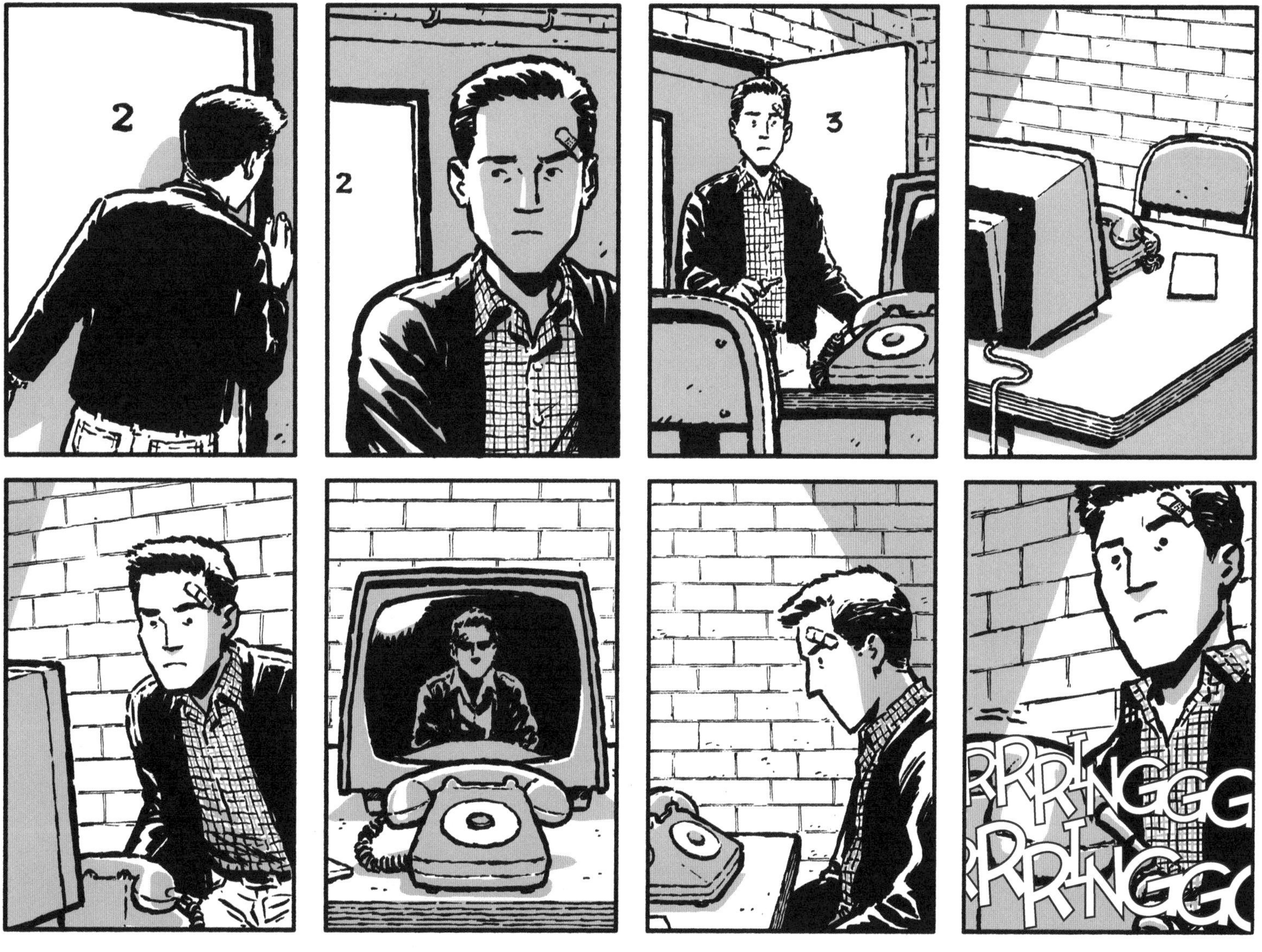
2
2
3
RRRINGGG
RRRINGG

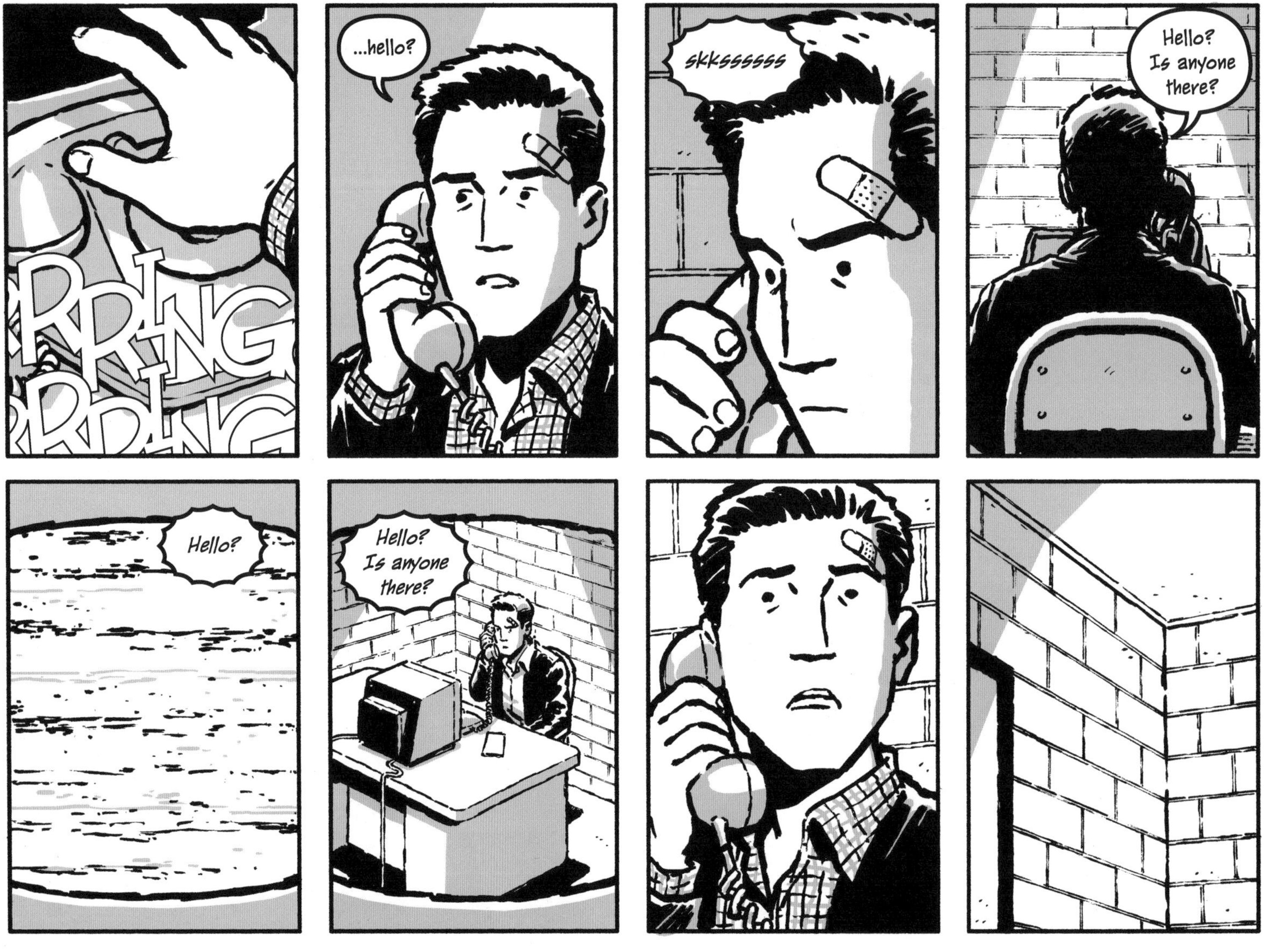
RRING
...hello?
skksssssss
Hello? Is anyone there?
Hello?
Hello? Is anyone there?

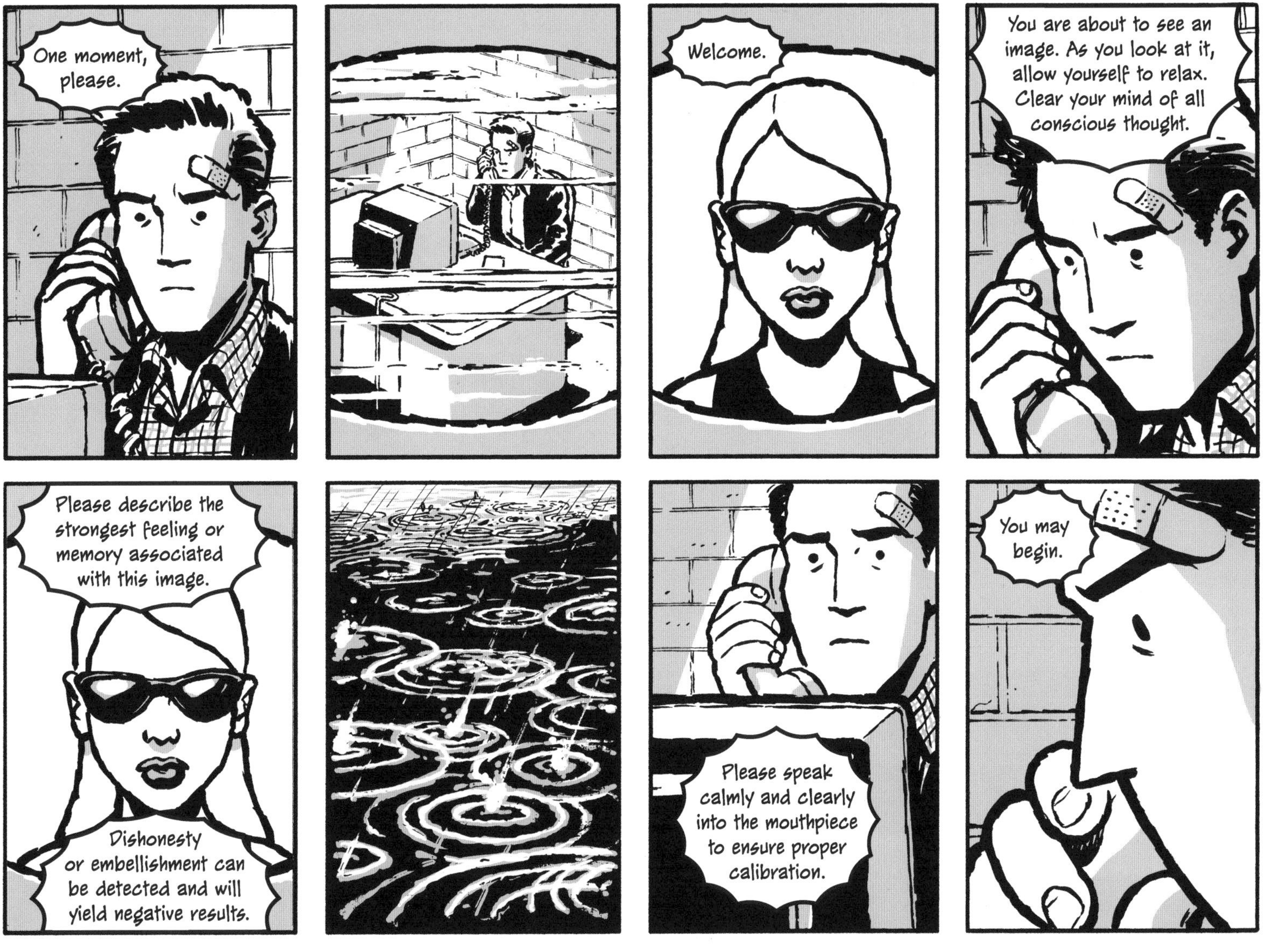
One moment, please.
Welcome.
You are about to see an image. As you look at it, allow yourself to relax. Clear your mind of all conscious thought.
Please describe the strongest feeling or memory associated with this image.
Dishonesty or embellishment can be detected and will yield negative results.
Please speak calmly and clearly into the mouthpiece to ensure proper calibration.
You may begin.

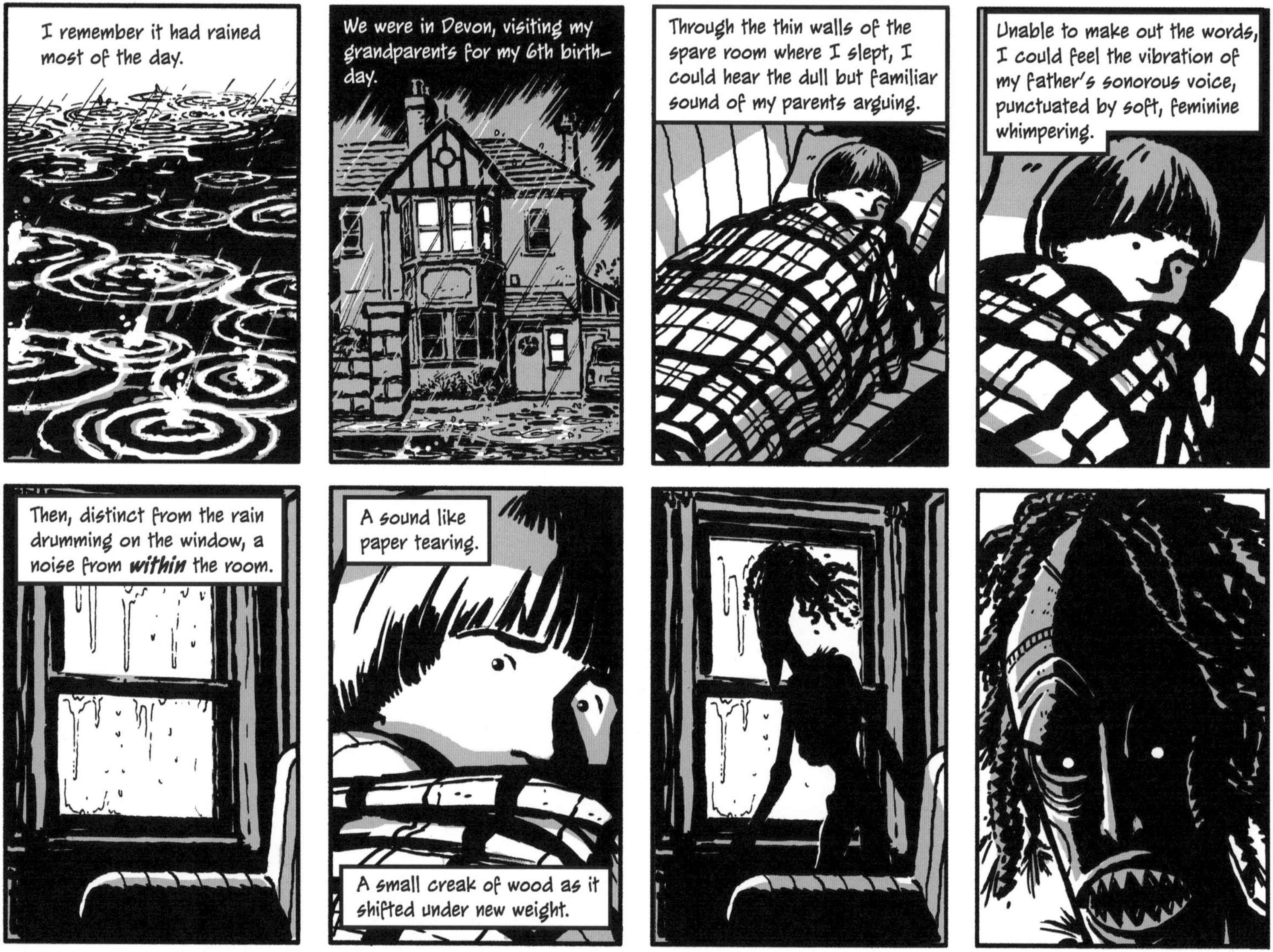
I remember it had rained most of the day.
We were in Devon, visiting my grandparents for my 6th birthday.
Through the thin walls of the spare room where I slept, I could hear the dull but familiar sound of my parents arguing.
Unable to make out the words, I could feel the vibration of my father's sonorous voice, punctuated by soft, feminine whimpering.
Then, distinct from the rain drumming on the window, a noise from *within* the room.
A sound like paper tearing.
A small creak of wood as it shifted under new weight.

I fled from the horror in the spare room, into the upstairs hallway.

From behind I heard a low, bestial growl and the first shambling steps.

Instead of seeking refuge in my parents' room, I ran for the stairs, hoping to reach the front door before the monstrous thing could follow.

Blind with tears, I bounded down the steps into the dark.

The wood had been recently polished and my feet slid out from under me.

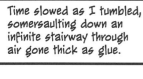

Time slowed as I tumbled, somersaulting down an infinite stairway through air gone thick as glue.

After what had seemed like hours of weightlessness I at last hit bottom.

KRAKK

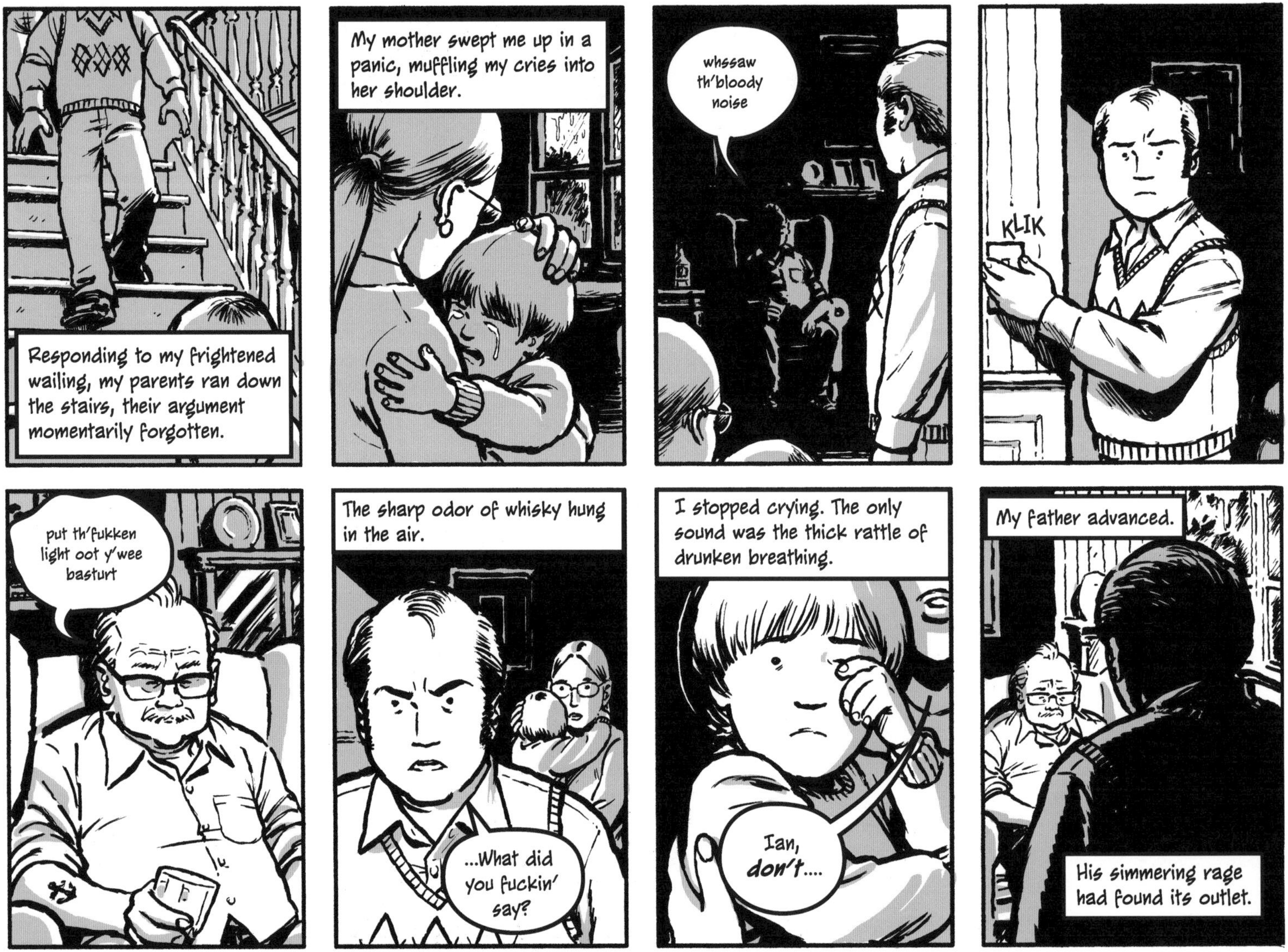
Responding to my frightened wailing, my parents ran down the stairs, their argument momentarily forgotten.
My mother swept me up in a panic, muffling my cries into her shoulder.
whssaw th'bloody noise
KLIK
put th'fukken light oot y'wee basturt
The sharp odor of whisky hung in the air.
...What did you fuckin' say?
I stopped crying. The only sound was the thick rattle of drunken breathing.
Ian, don't....
My father advanced.
His simmering rage had found its outlet.

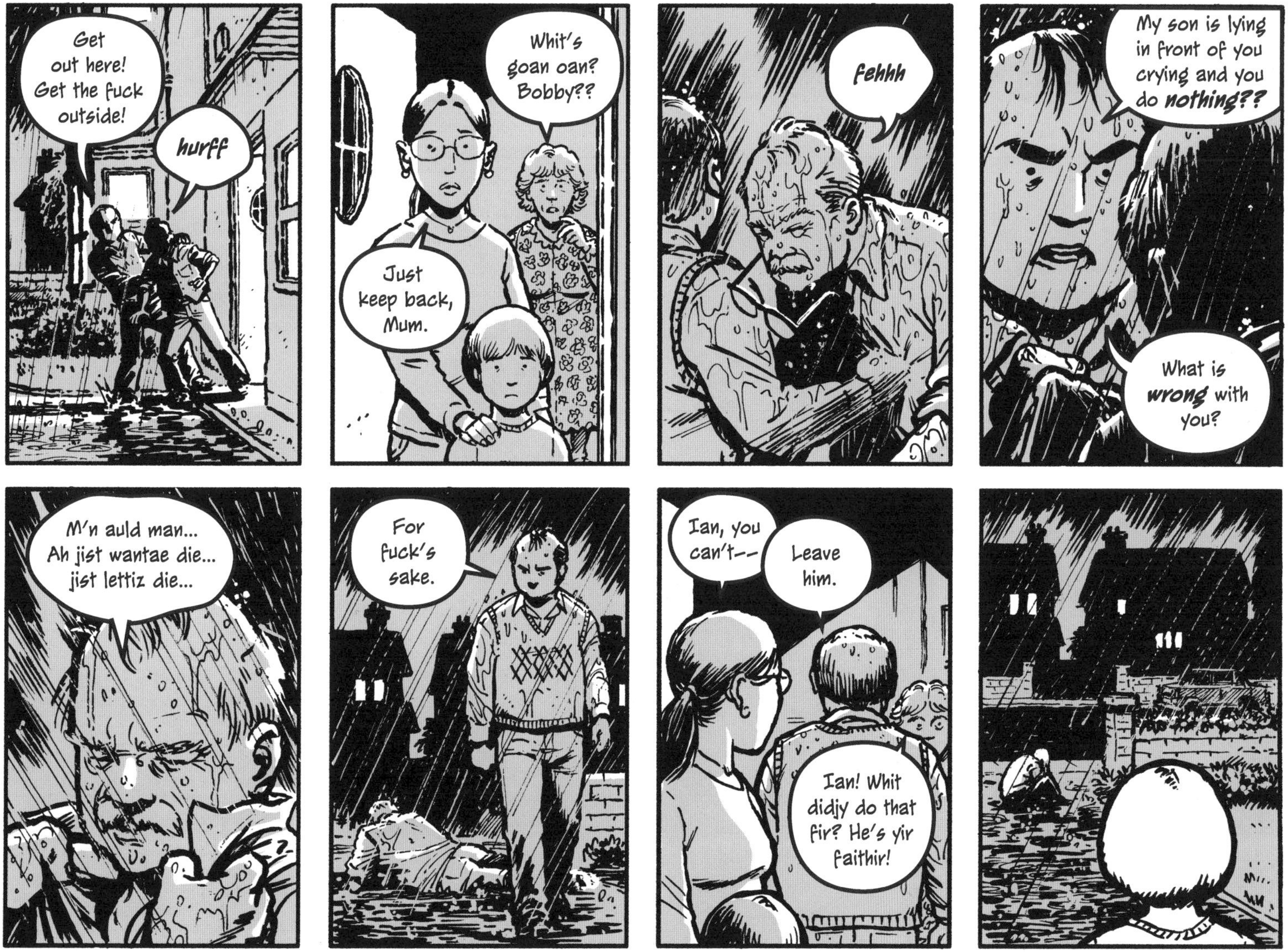
Get out here! Get the fuck outside!
hurff
Whit's goan oan? Bobby??
Just keep back, Mum.
fehhh
My son is lying in front of you crying and you do nothing??
What is wrong with you?
M'n auld man... Ah jist wantae die... jist lettiz die...
For fuck's sake.
Ian, you can't--
Leave him.
Ian! Whit didjy do that fir? He's yir faithir!

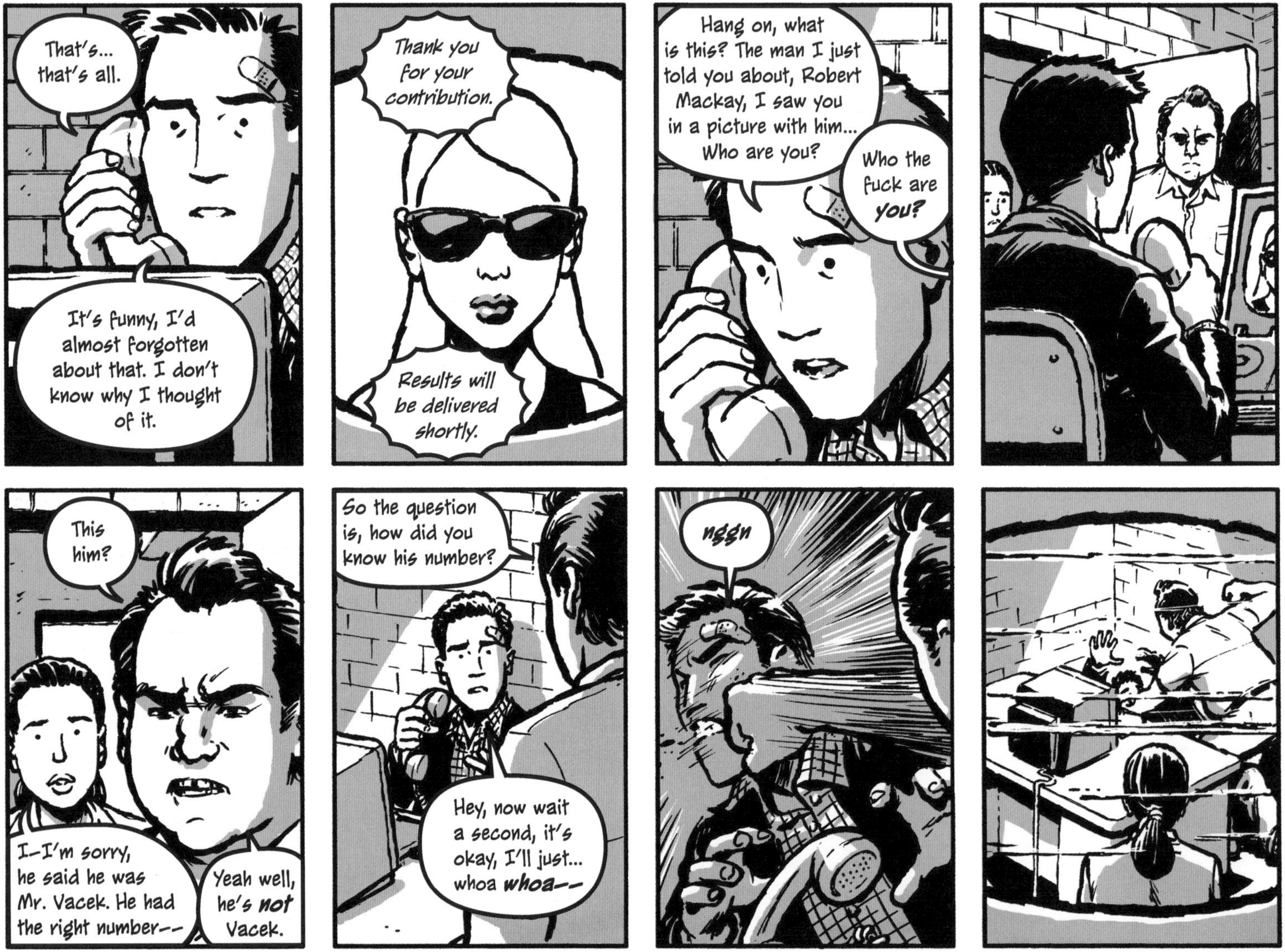
That's... that's all.
It's funny, I'd almost forgotten about that. I don't know why I thought of it.
Thank you for your contribution.
Results will be delivered shortly.
Hang on, what is this? The man I just told you about, Robert Mackay, I saw you in a picture with him... Who are you?
Who the fuck are *you?*
This him?
I-I'm sorry, he said he was Mr. Vacek. He had the right number--
Yeah well, he's *not* Vacek.
So the question is, how did you know his number?
Hey, now wait a second, it's okay, I'll just... whoa *whoa--*
nggn

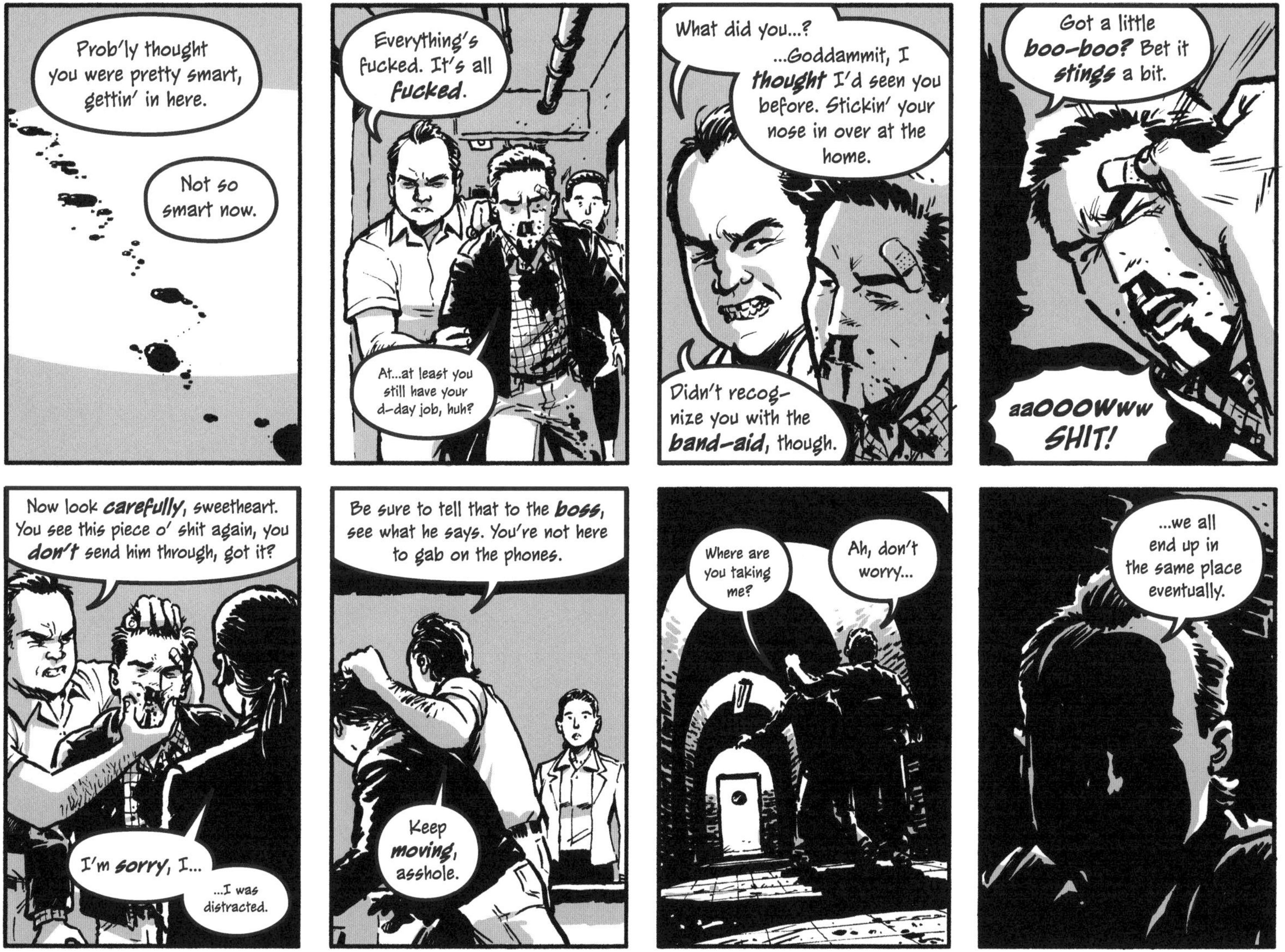
Prob'ly thought you were pretty smart, gettin' in here.
Not so smart now.
Everything's fucked. It's all fucked.
At...at least you still have your d-day job, huh?
What did you...?
...Goddammit, I thought I'd seen you before. Stickin' your nose in over at the home.
Didn't recog-nize you with the band-aid, though.
Got a little boo-boo? Bet it stings a bit.
aaOOOWWW SHIT!
Now look carefully, sweetheart. You see this piece o' shit again, you don't send him through, got it?
I'm sorry, I...
...I was distracted.
Be sure to tell that to the boss, see what he says. You're not here to gab on the phones.
Keep moving, asshole.
Where are you taking me?
Ah, don't worry...
...we all end up in the same place eventually.

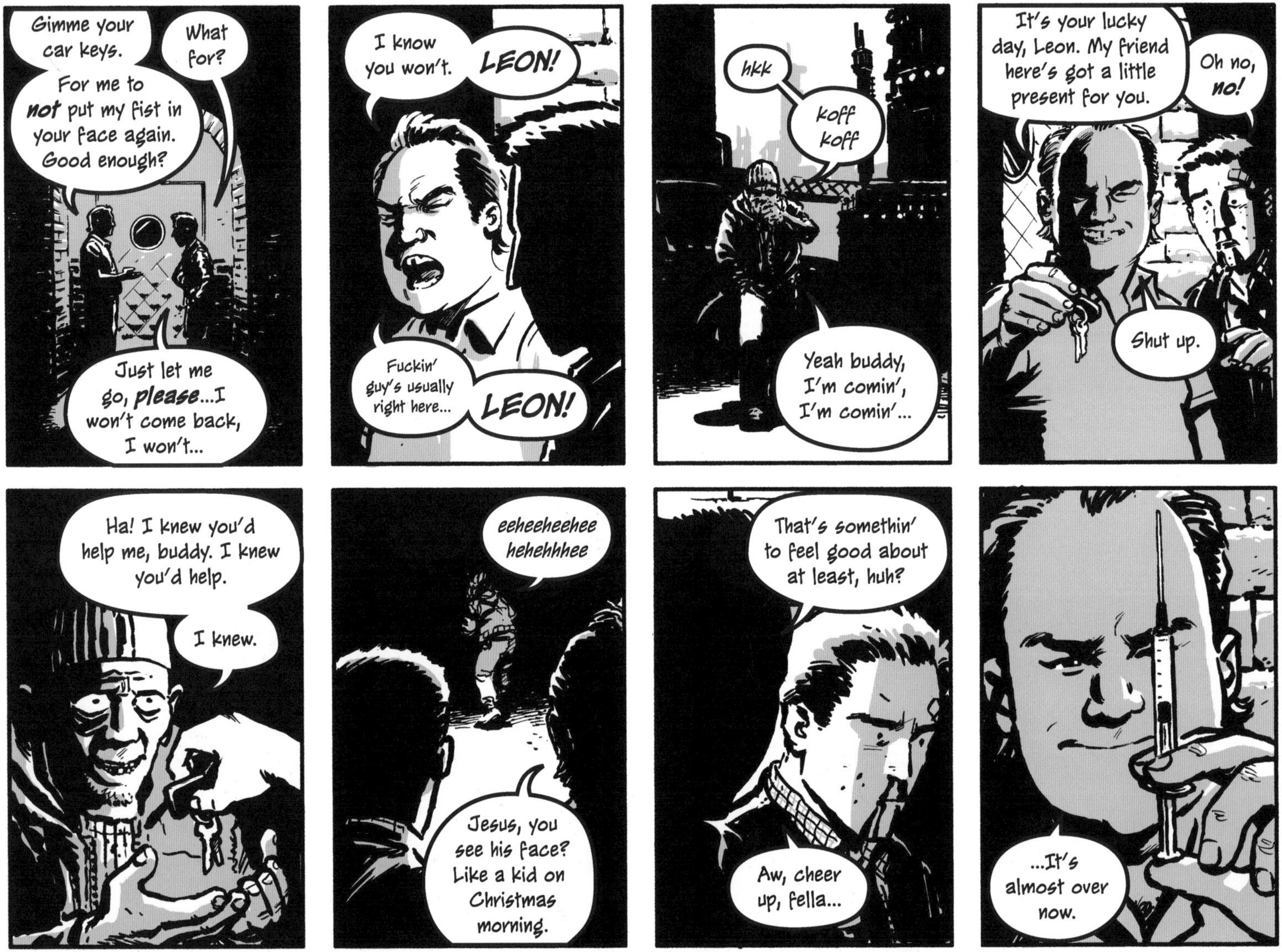

Gimme your car keys.
What for?
For me to **not** put my fist in your face again. Good enough?
Just let me go, **please**...I won't come back, I won't...
I know you won't.
LEON!
Fuckin' guy's usually right here...
LEON!
hkk
koff koff
Yeah buddy, I'm comin', I'm comin'...
It's your lucky day, Leon. My friend here's got a little present for you.
Oh no, **no!**
Shut up.
Ha! I knew you'd help me, buddy. I knew you'd help.
I knew.
eeheeheehee hehehhhee
Jesus, you see his face? Like a kid on Christmas morning.
That's somethin' to feel good about at least, huh?
Aw, cheer up, fella...
...It's almost over now.

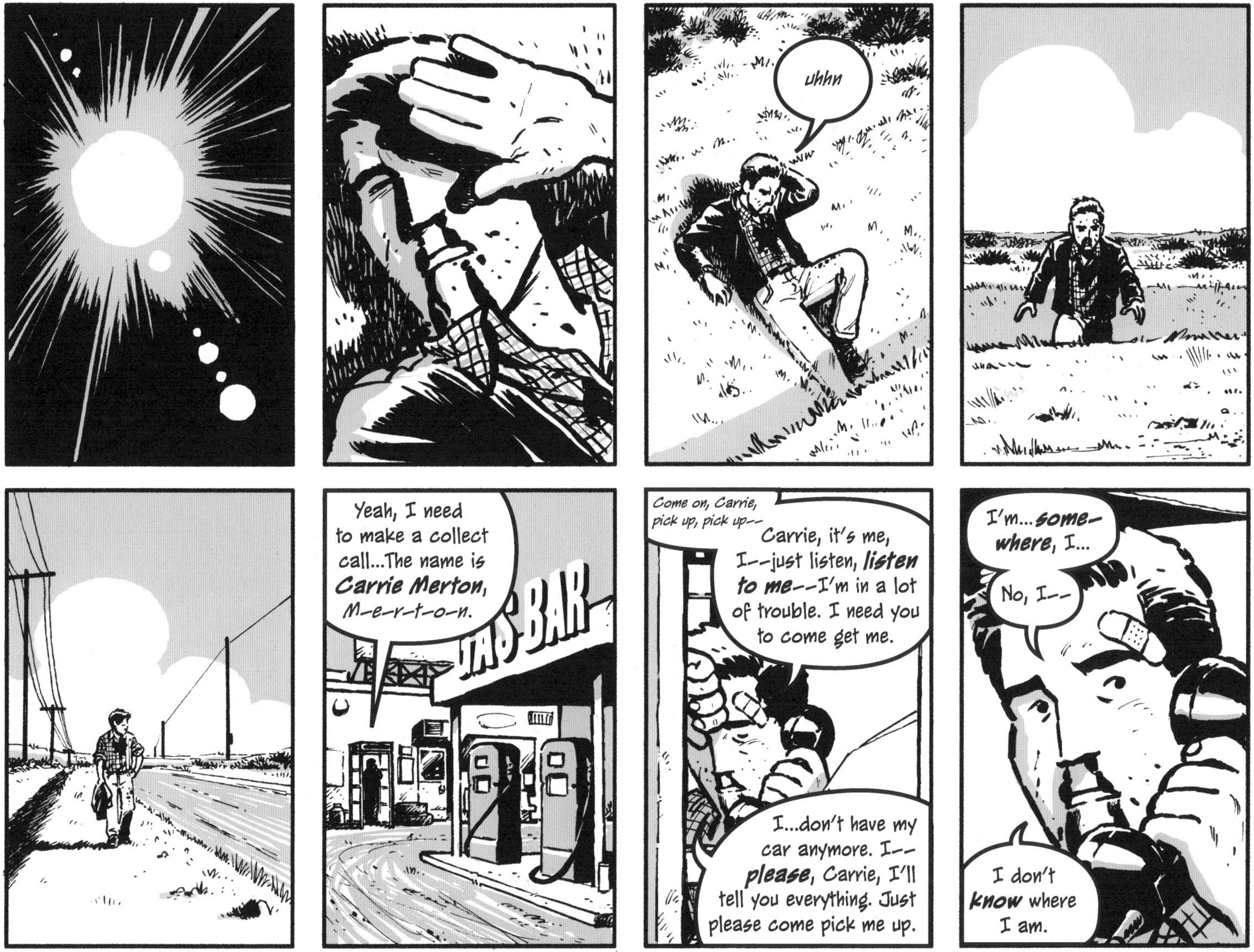
uhhn
Yeah, I need to make a collect call...The name is Carrie Merton, M-e-r-t-o-n.
Come on, Carrie, pick up, pick up--
Carrie, it's me, I--just listen, listen to me--I'm in a lot of trouble. I need you to come get me.
I...don't have my car anymore. I-- please, Carrie, I'll tell you everything. Just please come pick me up.
I'm...somewhere, I...
No, I--
I don't know where I am.

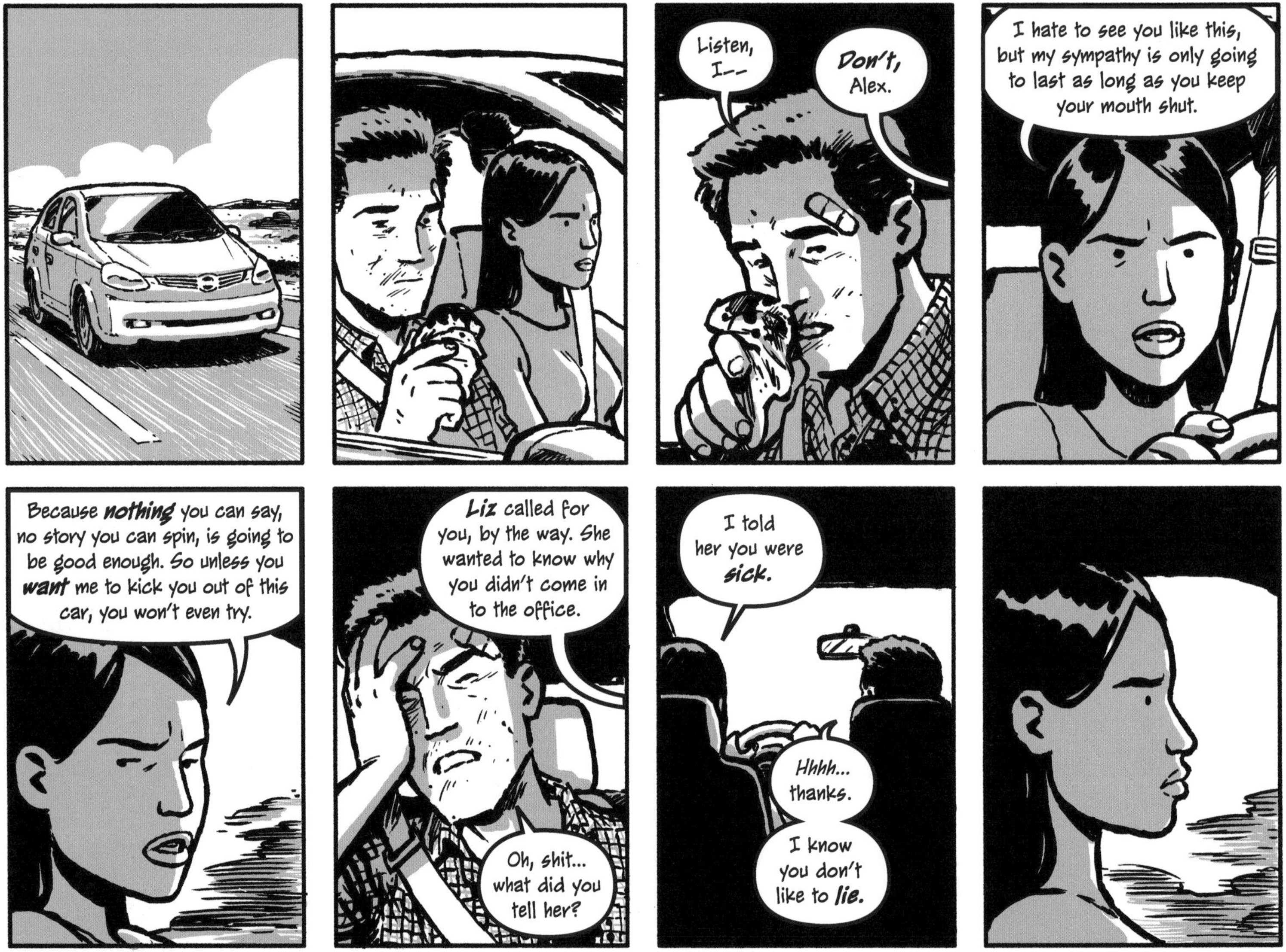
Listen, I--
Don't, Alex.
I hate to see you like this, but my sympathy is only going to last as long as you keep your mouth shut.
Because nothing you can say, no story you can spin, is going to be good enough. So unless you want me to kick you out of this car, you won't even try.
Liz called for you, by the way. She wanted to know why you didn't come in to the office.
Oh, shit... what did you tell her?
I told her you were sick.
Hhhh... thanks.
I know you don't like to lie.

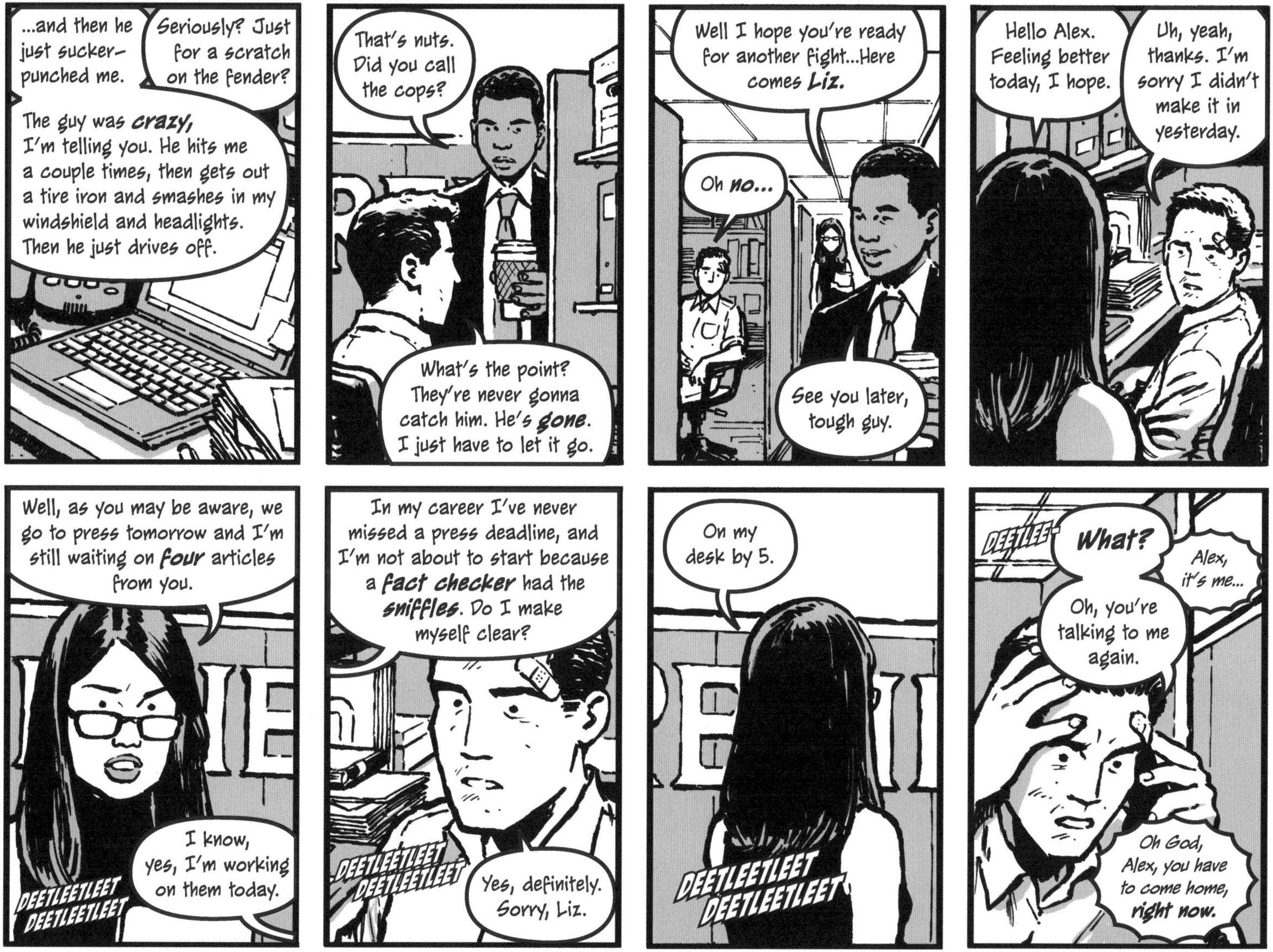

...and then he just sucker-punched me.
Seriously? Just for a scratch on the fender?
The guy was crazy, I'm telling you. He hits me a couple times, then gets out a tire iron and smashes in my windshield and headlights. Then he just drives off.
That's nuts. Did you call the cops?
What's the point? They're never gonna catch him. He's gone. I just have to let it go.
Well I hope you're ready for another fight...Here comes Liz.
Oh no...
See you later, tough guy.
Hello Alex. Feeling better today, I hope.
Uh, yeah, thanks. I'm sorry I didn't make it in yesterday.
Well, as you may be aware, we go to press tomorrow and I'm still waiting on four articles from you.
I know, yes, I'm working on them today.
DEETLEETLEET DEETLEETLEET
In my career I've never missed a press deadline, and I'm not about to start because a fact checker had the sniffles. Do I make myself clear?
DEETLEETLEET DEETLEETLEET
Yes, definitely. Sorry, Liz.
On my desk by 5.
DEETLEETLEET DEETLEETLEET
DEETLEE-
What?
Alex, it's me...
Oh, you're talking to me again.
Oh God, Alex, you have to come home, right now.

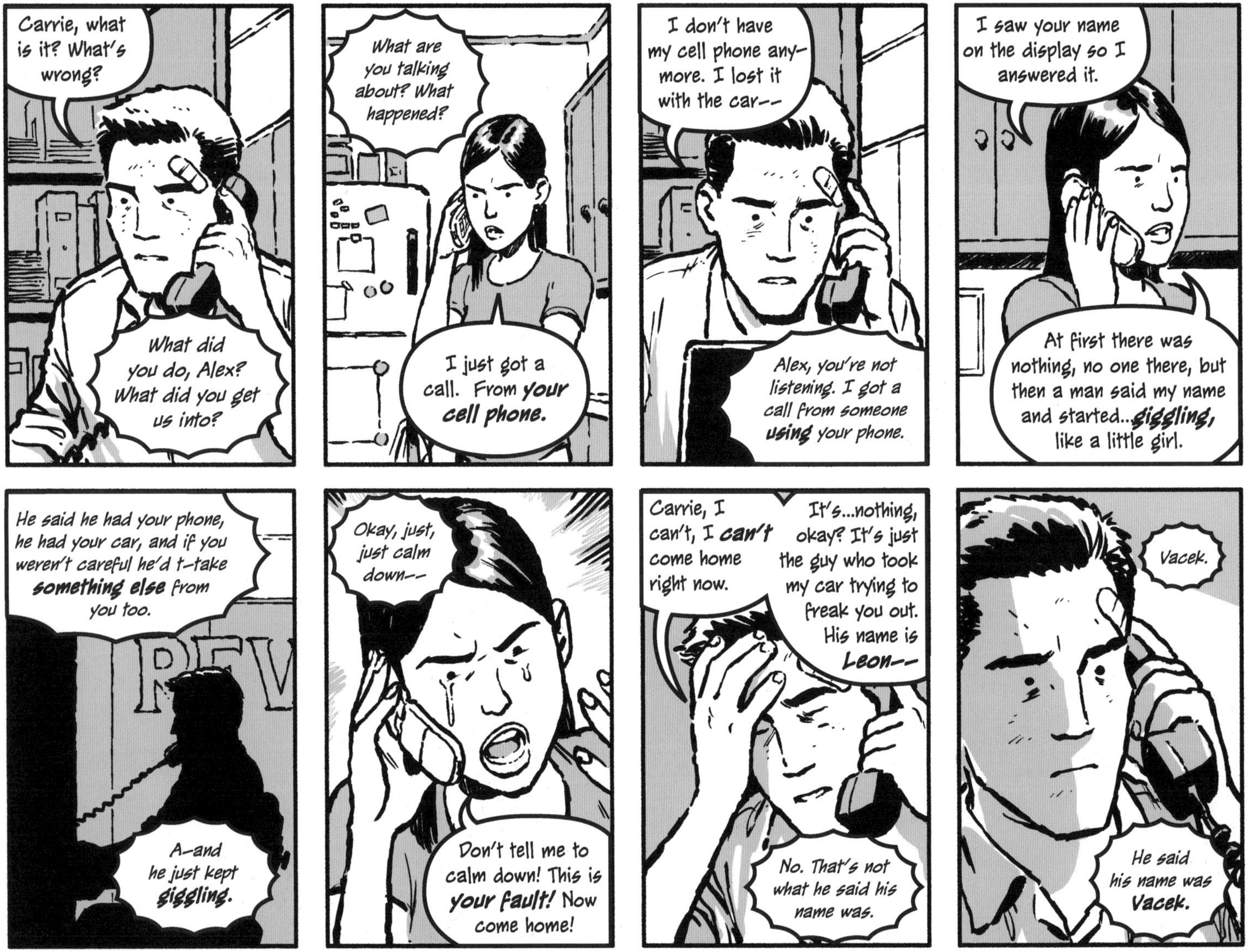
Carrie, what is it? What's wrong?
What did you do, Alex? What did you get us into?
What are you talking about? What happened?
I just got a call. From *your cell phone.*
I don't have my cell phone any-more. I lost it with the car--
Alex, you're not listening. I got a call from someone *using* your phone.
I saw your name on the display so I answered it.
At first there was nothing, no one there, but then a man said my name and started...*giggling,* like a little girl.
He said he had your phone, he had your car, and if you weren't careful he'd t-take *something else* from you too.
A-and he just kept *giggling.*
Okay, just, just calm down--
Don't tell me to calm down! This is *your fault!* Now come home!
Carrie, I can't, I *can't* come home right now.
It's...nothing, okay? It's just the guy who took my car trying to freak you out. His name is *Leon--*
No. That's not what he said his name was.
Vacek.
He said his name was *Vacek.*

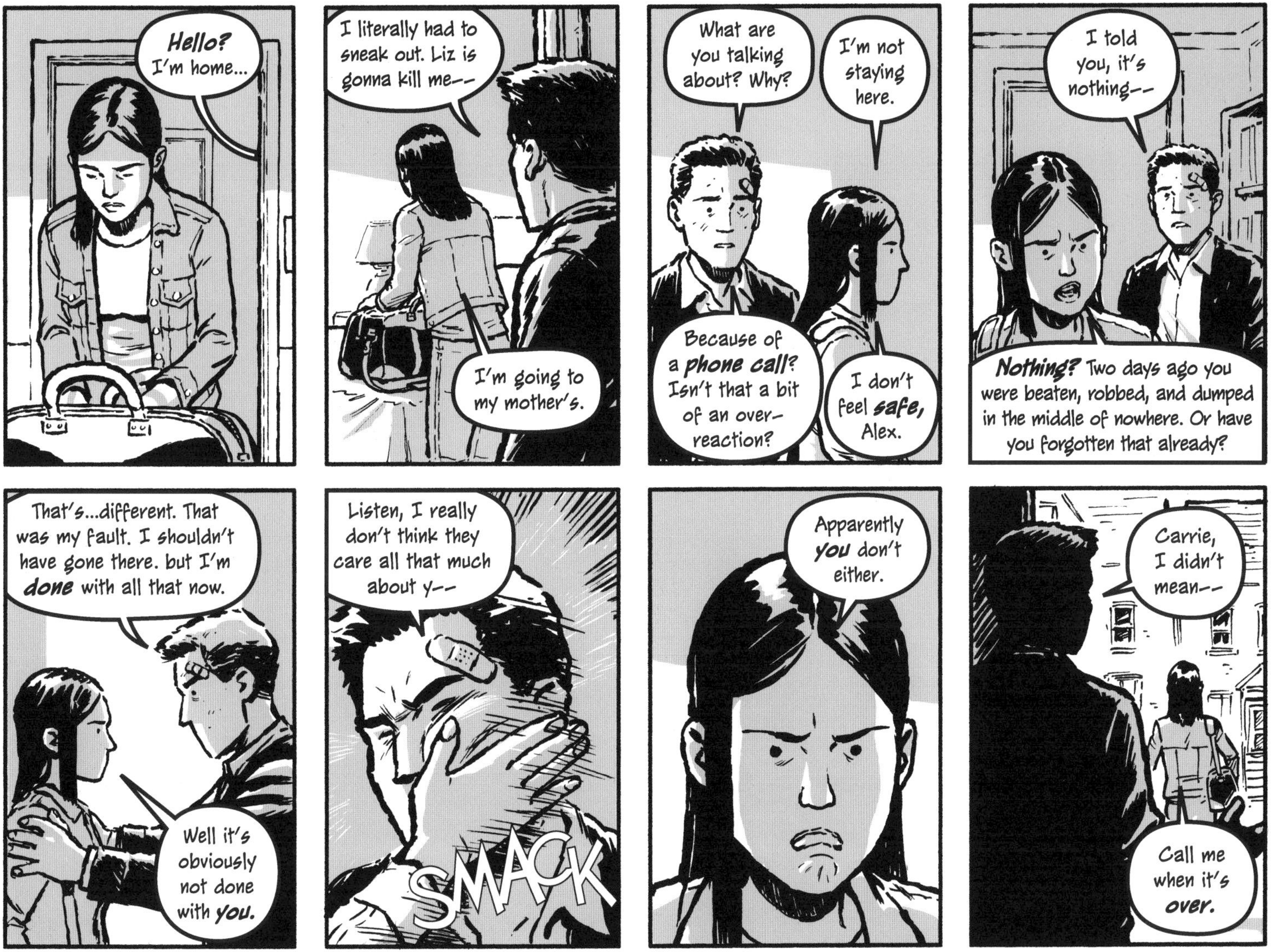
Hello? I'm home...
I literally had to sneak out. Liz is gonna kill me--
I'm going to my mother's.
What are you talking about? Why?
I'm not staying here.
Because of a phone call? Isn't that a bit of an over-reaction?
I don't feel safe, Alex.
I told you, it's nothing--
Nothing? Two days ago you were beaten, robbed, and dumped in the middle of nowhere. Or have you forgotten that already?
That's...different. That was my fault. I shouldn't have gone there. but I'm done with all that now.
Well it's obviously not done with you.
Listen, I really don't think they care all that much about y--
SMACK
Apparently you don't either.
Carrie, I didn't mean--
Call me when it's over.

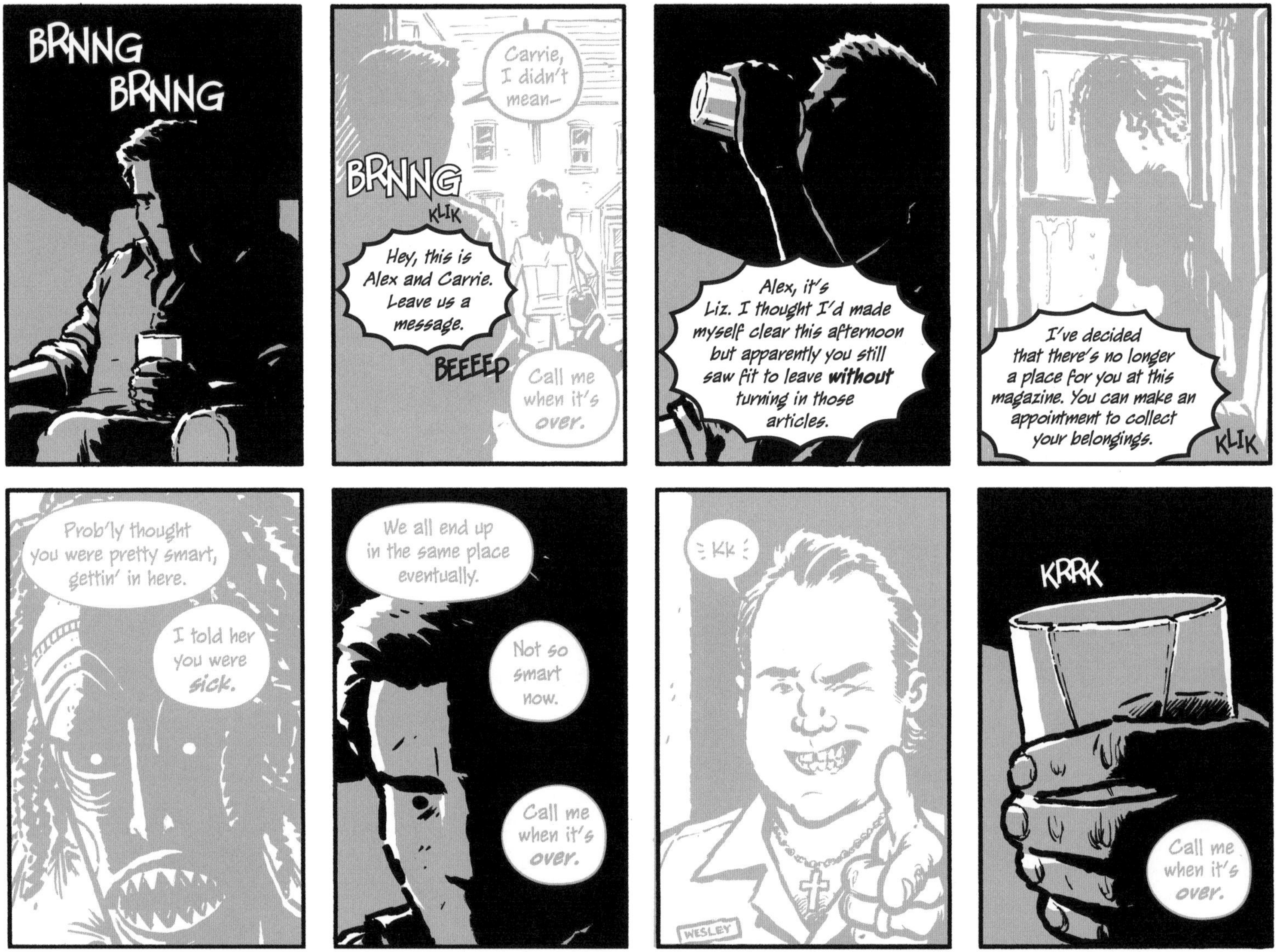
BRNNG BRNNG
Carrie, I didn't mean—
BRNNG
KLIK
Hey, this is Alex and Carrie. Leave us a message.
BEEEEP
Call me when it's over.
Alex, it's Liz. I thought I'd made myself clear this afternoon but apparently you still saw fit to leave without turning in those articles.
I've decided that there's no longer a place for you at this magazine. You can make an appointment to collect your belongings.
KLIK
Prob'ly thought you were pretty smart, gettin' in here.
I told her you were sick.
We all end up in the same place eventually.
Not so smart now.
Call me when it's over.
Kk
WESLEY
KRRK
Call me when it's over.

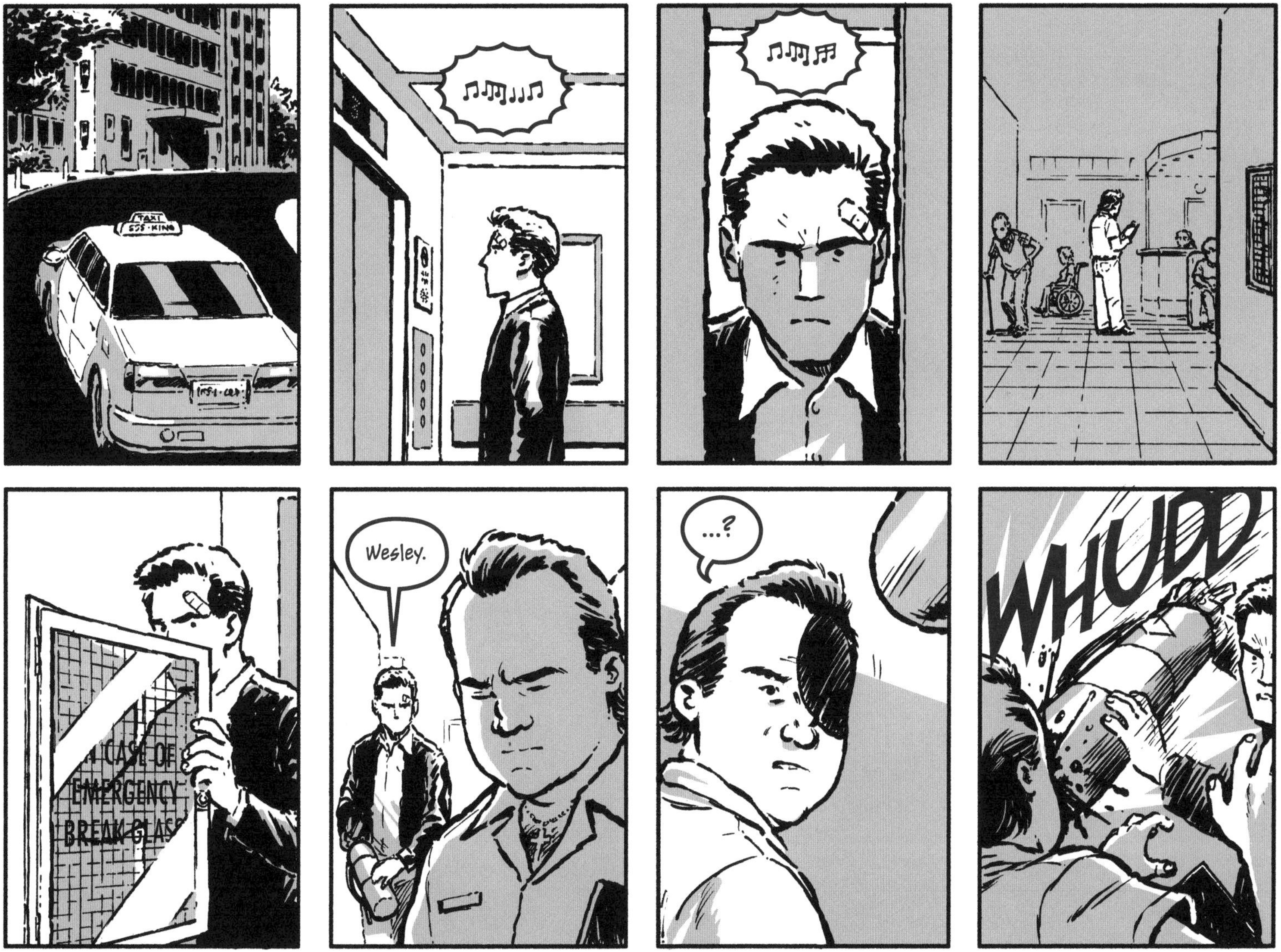
N CASE OF
EMERGENCY
BREAK GLAS
Wesley.
...?
WHUDD

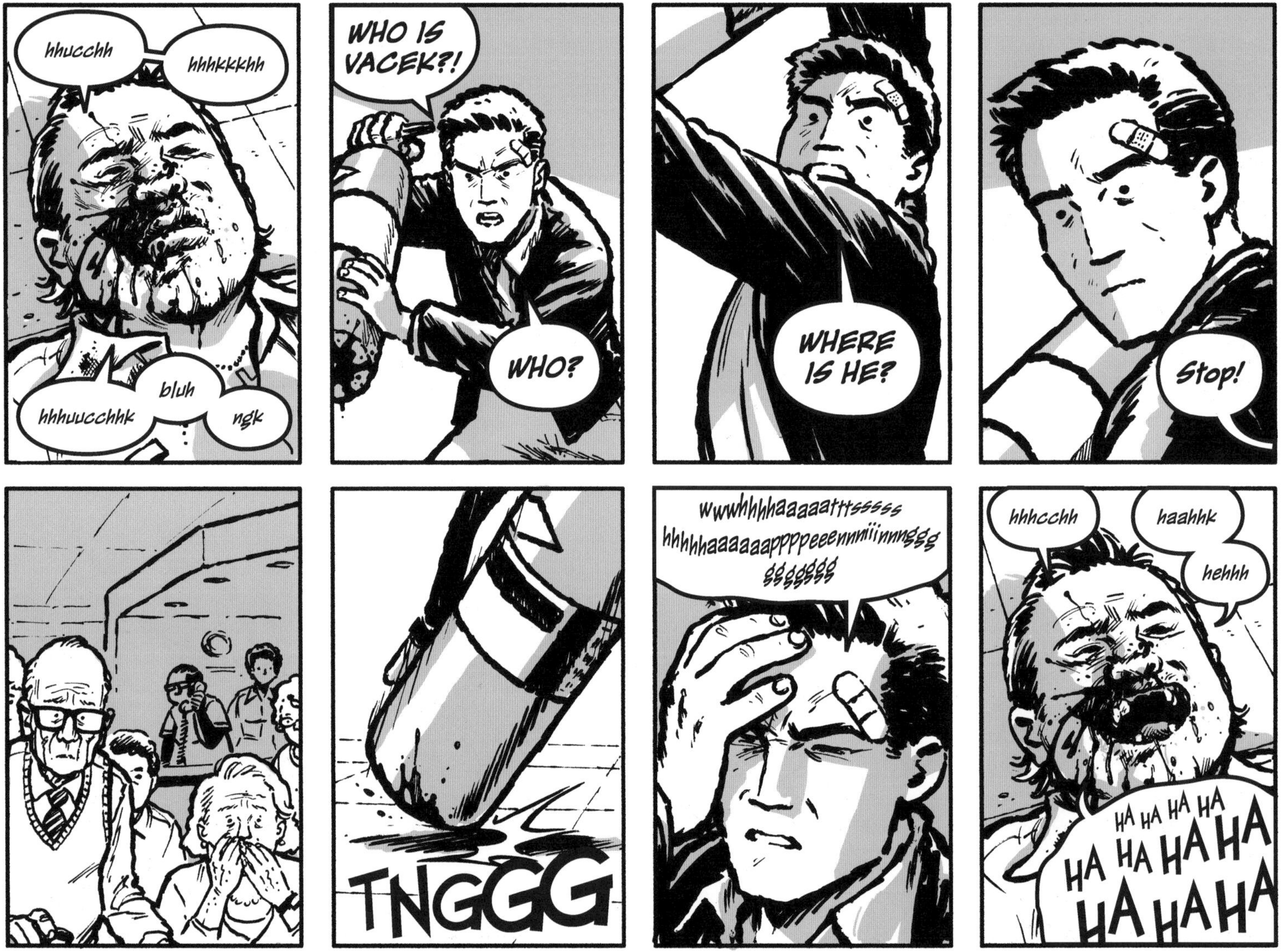
hhucchh
hhhkkkhh
hhhuucchhk
bluh
ngk
WHO IS VACEK?!
WHO?
WHERE IS HE?
Stop!
TNGGG
wwwhhhhaaaaatttsssss hhhhhaaaaaappppeeennnniiinnnggg gggggg
hhhcchh
haahhk
hehhh
HA HA HA HA HA HA HA HA HA HA HA HA

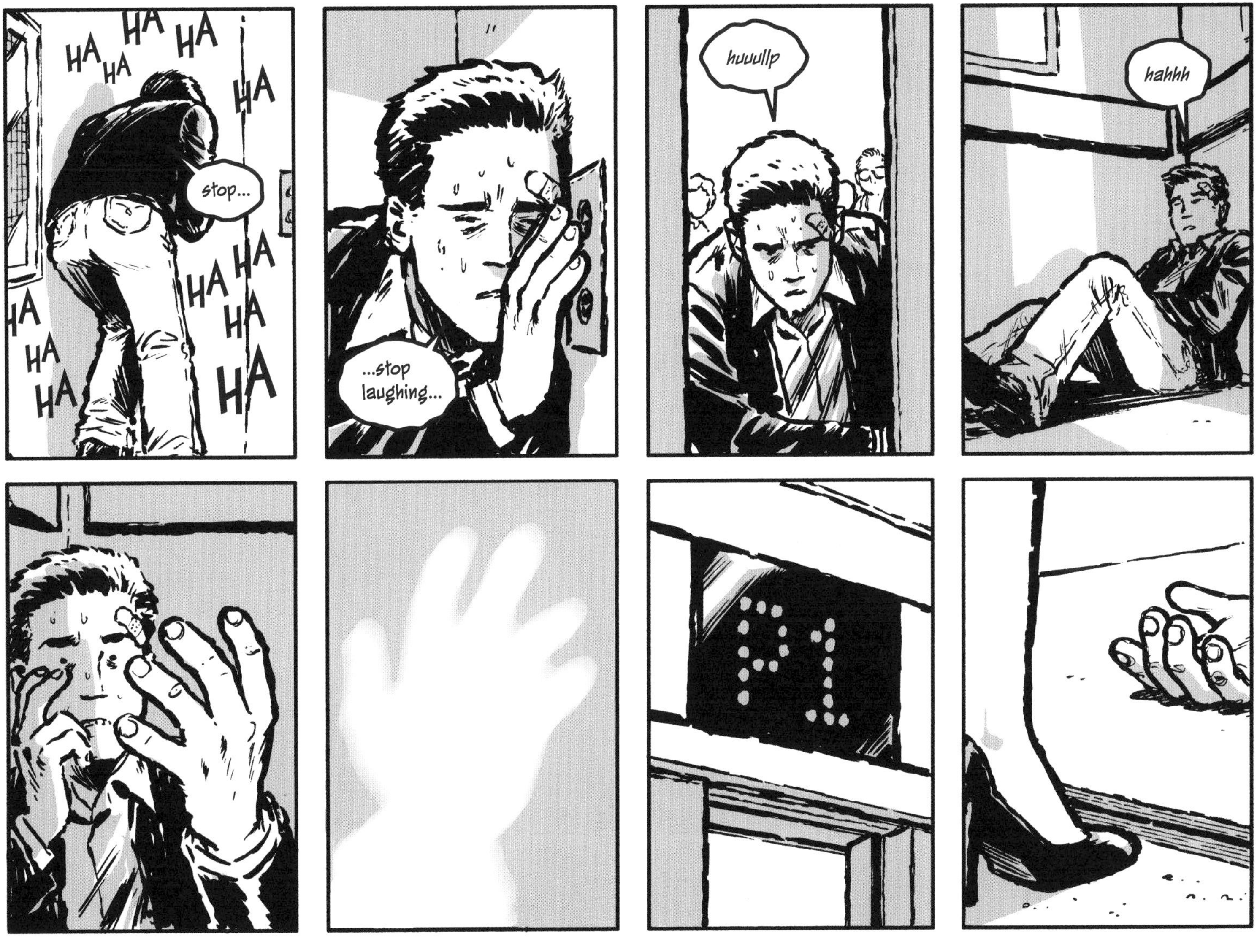
HA HA HA HA
HA
stop...
HA HA HA HA
HA HA HA
...stop laughing...
huuullp
hahhh

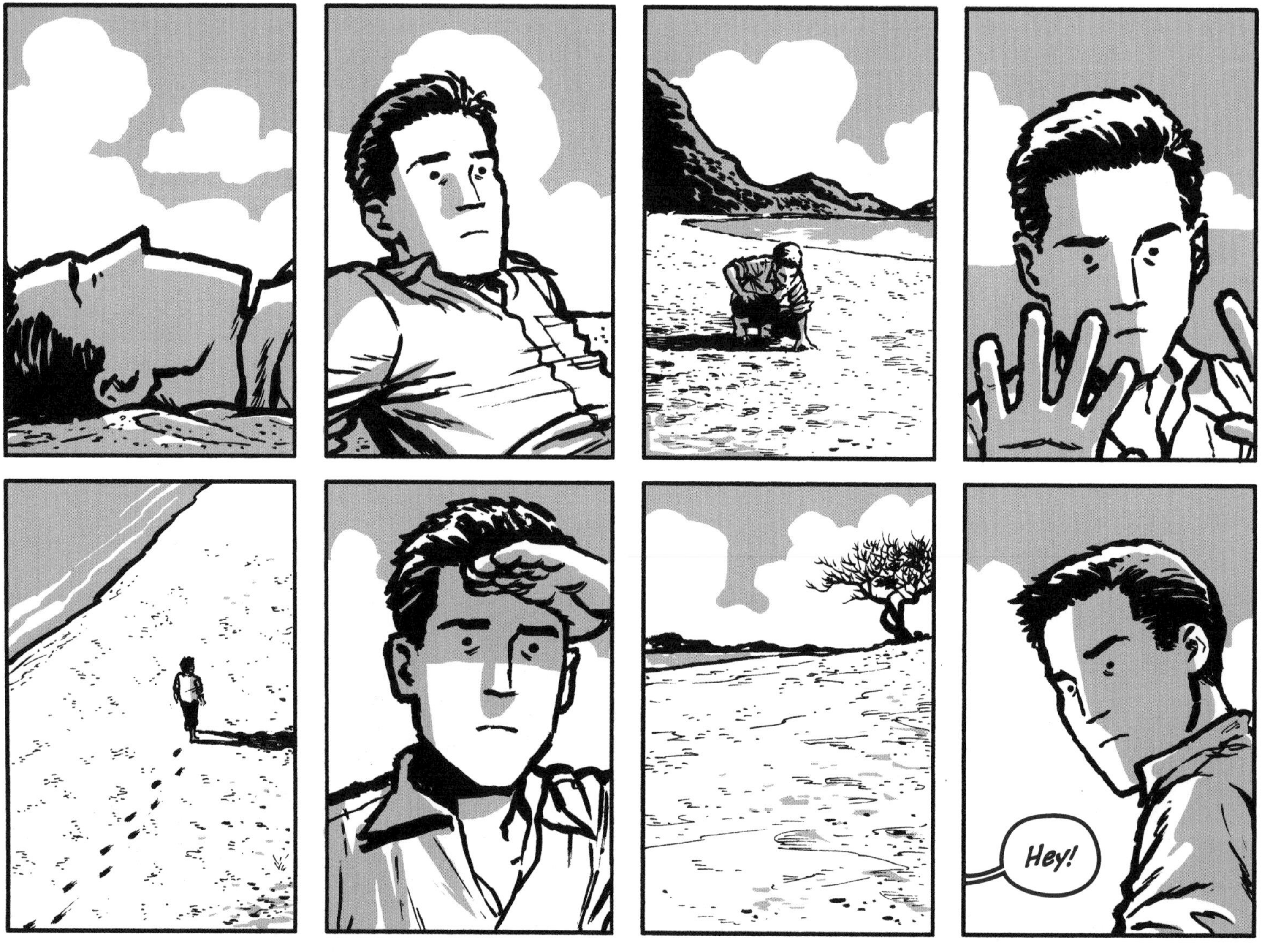
Hey!

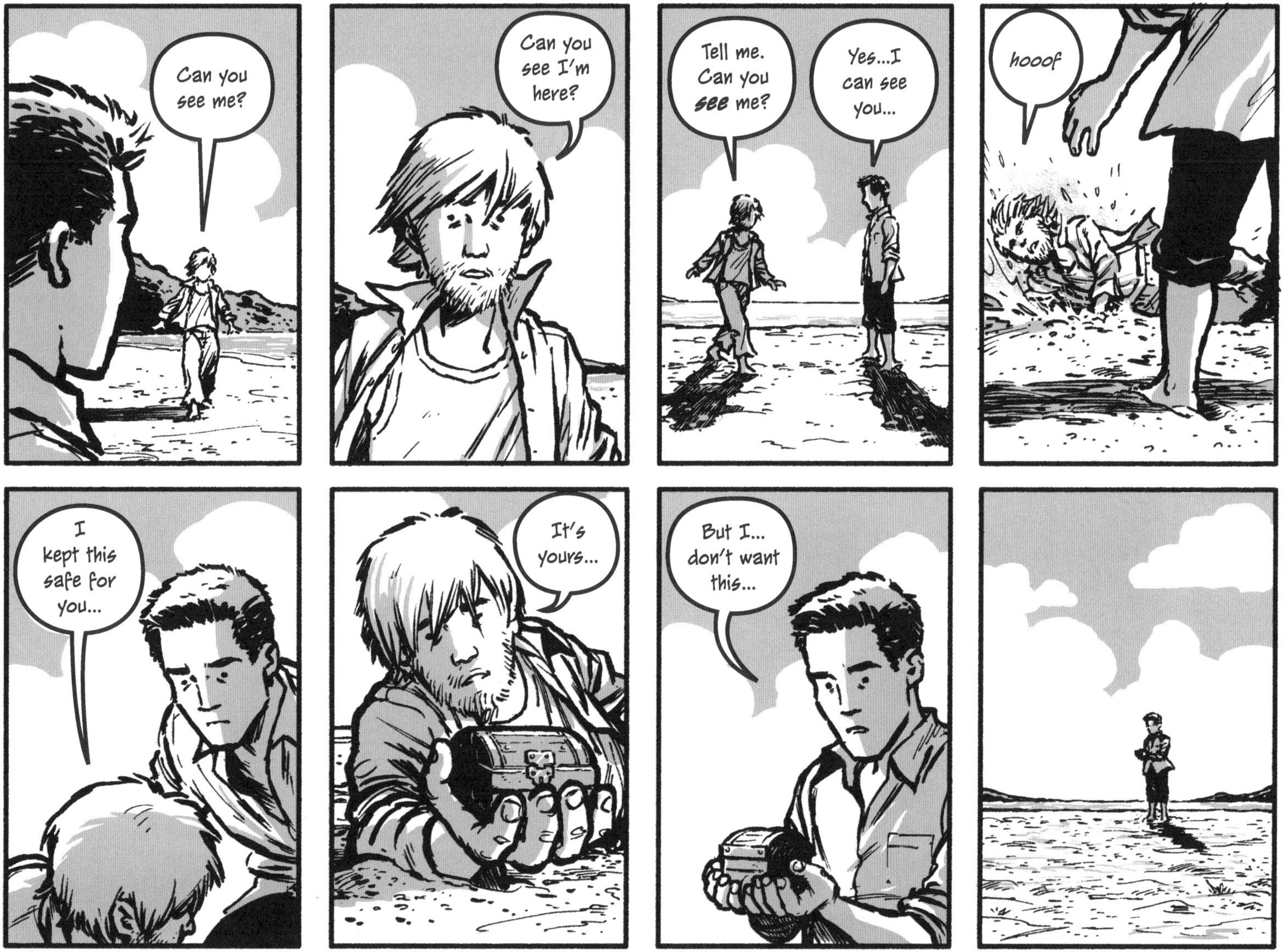
Can you see me?
Can you see I'm here?
Tell me. Can you see me?
Yes...I can see you...
hooof
I kept this safe for you...
It's yours...
But I... don't want this...

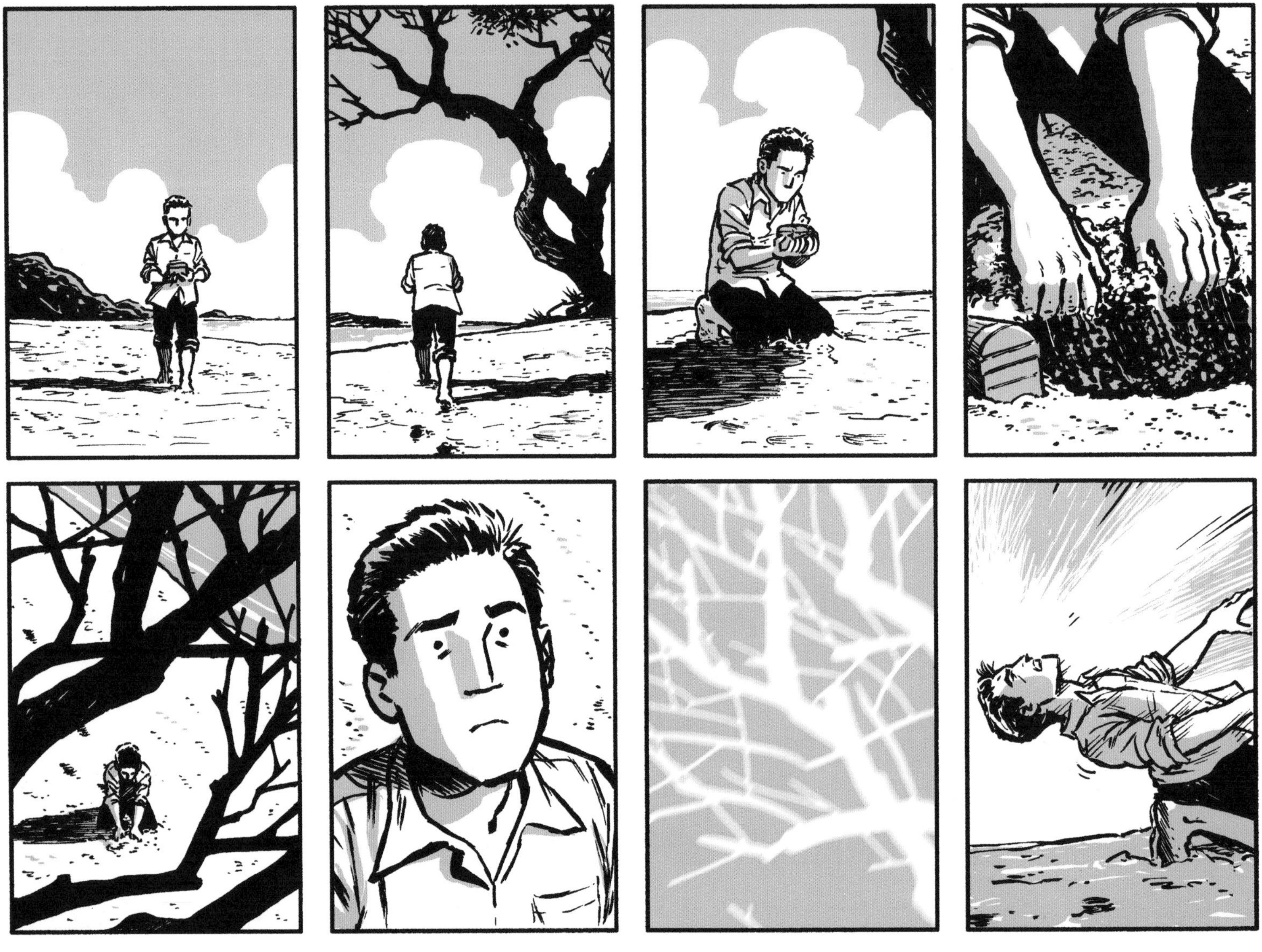

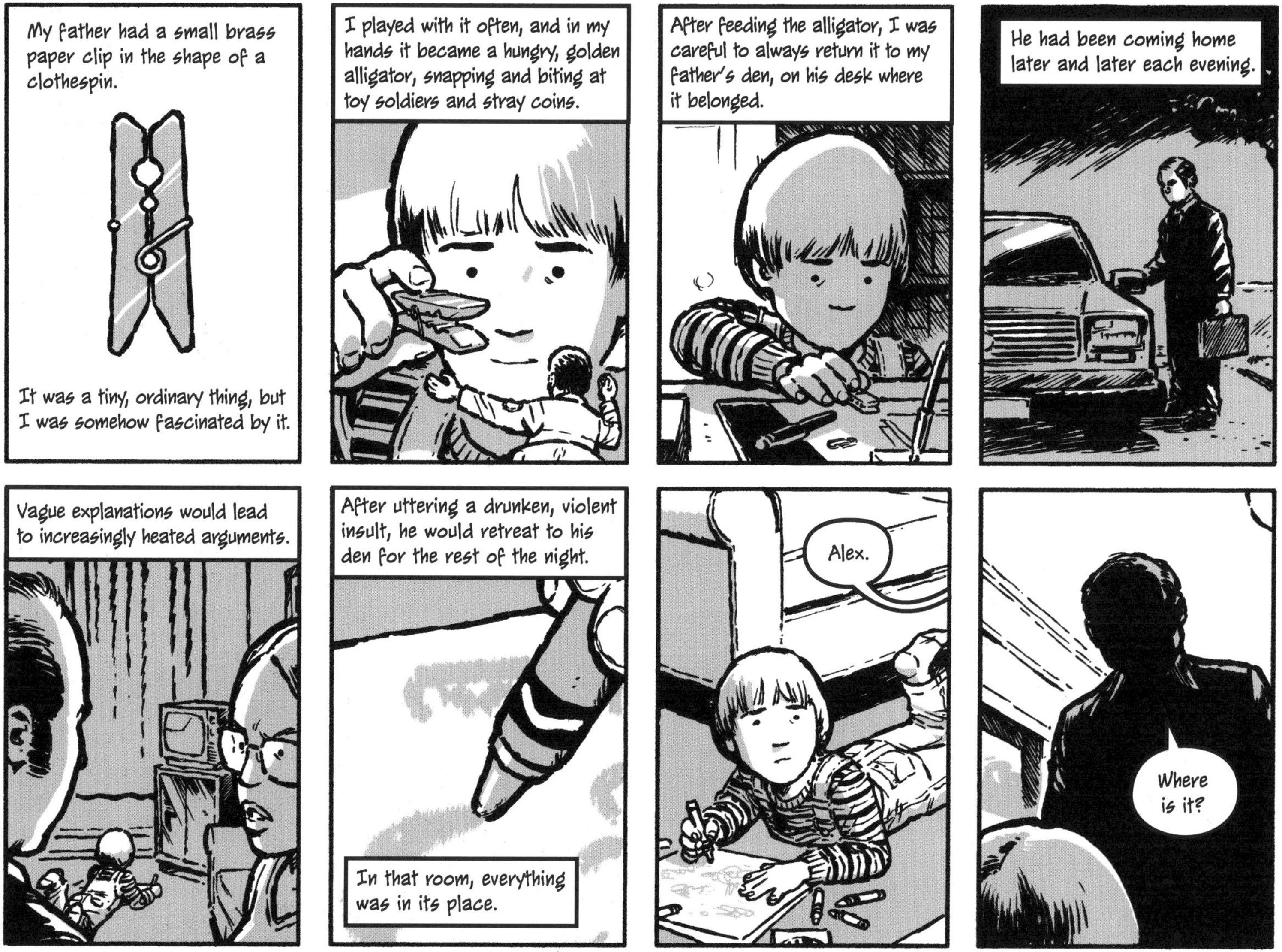
My father had a small brass paper clip in the shape of a clothespin.
It was a tiny, ordinary thing, but I was somehow fascinated by it.
I played with it often, and in my hands it became a hungry, golden alligator, snapping and biting at toy soldiers and stray coins.
After feeding the alligator, I was careful to always return it to my father's den, on his desk where it belonged.
He had been coming home later and later each evening.
Vague explanations would lead to increasingly heated arguments.
After uttering a drunken, violent insult, he would retreat to his den for the rest of the night.
In that room, everything was in its place.
Alex.
Where is it?

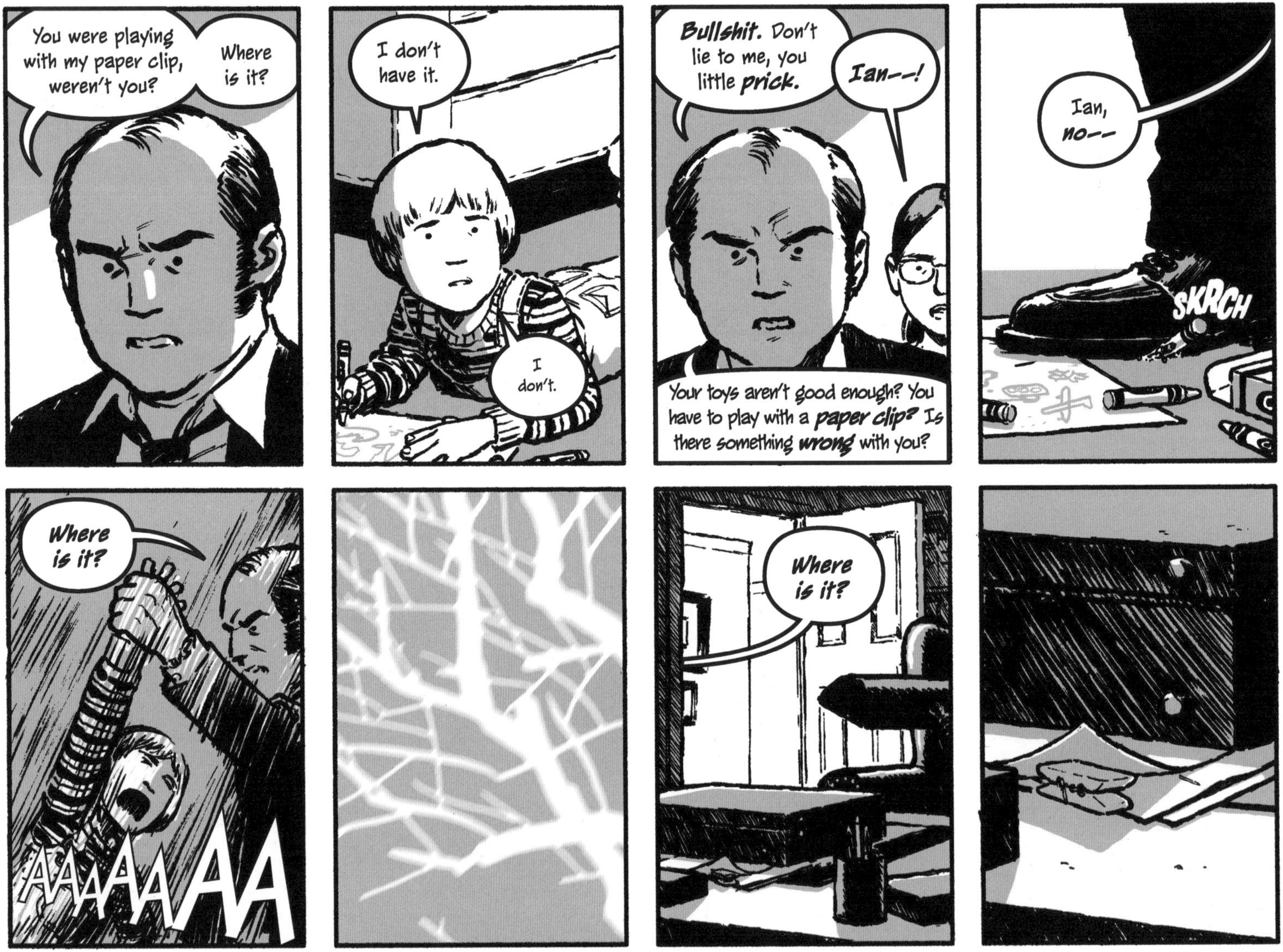
You were playing with my paper clip, weren't you?
Where is it?
I don't have it.
I don't.
Bullshit. Don't lie to me, you little prick.
Ian--!
Your toys aren't good enough? You have to play with a paper clip? Is there something wrong with you?
Ian, no--
SKRCH
Where is it?
AAAAAAAA
Where is it?

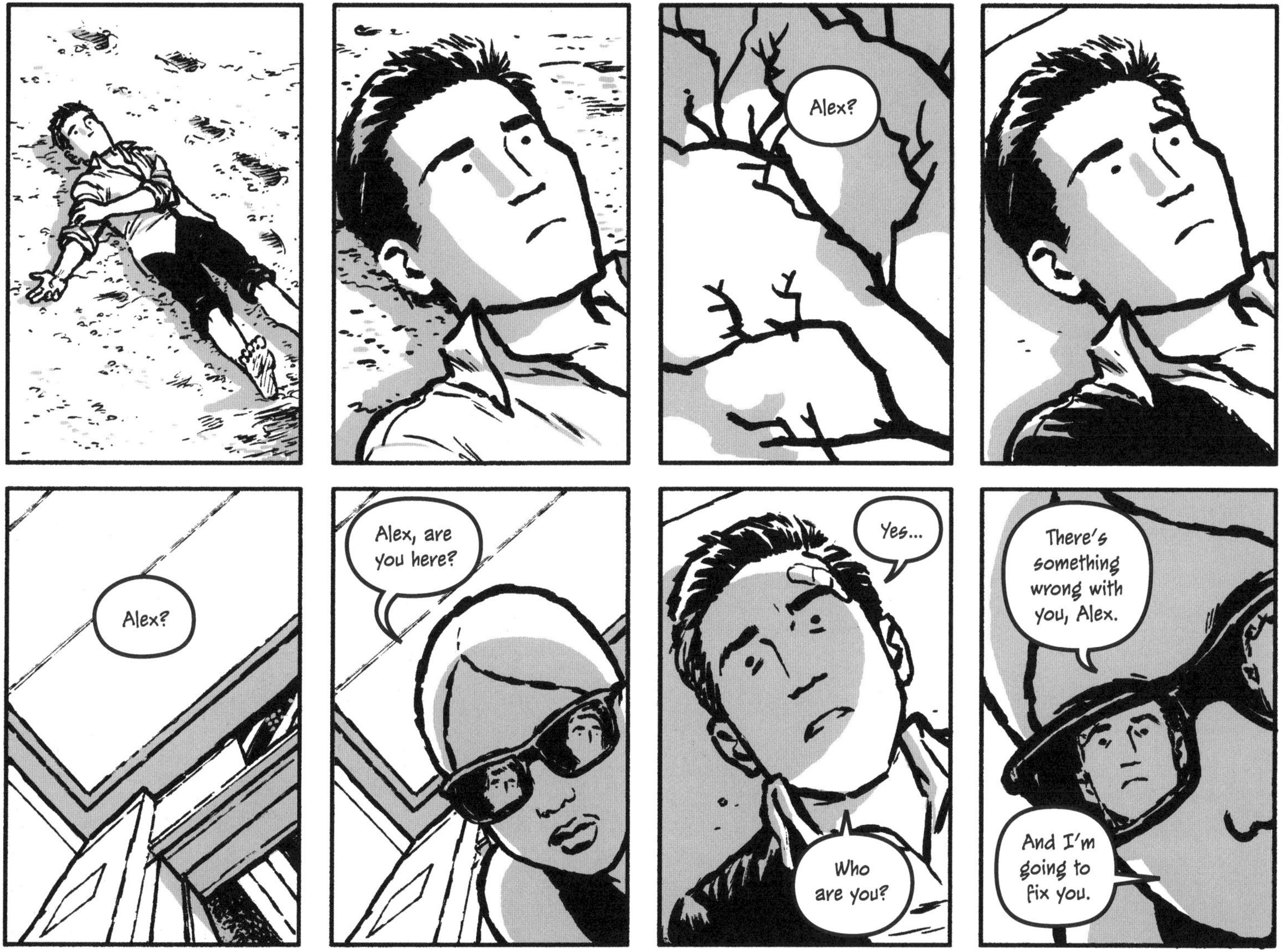
Alex?
Alex?
Alex, are you here?
Yes...
Who are you?
There's something wrong with you, Alex.
And I'm going to fix you.

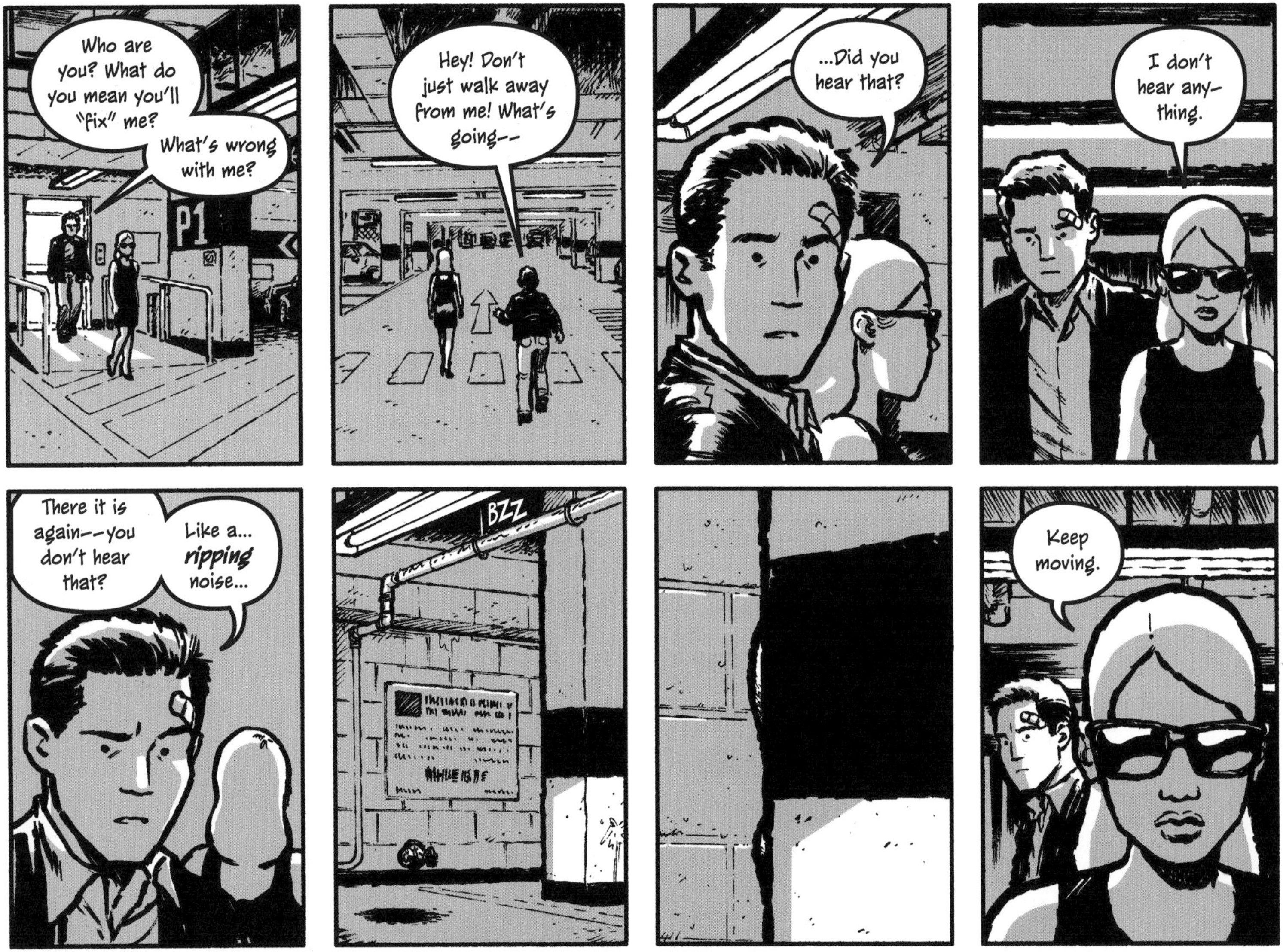
Who are you? What do you mean you'll "fix" me?
What's wrong with me?
Hey! Don't just walk away from me! What's going--
...Did you hear that?
I don't hear any-thing.
There it is again--you don't hear that?
Like a... *ripping* noise...
BZZ
Keep moving.

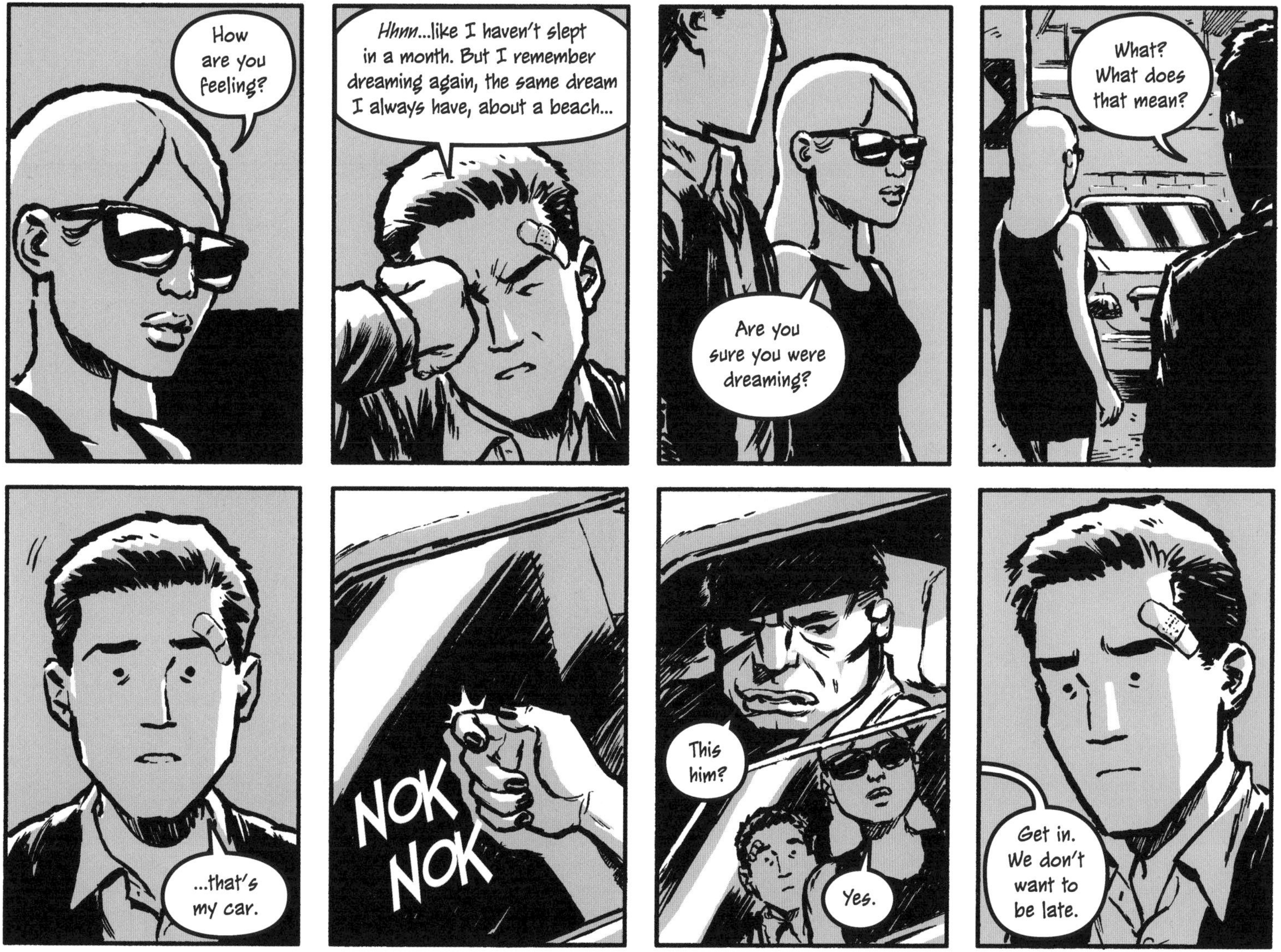
How are you feeling?
Hhnn...like I haven't slept in a month. But I remember dreaming again, the same dream I always have, about a beach...
Are you sure you were dreaming?
What? What does that mean?
...that's my car.
NOK NOK
This him?
Yes.
Get in. We don't want to be late.

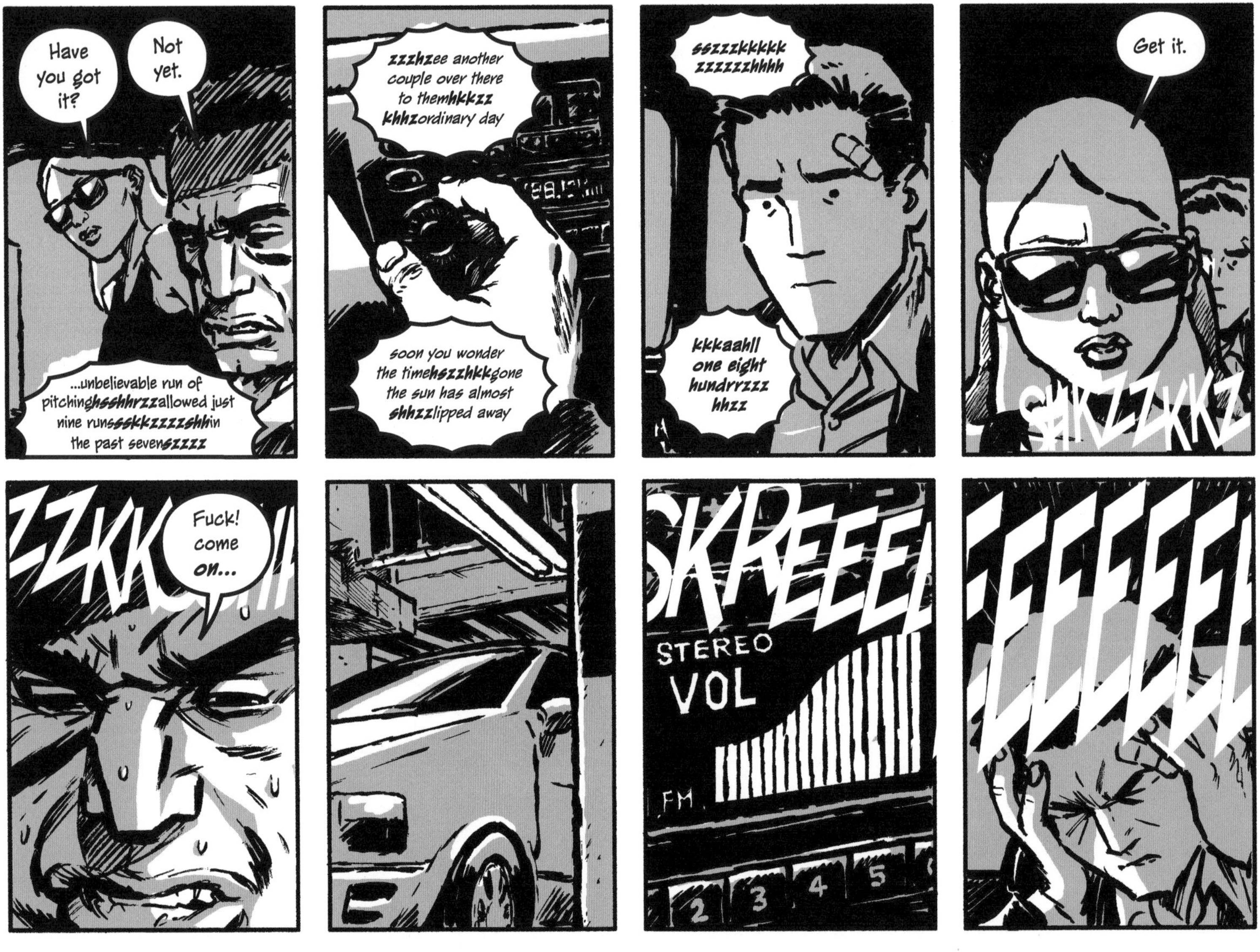

Have you got it?
Not yet.
...unbelievable run of pitchinghsshhrzzallowed just nine runssskkzzzzzshhin the past sevenszzzz
zzzhzee another couple over there to themhkkzz khhzordinary day
soon you wonder the timehszzhkkgone the sun has almost shhzzlipped away
sszzzkkkkk zzzzzzhhhh
kkkaahll one eight hundrrzzz hhzz
Get it.
SHKZZZKKZ
ZZKK
Fuck! come on...
SKREEEEL
STEREO
VOL
FM
2 3 4 5
EEEEEEL

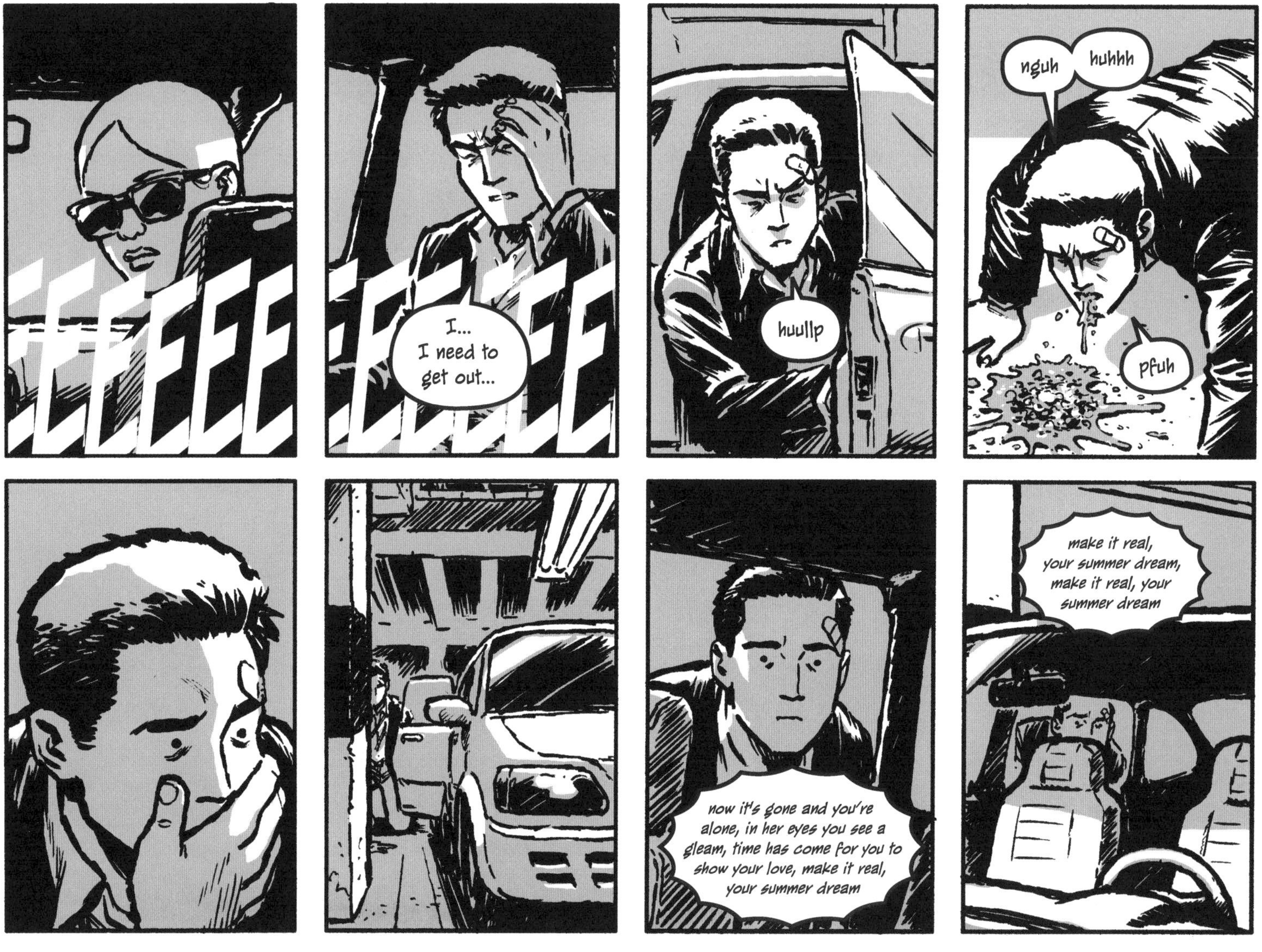
EEEEE
EEEEE
I... I need to get out...
huullp
nguh
huhhh
pfuh
now it's gone and you're alone, in her eyes you see a gleam, time has come for you to show your love, make it real, your summer dream
make it real, your summer dream, make it real, your summer dream

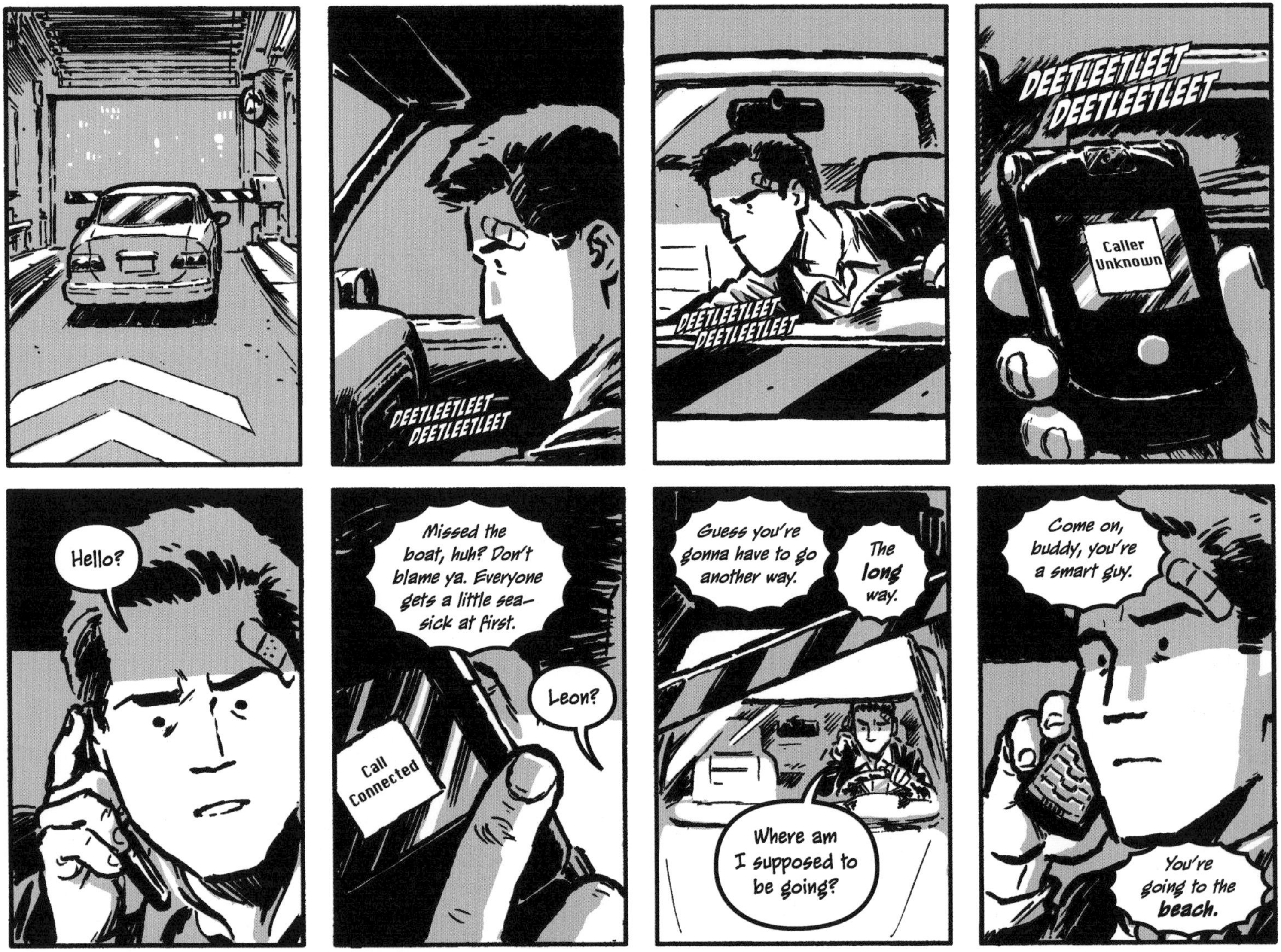
DEETLEETLEET
DEETLEETLEET
DEETLEETLEET
DEETLEETLEET
DEETLEETLEET
DEETLEETLEET
Caller Unknown
Hello?
Missed the boat, huh? Don't blame ya. Everyone gets a little sea-sick at first.
Call Connected
Leon?
Guess you're gonna have to go another way.
The long way.
Where am I supposed to be going?
Come on, buddy, you're a smart guy.
You're going to the beach.

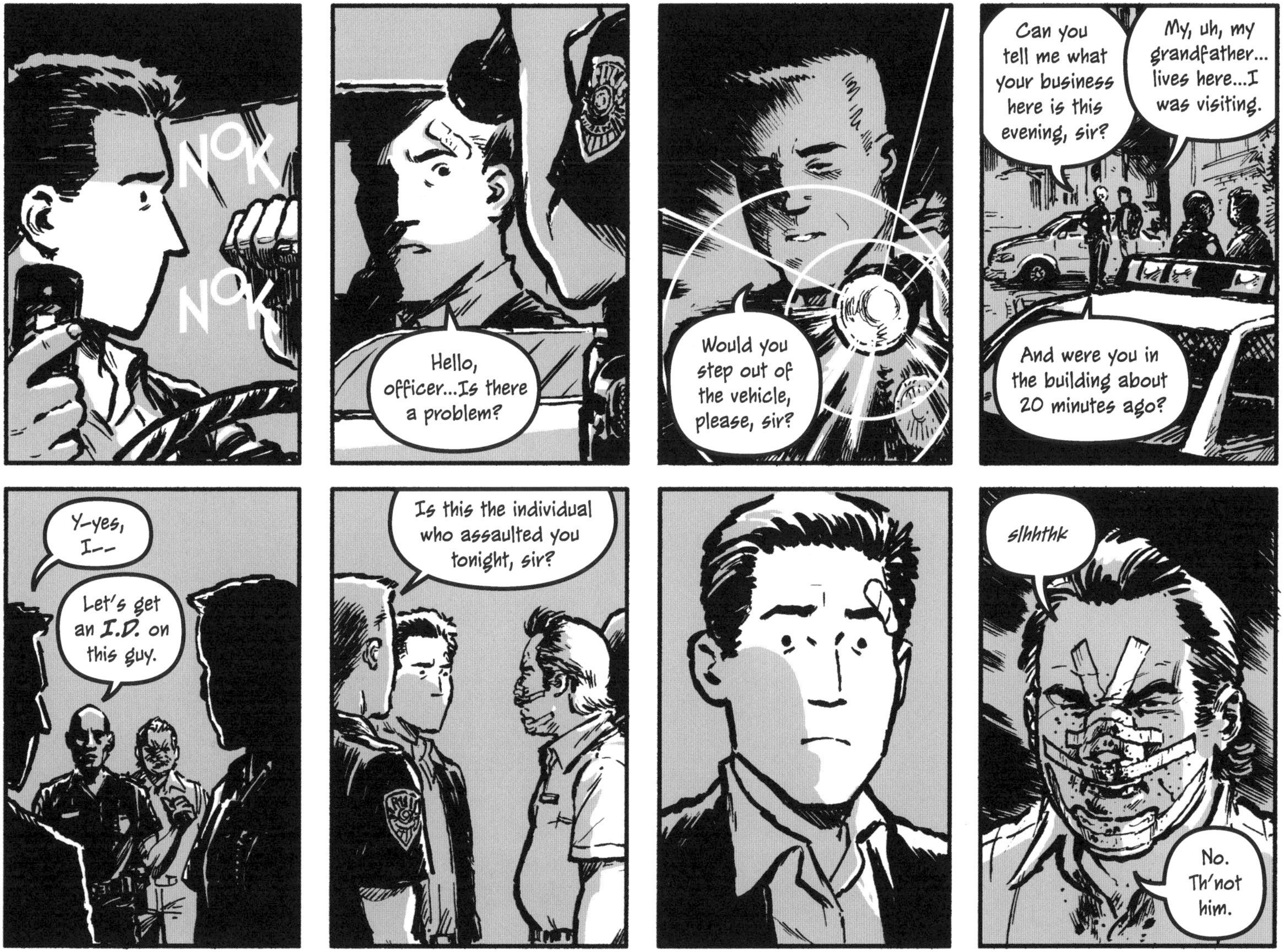
NOK
NOK
Hello, officer...Is there a problem?
Would you step out of the vehicle, please, sir?
Can you tell me what your business here is this evening, sir?
My, uh, my grandfather... lives here...I was visiting.
And were you in the building about 20 minutes ago?
Y-yes, I--
Let's get an I.D. on this guy.
Is this the individual who assaulted you tonight, sir?
slhhthk
No. Th'not him.

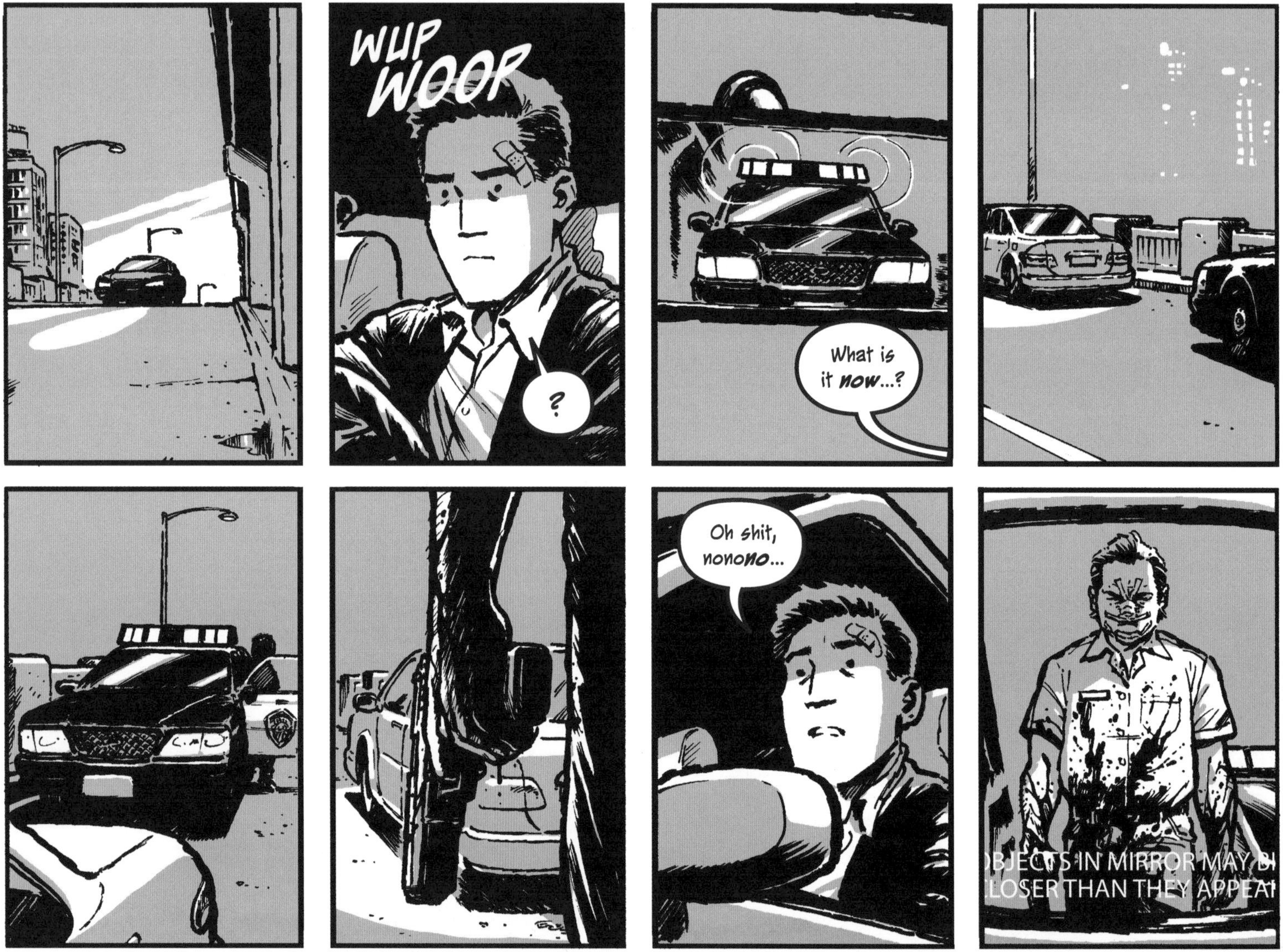
WUP
WOOP
?
What is it now...?
Oh shit, nononO...
OBJECTS IN MIRROR MAY BE
CLOSER THAN THEY APPEAR

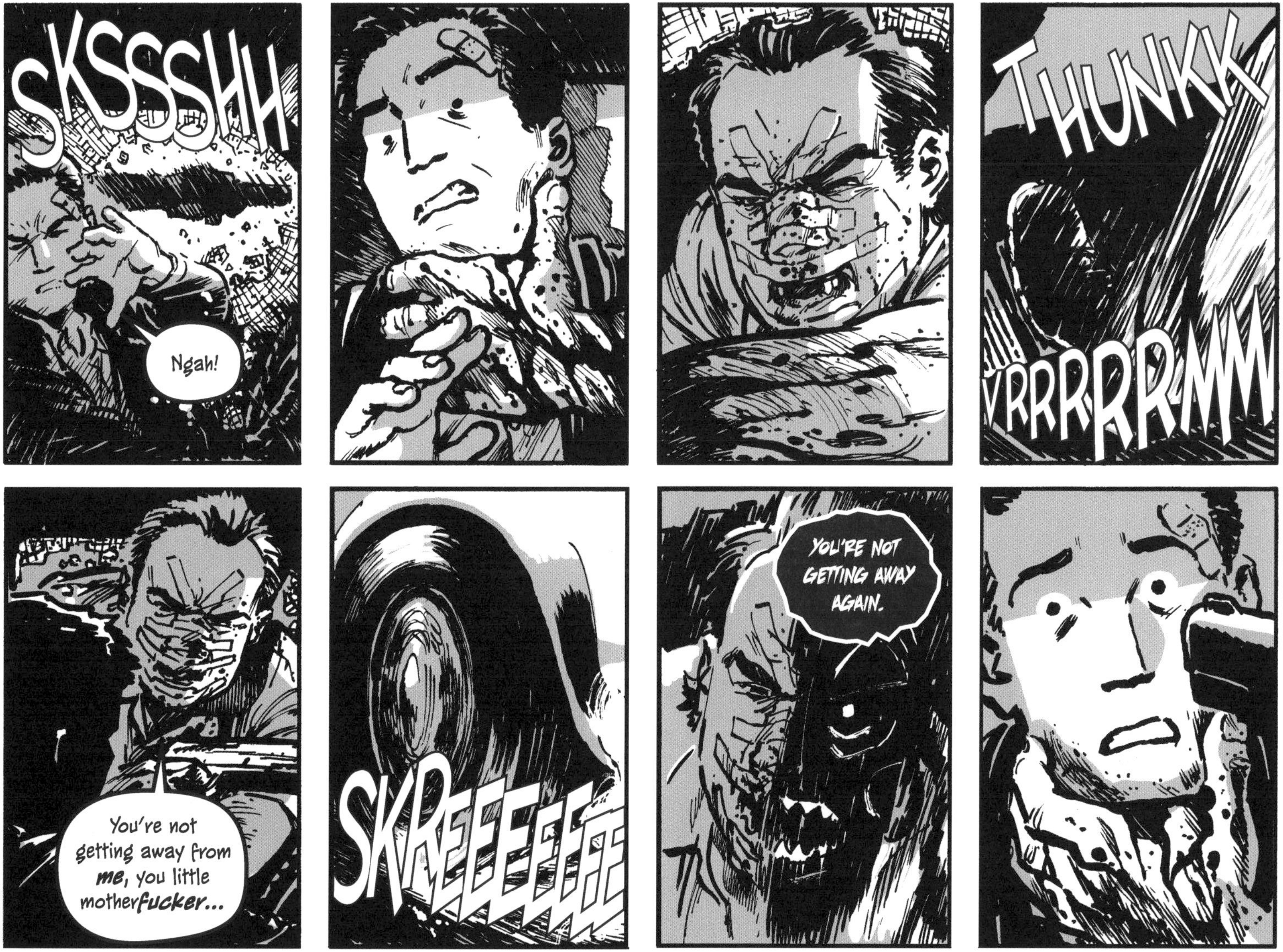
SKSSSHH
Ngah!
THUNKK
VRRRRRRMM
You're not getting away from *me*, you little mother*fucker*...
SKREEEEEEE
YOU'RE NOT GETTING AWAY AGAIN.

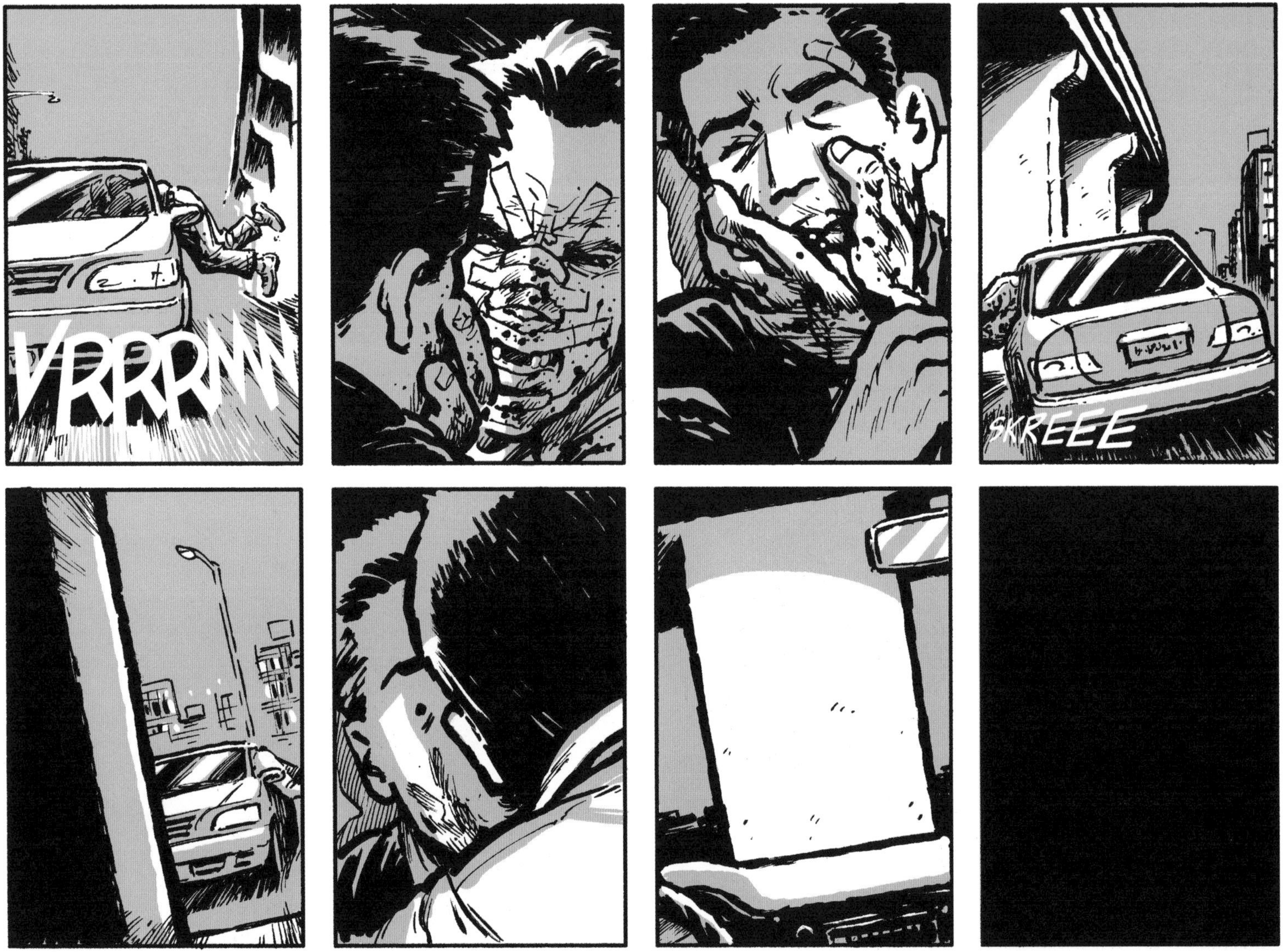

VRRRMM
SKREEE

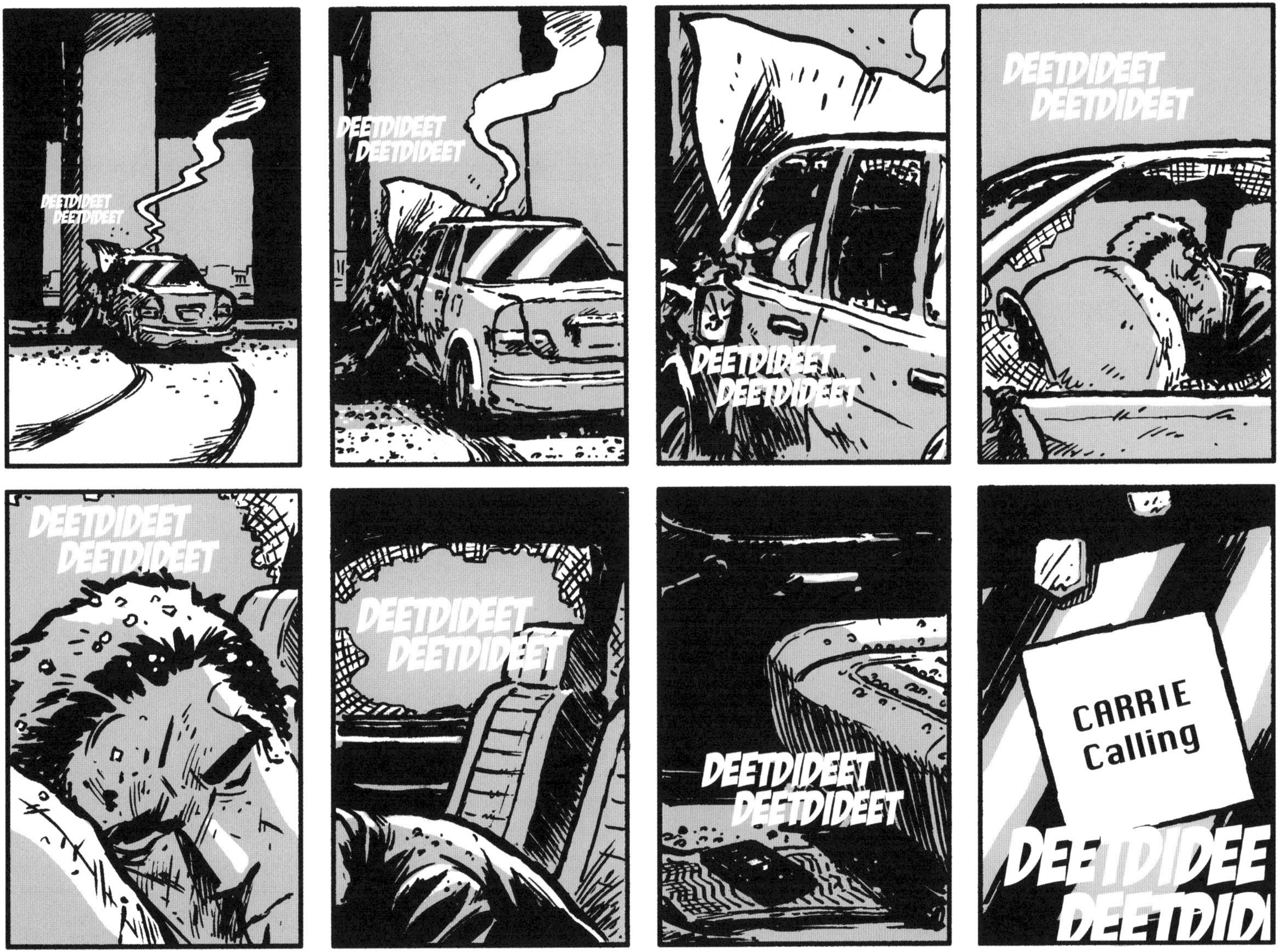
DEETDIDEET DEETDIDEET
DEETDIDEET DEETDIDEET
DEETDIDEET DEETDIDEET
DEETDIDEET DEETDIDEET
DEETDIDEET DEETDIDEET
DEETDIDEET DEETDIDEET
DEETDIDEET DEETDIDEET
CARRIE Calling
DEETDIDEE DEETDIDI

62

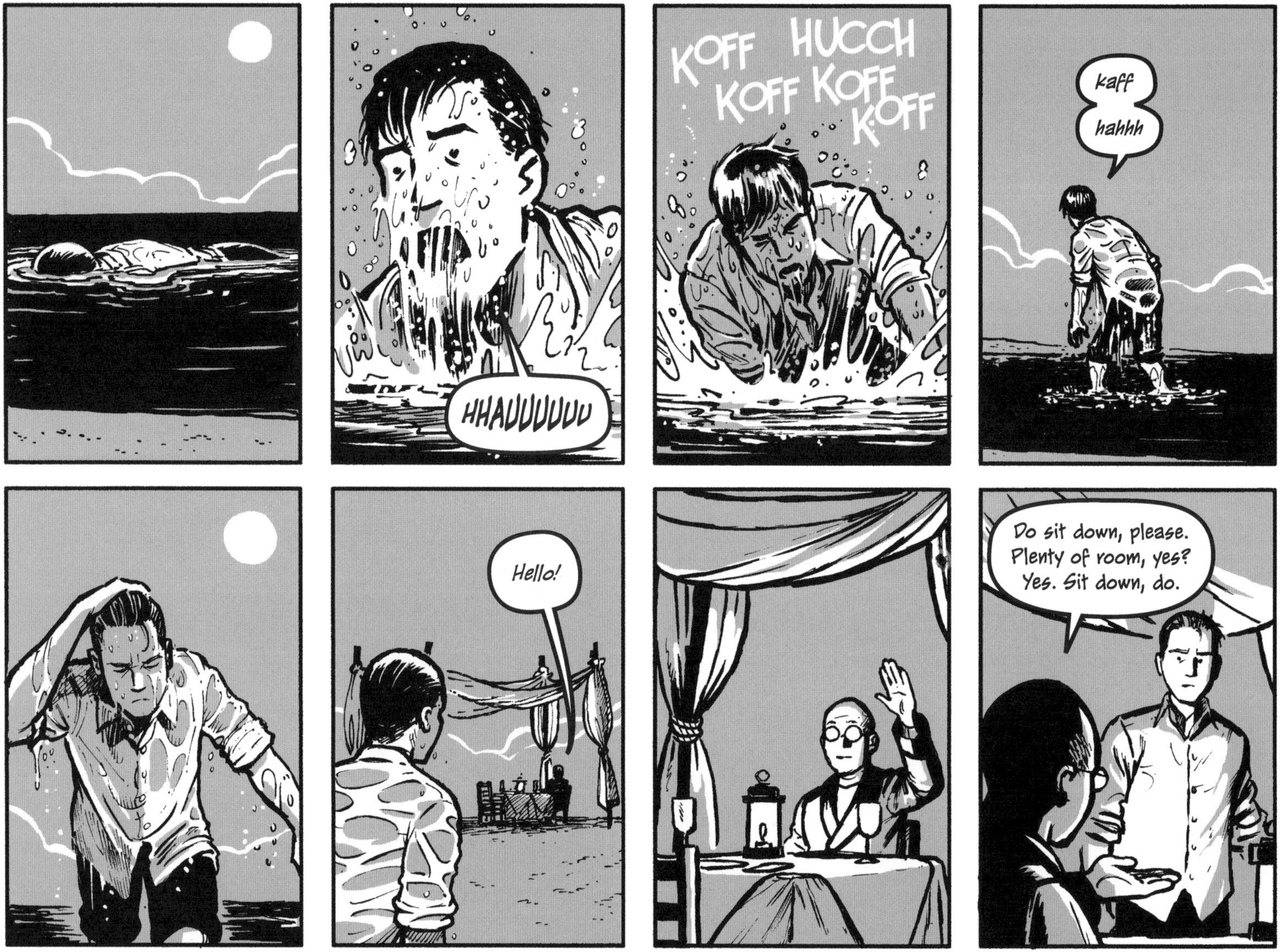
HHAUUUUUU
KOFF HUCCH
KOFF KOFF
KOFF
kaff
hahhh
Hello!
Do sit down, please. Plenty of room, yes? Yes. Sit down, do.

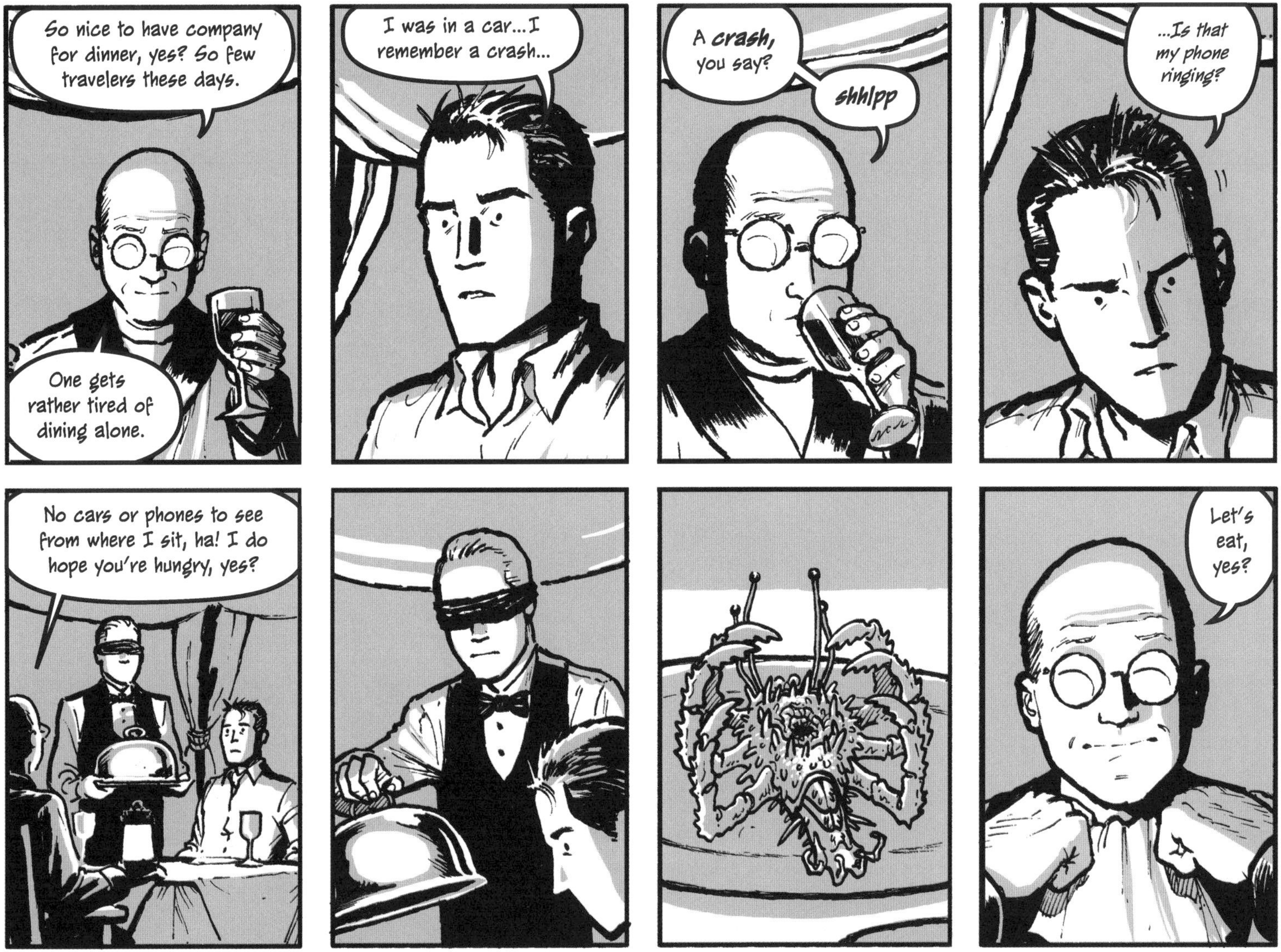

So nice to have company for dinner, yes? So few travelers these days.
One gets rather tired of dining alone.
I was in a car...I remember a crash...
A crash, you say?
shhlpp
...Is that my phone ringing?
No cars or phones to see from where I sit, ha! I do hope you're hungry, yes?
Let's eat, yes?

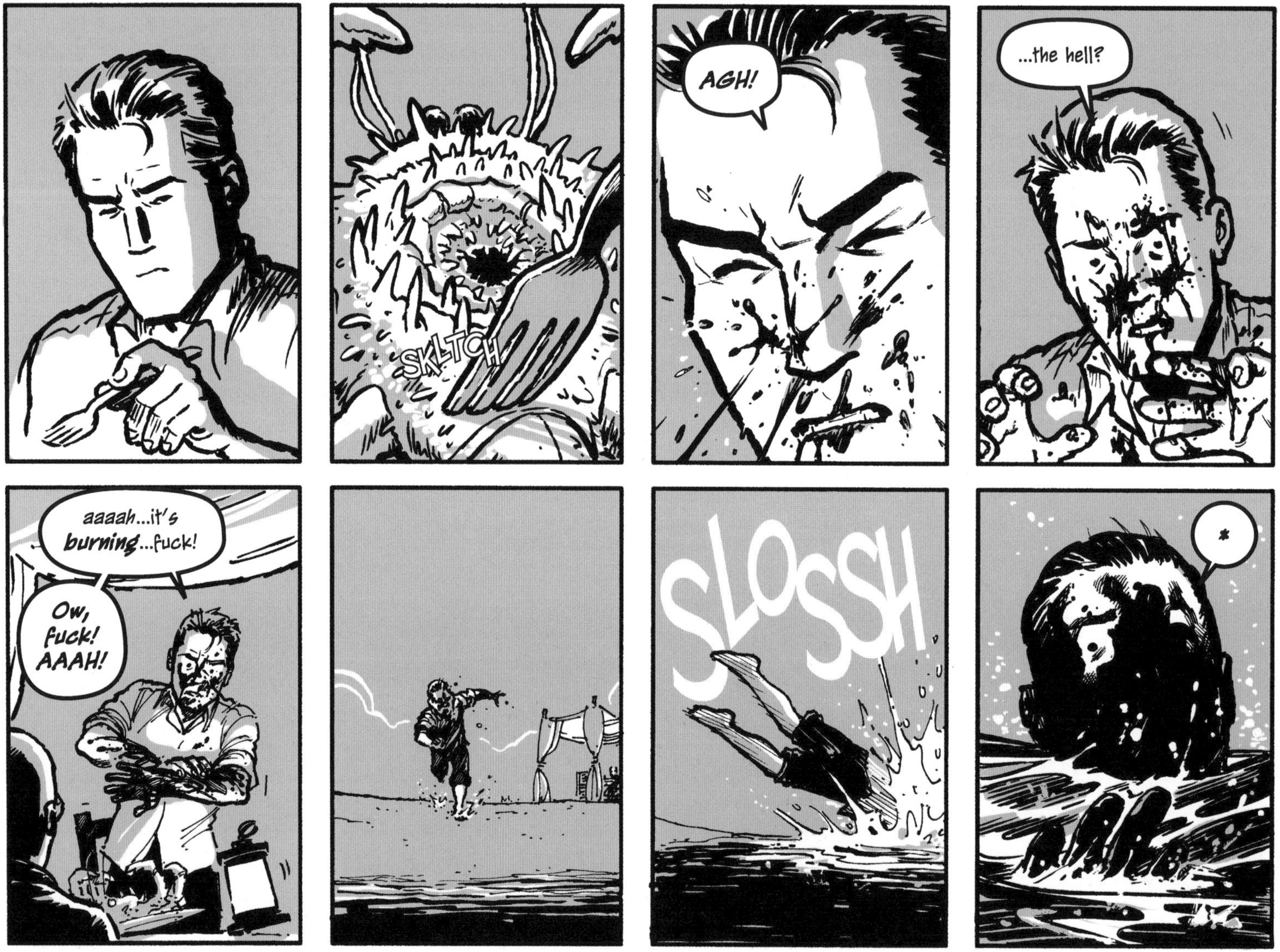
SKLTCH
AGH!
...the hell?
aaaah...it's **burning**...fuck!
Ow, fuck! AAAH!
SLOSSH
*

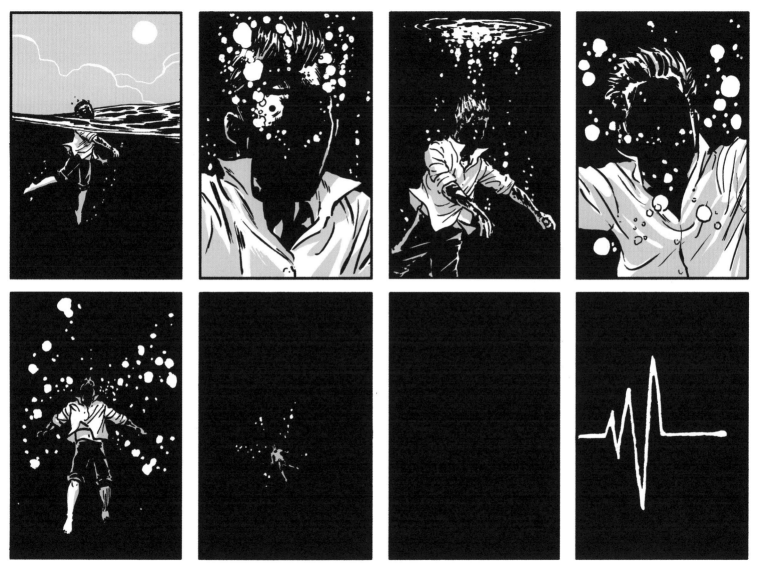

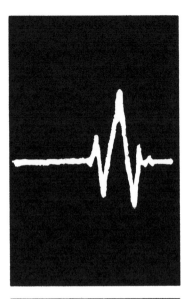

Alex? Alex, are you awake?

Hi.

They, uh, they called me...My number was in your phone.

I called you last night. I guess you'd, uh, you were already...

...you didn't answer.

Alex, what are you doing?

Look at you. You've lost your job. You've lost *me.* You nearly *killed yourself.*

What's it all for?

Is it really worth this?

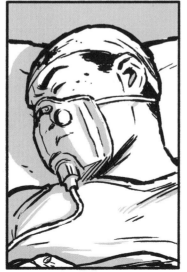

Excuse me, miss, I'm afraid I have to ask you to leave...

...The *police* are here.

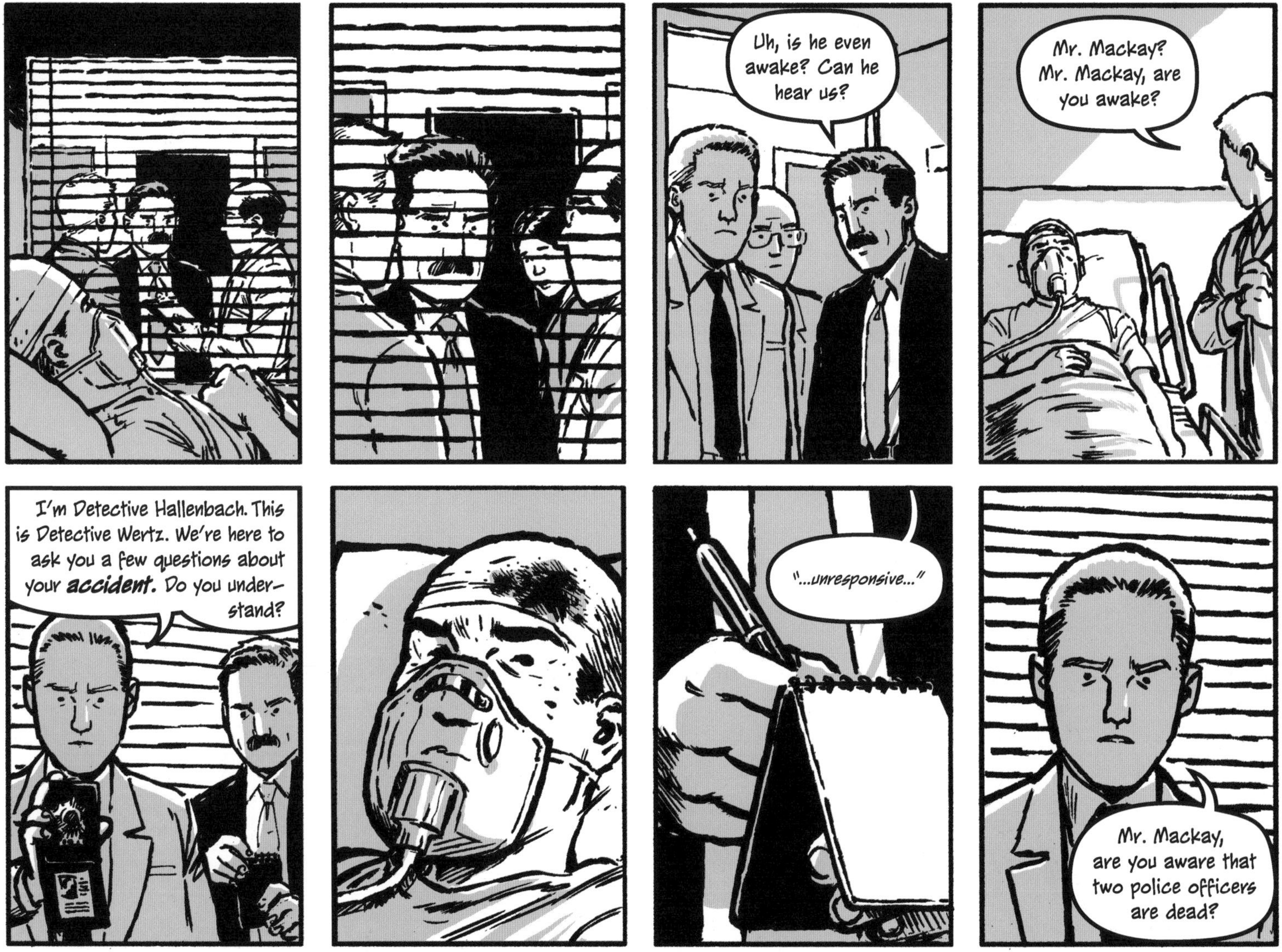
Uh, is he even awake? Can he hear us?
Mr. Mackay? Mr. Mackay, are you awake?
I'm Detective Hallenbach. This is Detective Wertz. We're here to ask you a few questions about your **accident.** Do you understand?
"...unresponsive..."
Mr. Mackay, are you aware that two police officers are dead?

Two patrolmen were responding to an **assault** at Glendale Acres Retirement Community.

As we understand it, you had a relative living there?

Roughly thirty minutes after the officers arrived on the scene, their **bodies** were found--

"...torn to pieces."

Their squad car was found abandoned several miles away, very near the scene of your accident.

We found the service weapon of one of the deceased officers in the front seat of your car.

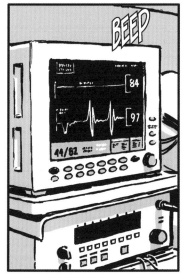

BEEP

84
97
44/62

This makes you a person of **great interest**, Mr. Mackay--

BEEP

"Hey, Doc, is he all right?"

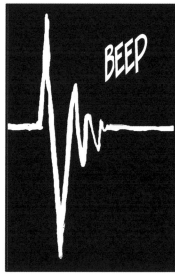

BEEP

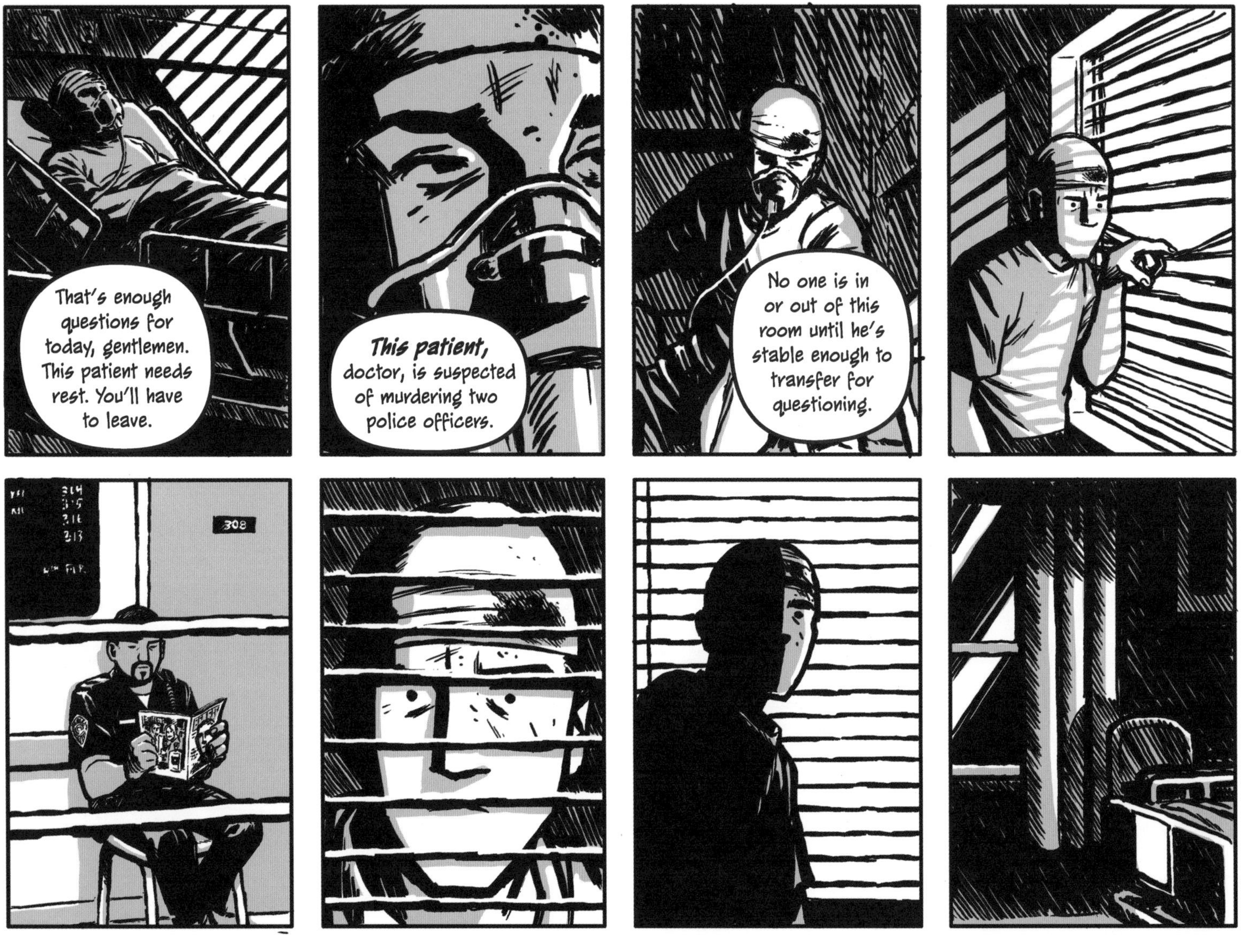
That's enough questions for today, gentlemen. This patient needs rest. You'll have to leave.
This patient, doctor, is suspected of murdering two police officers.
No one is in or out of this room until he's stable enough to transfer for questioning.
308

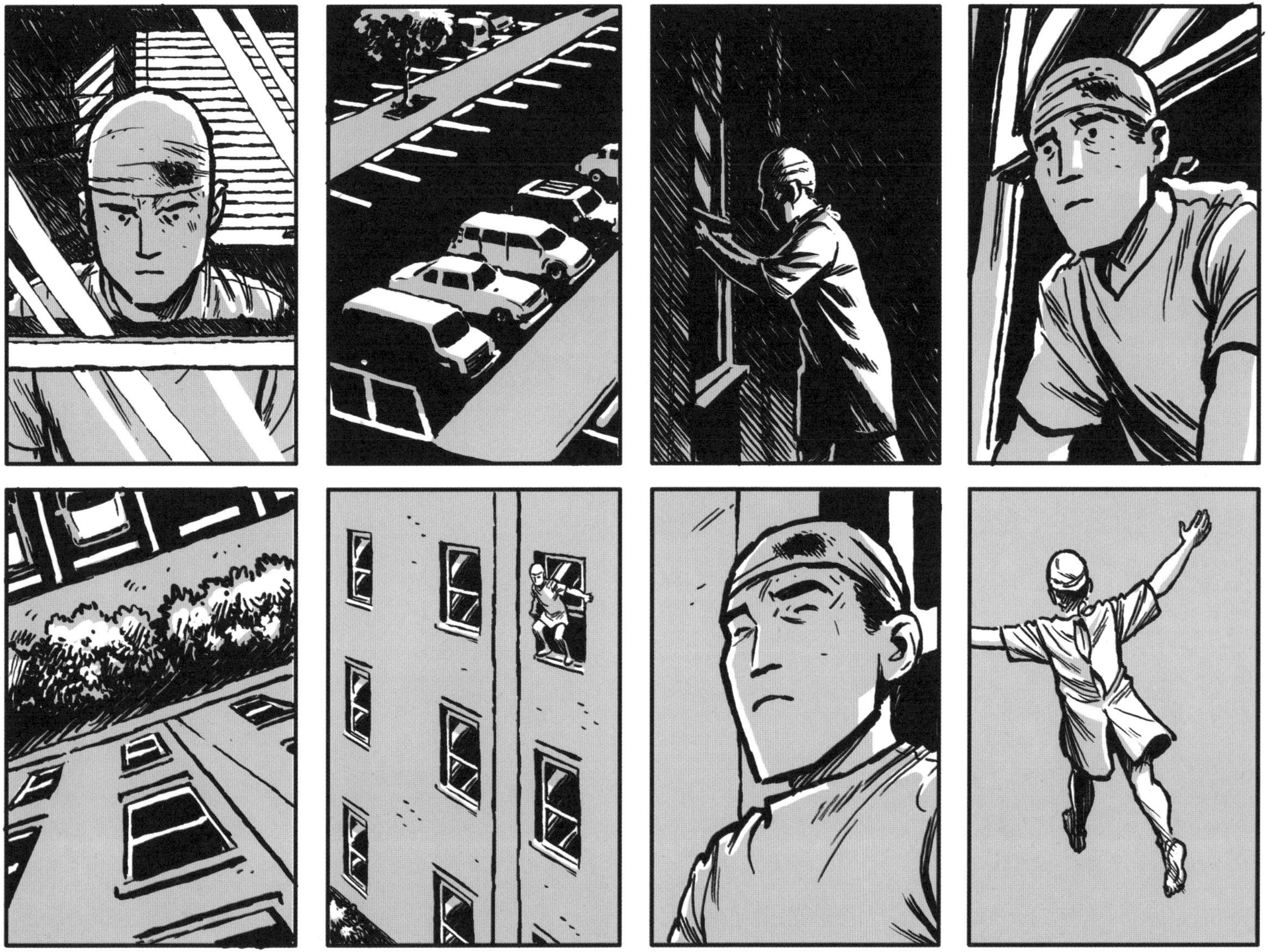

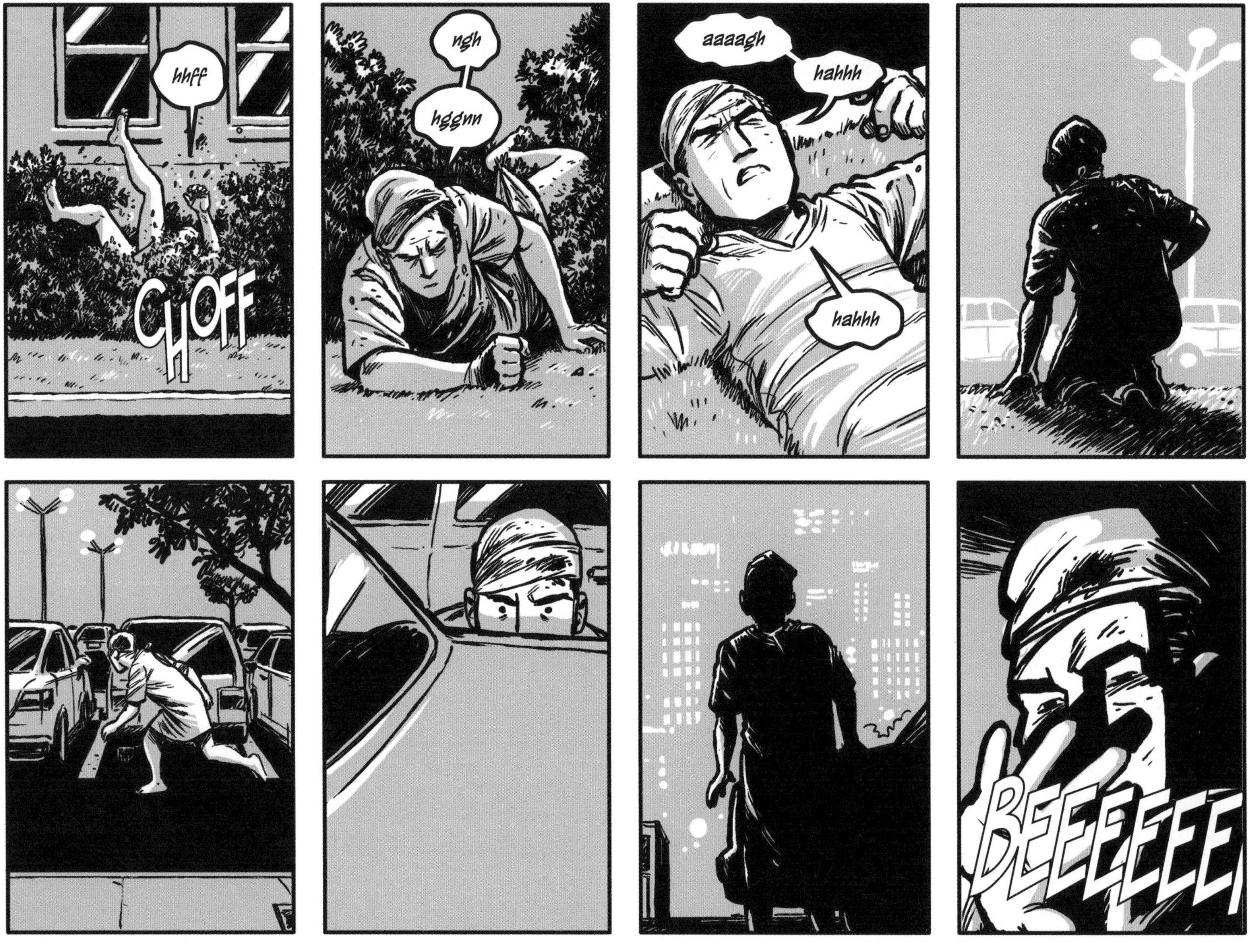
hhff
CHOFF
ngh
hggnn
aaaagh
hahhh
hahhh
BEEEEEE

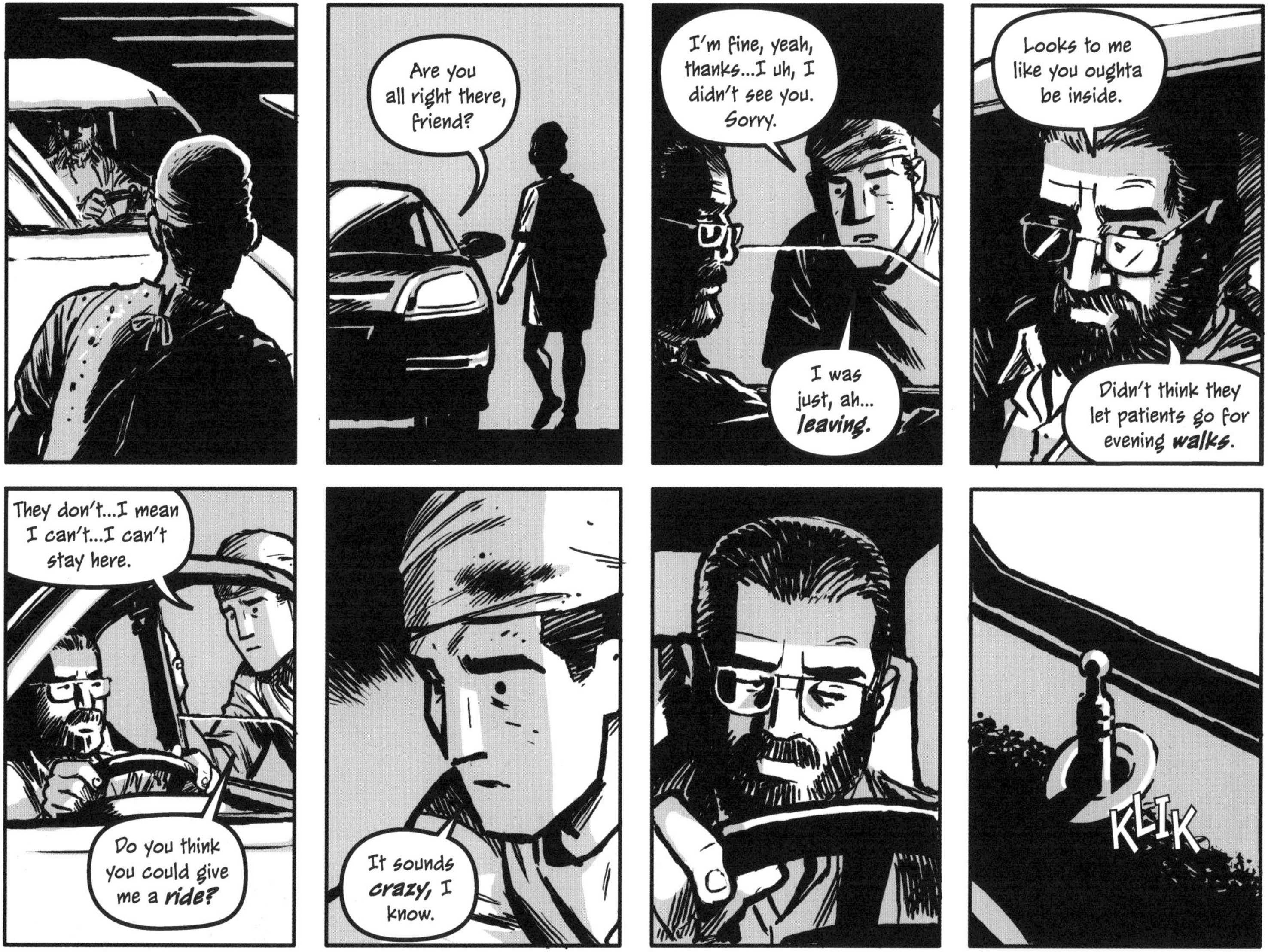
Are you all right there, friend?
I'm fine, yeah, thanks...I uh, I didn't see you. Sorry.
I was just, ah... leaving.
Looks to me like you oughta be inside.
Didn't think they let patients go for evening walks.
They don't...I mean I can't...I can't stay here.
Do you think you could give me a ride?
It sounds crazy, I know.
KLIK

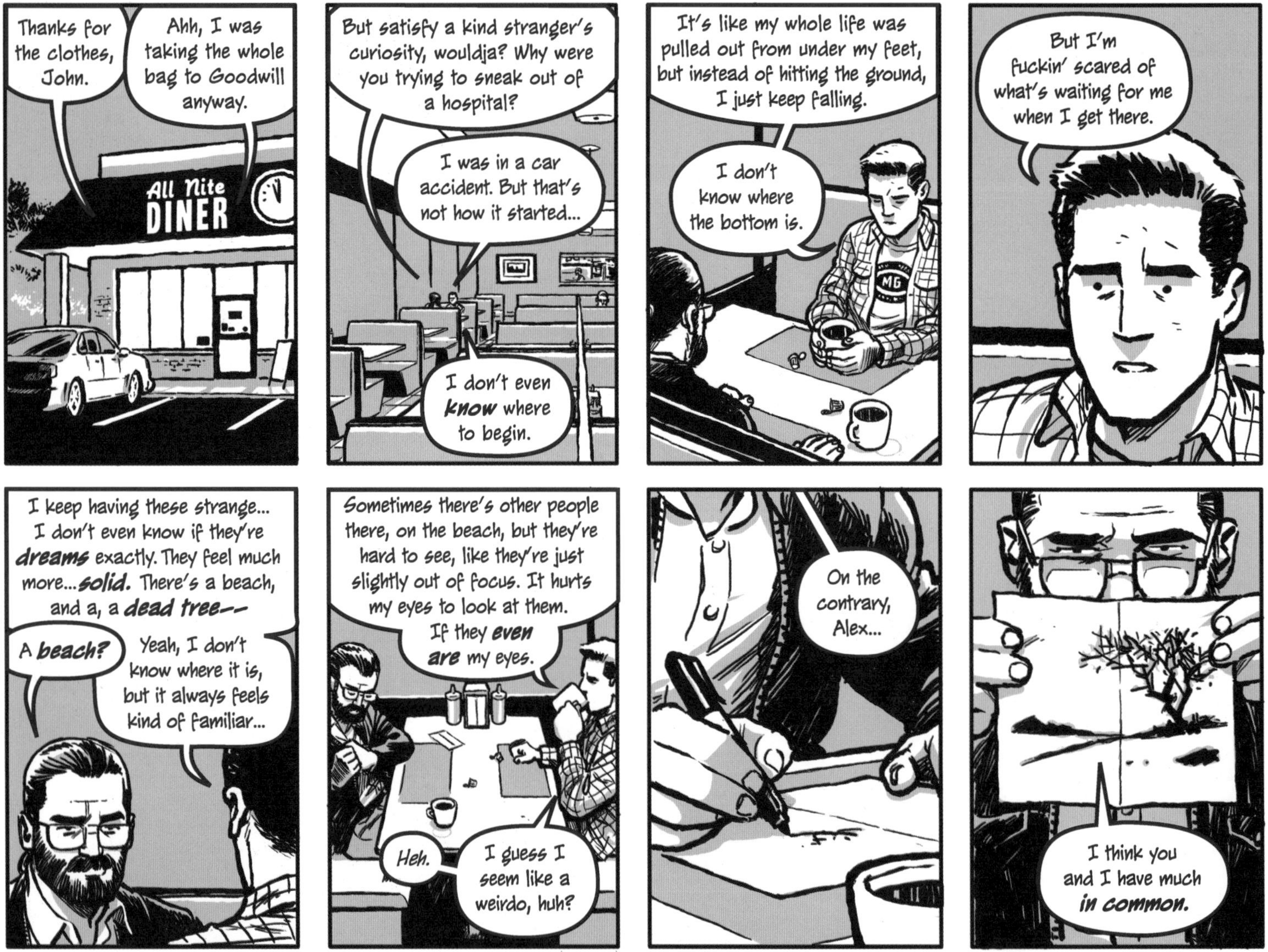

Thanks for the clothes, John.
Ahh, I was taking the whole bag to Goodwill anyway.
All Nite DINER
But satisfy a kind stranger's curiosity, wouldja? Why were you trying to sneak out of a hospital?
I was in a car accident. But that's not how it started...
I don't even **know** where to begin.
It's like my whole life was pulled out from under my feet, but instead of hitting the ground, I just keep falling.
I don't know where the bottom is.
But I'm fuckin' scared of what's waiting for me when I get there.
I keep having these strange... I don't even know if they're ***dreams*** exactly. They feel much more...***solid.*** There's a beach, and a, a ***dead tree--***
A ***beach?***
Yeah, I don't know where it is, but it always feels kind of familiar...
Sometimes there's other people there, on the beach, but they're hard to see, like they're just slightly out of focus. It hurts my eyes to look at them.
If they ***even are*** my eyes.
Heh.
I guess I seem like a weirdo, huh?
On the contrary, Alex...
I think you and I have much ***in common.***

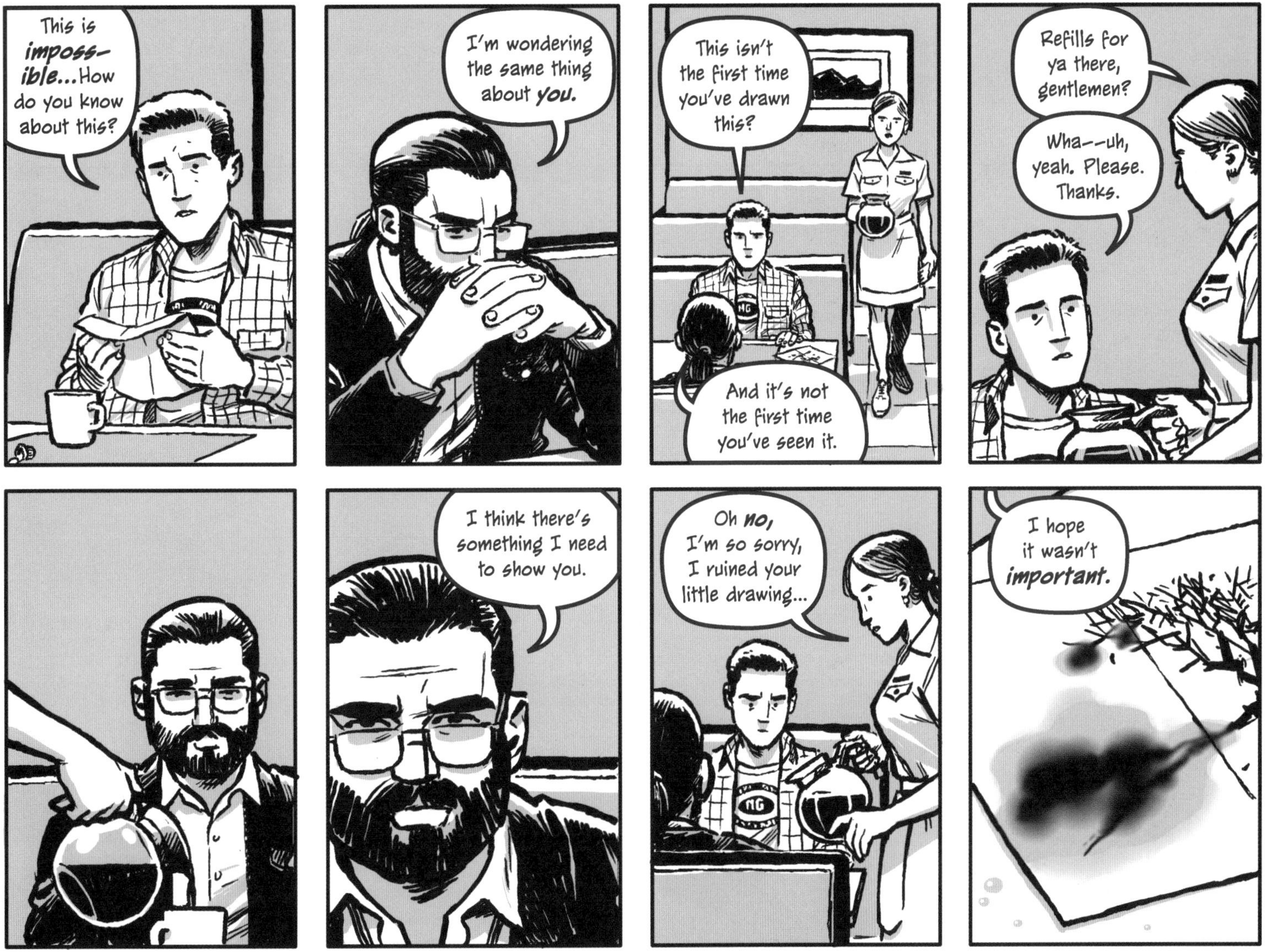
This is **imposs-ible...** How do you know about this?
I'm wondering the same thing about **you.**
This isn't the first time you've drawn this?
And it's not the first time you've seen it.
Refills for ya there, gentlemen?
Wha--uh, yeah. Please. Thanks.
I think there's something I need to show you.
Oh **no,** I'm so sorry, I ruined your little drawing...
I hope it wasn't **important.**

...for your busy lifestyle.

Thanks, Mom!

And how was everything this evening?

Have A Nice Day!

Fine, thanks. Great.

City police have issued an alert this evening after a suspect in the brutal slaying of two officers escaped from Westboro Hospital.

Alex Mackay, seen here in a recent photograph, was under supervision after being involved in a car accident near the scene of the killings.

Mackay was able to escape custody earlier this evening, and is now at large.

PECT IN POLICE MUR

Police advise that he is to be considered ex-tremely dangerous, and ask that any information be reported immediately.

Hope we see you again real soon!

Well?

Are you coming, or what?

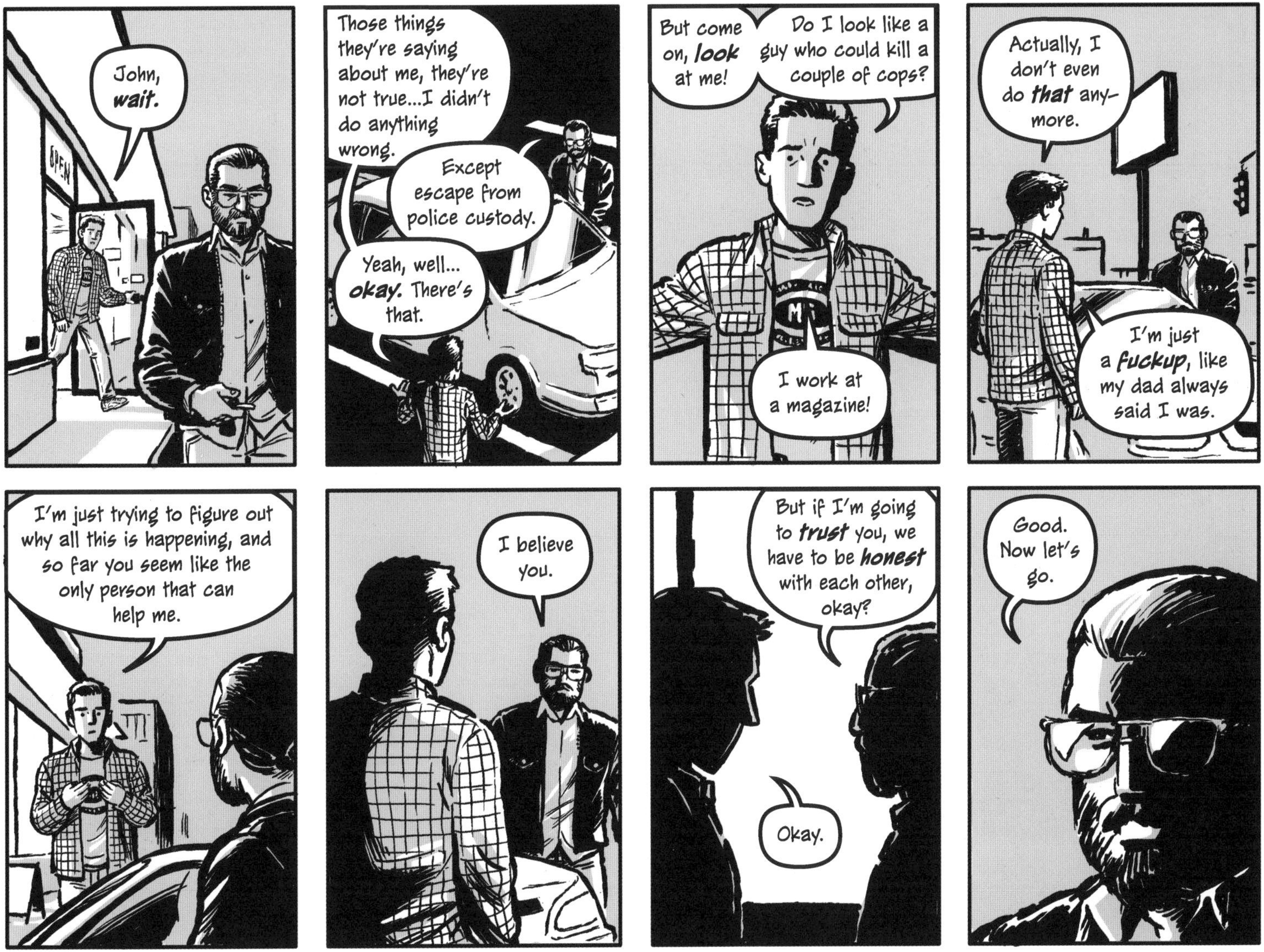

John, *wait.*
Those things they're saying about me, they're not true...I didn't do anything wrong.
Except escape from police custody.
Yeah, well... *okay.* There's that.
But come on, *look* at me!
Do I look like a guy who could kill a couple of cops?
I work at a magazine!
Actually, I don't even do *that* anymore.
I'm just a *fuckup,* like my dad always said I was.
I'm just trying to figure out why all this is happening, and so far you seem like the only person that can help me.
I believe you.
But if I'm going to *trust* you, we have to be *honest* with each other, okay?
Okay.
Good. Now let's go.

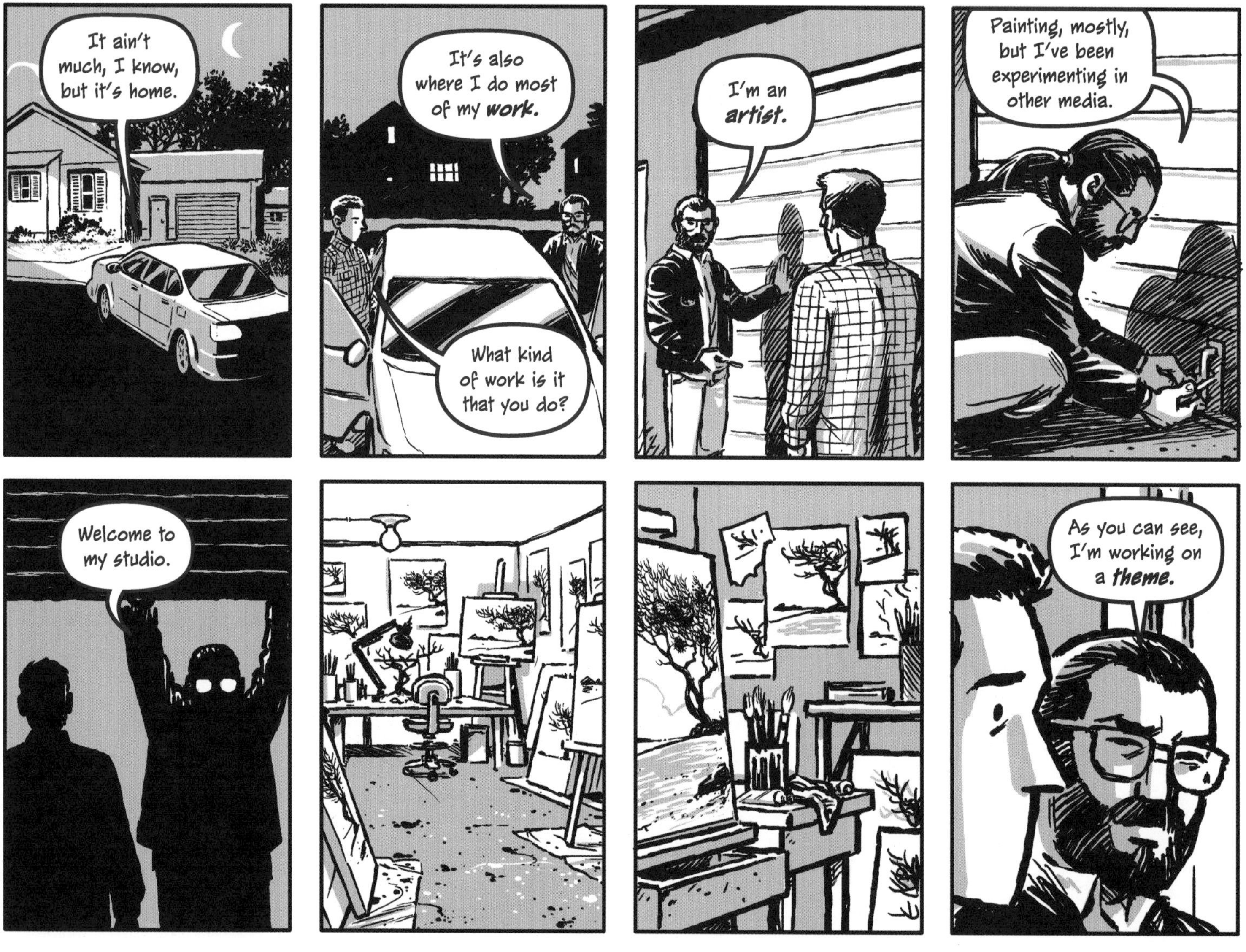
It ain't much, I know, but it's home.
It's also where I do most of my *work.*
What kind of work is it that you do?
I'm an *artist.*
Painting, mostly, but I've been experimenting in other media.
Welcome to my studio.
As you can see, I'm working on a *theme.*

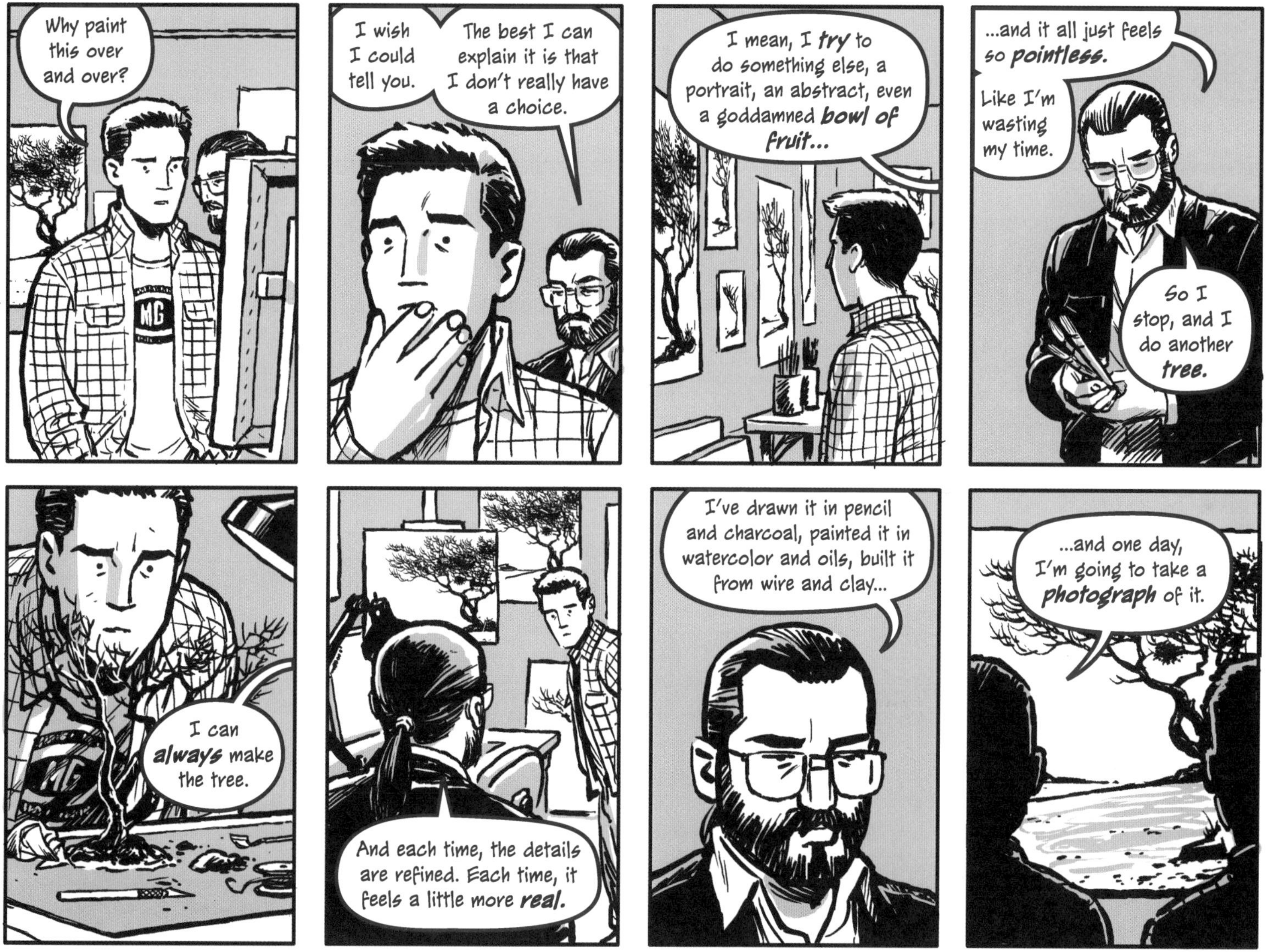
Why paint this over and over?
I wish I could tell you.
The best I can explain it is that I don't really have a choice.
I mean, I try to do something else, a portrait, an abstract, even a goddamned bowl of fruit...
...and it all just feels so pointless.
Like I'm wasting my time.
So I stop, and I do another tree.
I can always make the tree.
And each time, the details are refined. Each time, it feels a little more real.
I've drawn it in pencil and charcoal, painted it in watercolor and oils, built it from wire and clay...
...and one day, I'm going to take a photograph of it.

I was never a particularly good student. Having no care or aptitude for math and science, I spent most of my days lost in private thought, oblivious to the lesson.

The only class that held my attention was Creative Writing. My teacher, Mrs. Lamb, was more than happy to spend extra time with me after the bell, encouraging my interest.

She remarked that I had great "potential."

Eager for her approval but lacking any ideas of my own, I turned in a story plagiarized from a science-fiction anthology she was unlikely to have read.

The ruse worked, and she was impressed with the sophistication of my prose. She handed out copies of the story to the class the next day.

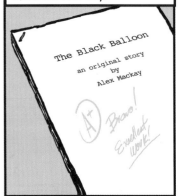

The Black Balloon
an original story
by
Alex Mackay

A+ Bravo!
Excellent work!

My parents had been divorced for almost a year, and weekends I spent with my father. Usually we would go see a movie, an activity that allowed us to be in each other's company, but avoid talking.

Each week we would alternate who chose the movie. Our tastes rarely matched, and one of us would sit through the other's selection in silent resentment.

The silence would almost always extend to dinner, which was invariably spaghetti or a similar bachelor's recipe.

How's school going?

It's okay, I guess. I don't really pay much attention.

Christ.

You're just like your fuckin' mother.

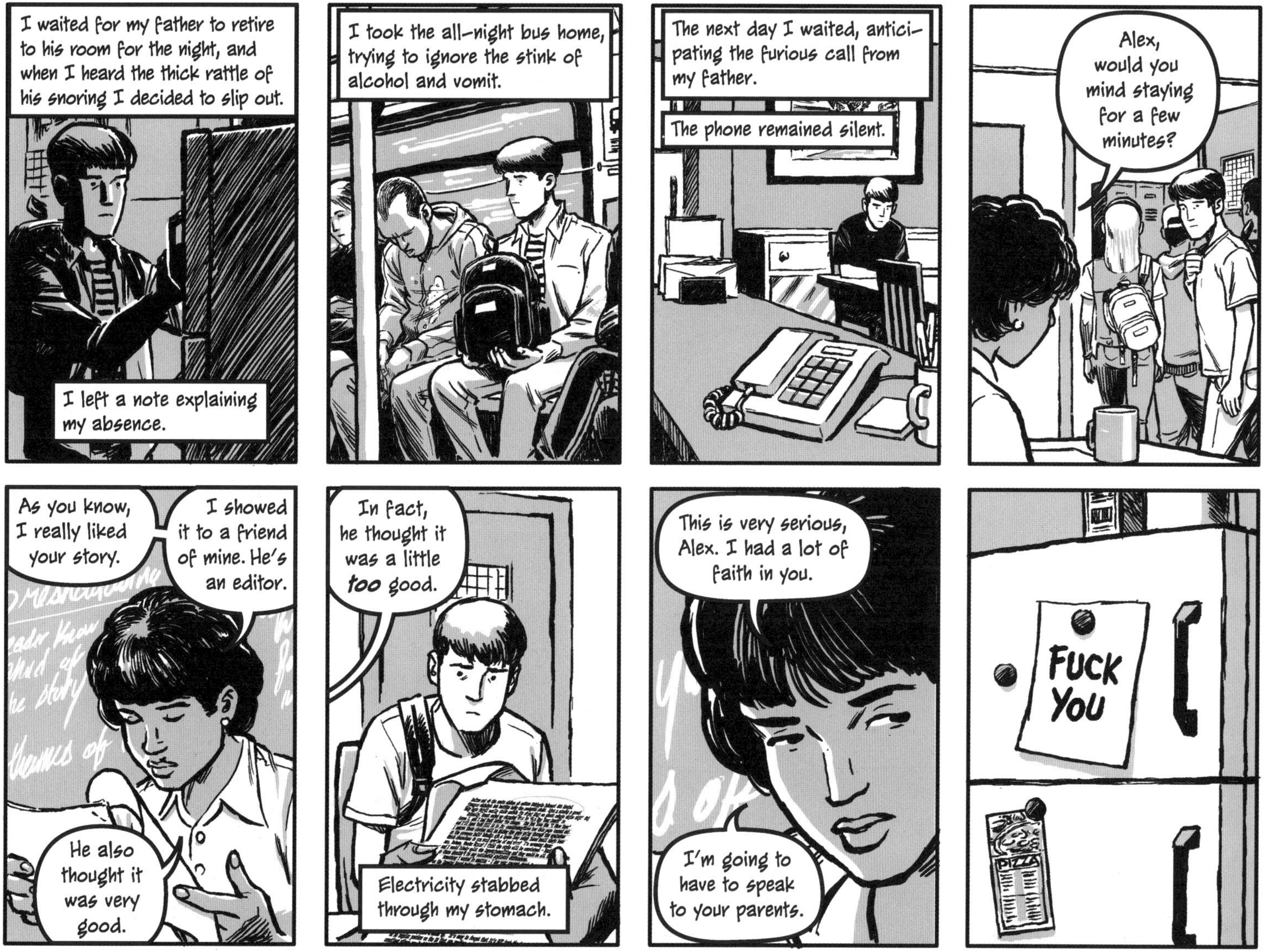

I waited for my father to retire to his room for the night, and when I heard the thick rattle of his snoring I decided to slip out.
I left a note explaining my absence.
I took the all-night bus home, trying to ignore the stink of alcohol and vomit.
The next day I waited, anticipating the furious call from my father.
The phone remained silent.
Alex, would you mind staying for a few minutes?
As you know, I really liked your story.
I showed it to a friend of mine. He's an editor.
He also thought it was very good.
In fact, he thought it was a little *too* good.
Electricity stabbed through my stomach.
This is very serious, Alex. I had a lot of faith in you.
I'm going to have to speak to your parents.
FUCK YOU
PIZZA

81

My mother was unavailable, so it was my father who came to school to collect me.

Mrs. Lamb explained what I had done, and expressed her disappointment to my father, who sat and listened, silent and inscrutable.

The only time he addressed me directly was to tell me we were leaving.

So was your little note on my fridge an original composition, or did you cheat on that one too?

Like you're one to talk about *cheating.*

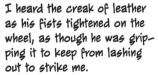

I heard the creak of leather as his fists tightened on the wheel, as though he was gripping it to keep from lashing out to strike me.

You know, for such a stupid kid you've got a real smart mouth.

That's going to get you into trouble one day.

82

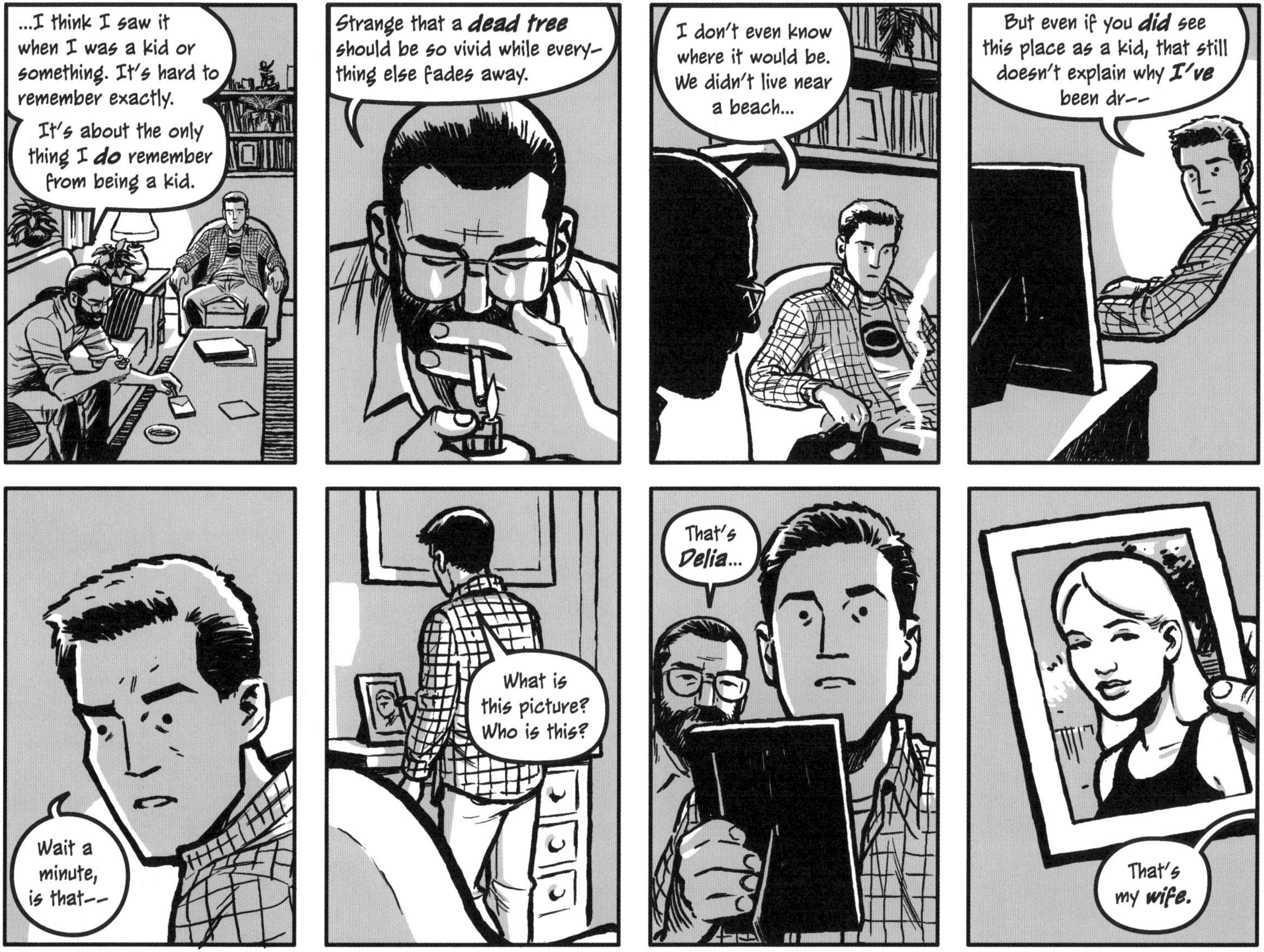
...I think I saw it when I was a kid or something. It's hard to remember exactly.
It's about the only thing I do remember from being a kid.
Strange that a dead tree should be so vivid while every-thing else fades away.
I don't even know where it would be. We didn't live near a beach...
But even if you did see this place as a kid, that still doesn't explain why I've been dr--
Wait a minute, is that--
What is this picture? Who is this?
That's Delia...
That's my wife.

83

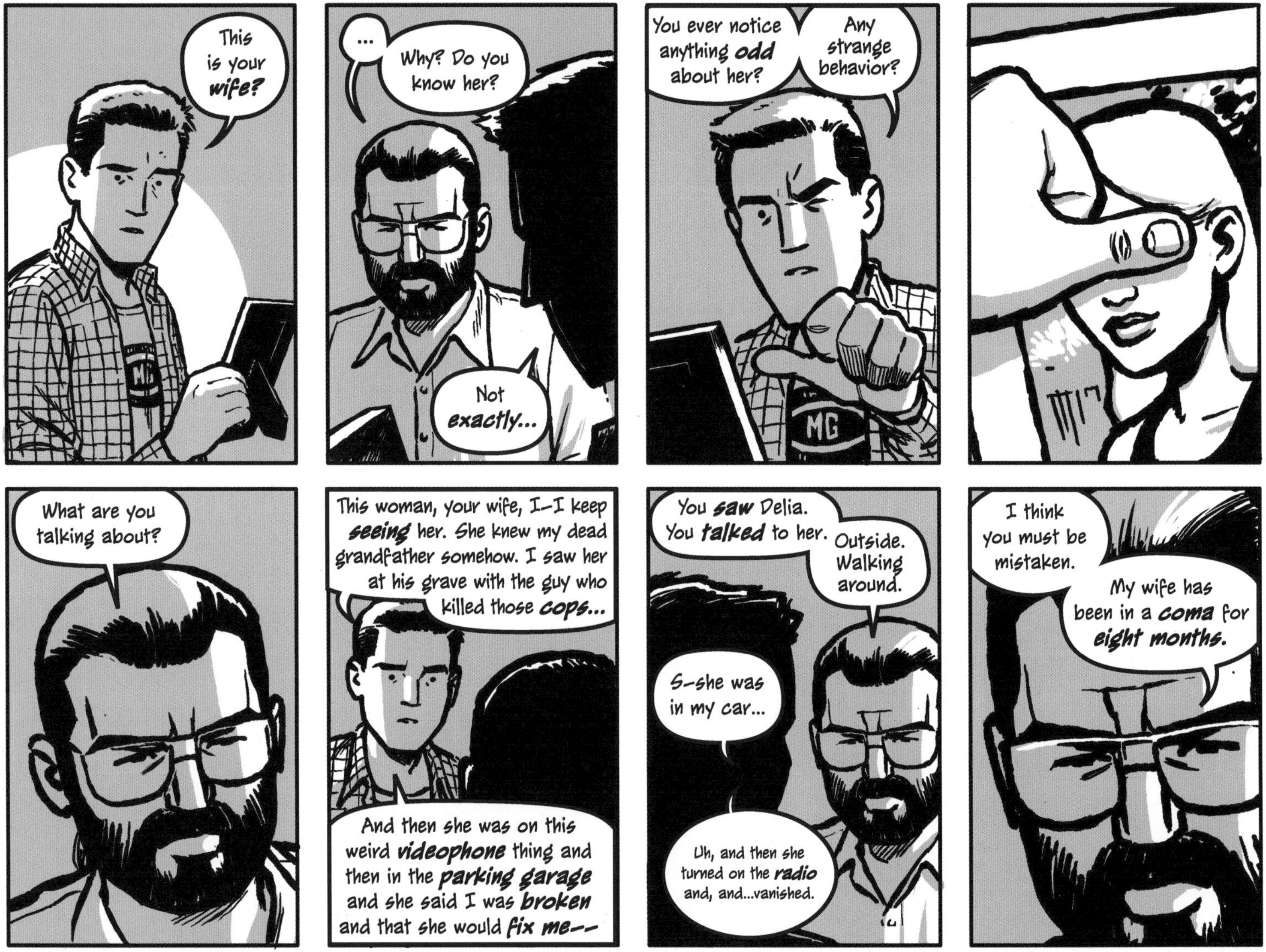
This is your wife?
...
Why? Do you know her?
Not exactly...
You ever notice anything odd about her?
Any strange behavior?
What are you talking about?
This woman, your wife, I–I keep seeing her. She knew my dead grandfather somehow. I saw her at his grave with the guy who killed those cops...
And then she was on this weird videophone thing and then in the parking garage and she said I was broken and that she would fix me––
You saw Delia. You talked to her.
Outside. Walking around.
S–she was in my car...
Uh, and then she turned on the radio and, and...vanished.
I think you must be mistaken.
My wife has been in a coma for eight months.

The accident was last fall.

We'd decided to go on a cycling trip together.

I was having a dry spell with my painting, and she thought the mountain air would be good for me.

She looked prettier without her helmet, but she

lost

her

grip

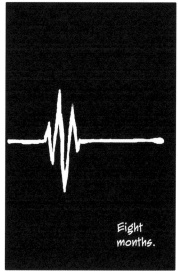

Eight months.

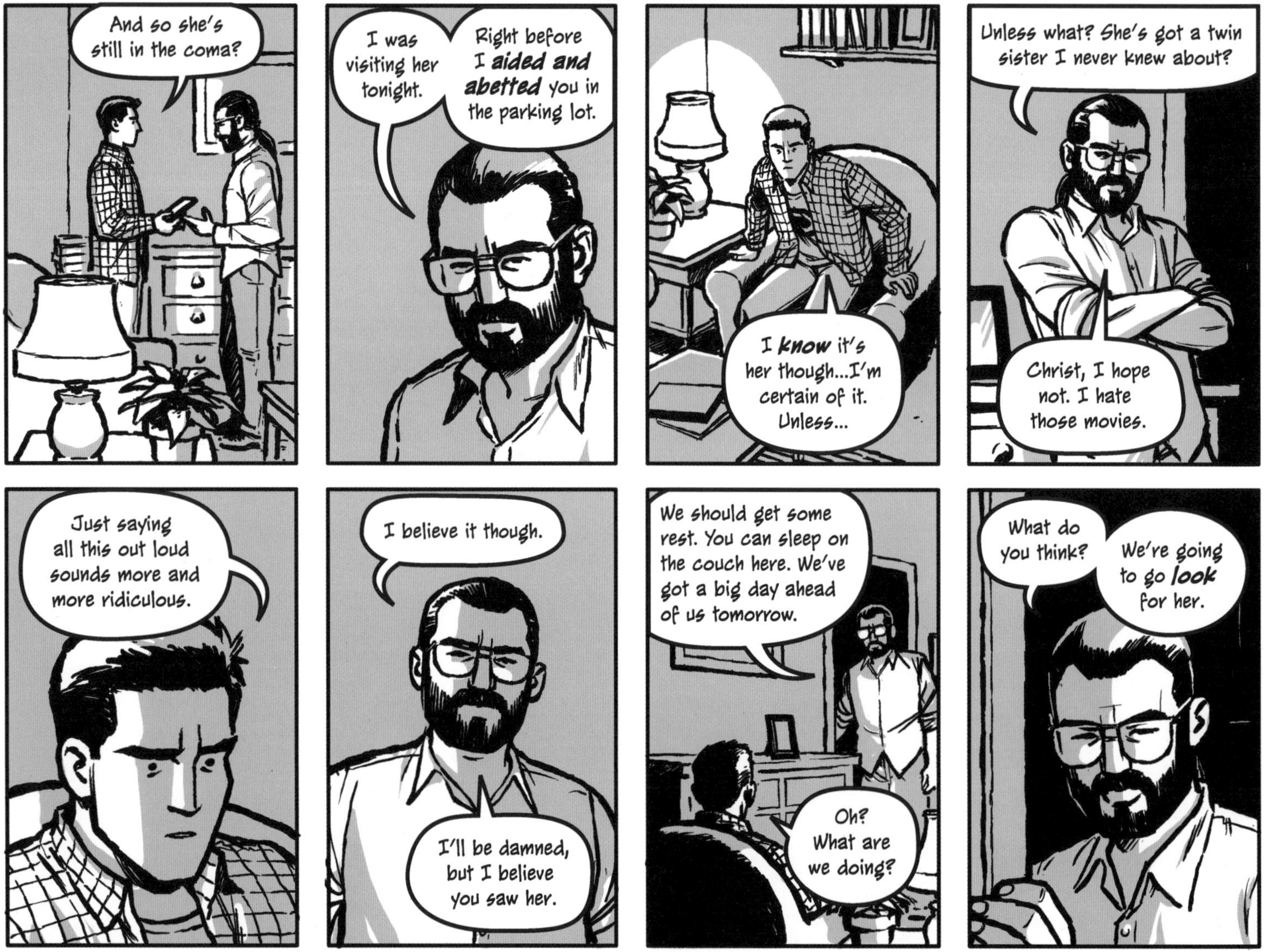
And so she's still in the coma?
I was visiting her tonight.
Right before I aided and abetted you in the parking lot.
I know it's her though...I'm certain of it. Unless...
Unless what? She's got a twin sister I never knew about?
Christ, I hope not. I hate those movies.
Just saying all this out loud sounds more and more ridiculous.
I believe it though.
I'll be damned, but I believe you saw her.
We should get some rest. You can sleep on the couch here. We've got a big day ahead of us tomorrow.
Oh? What are we doing?
What do you think?
We're going to go look for her.

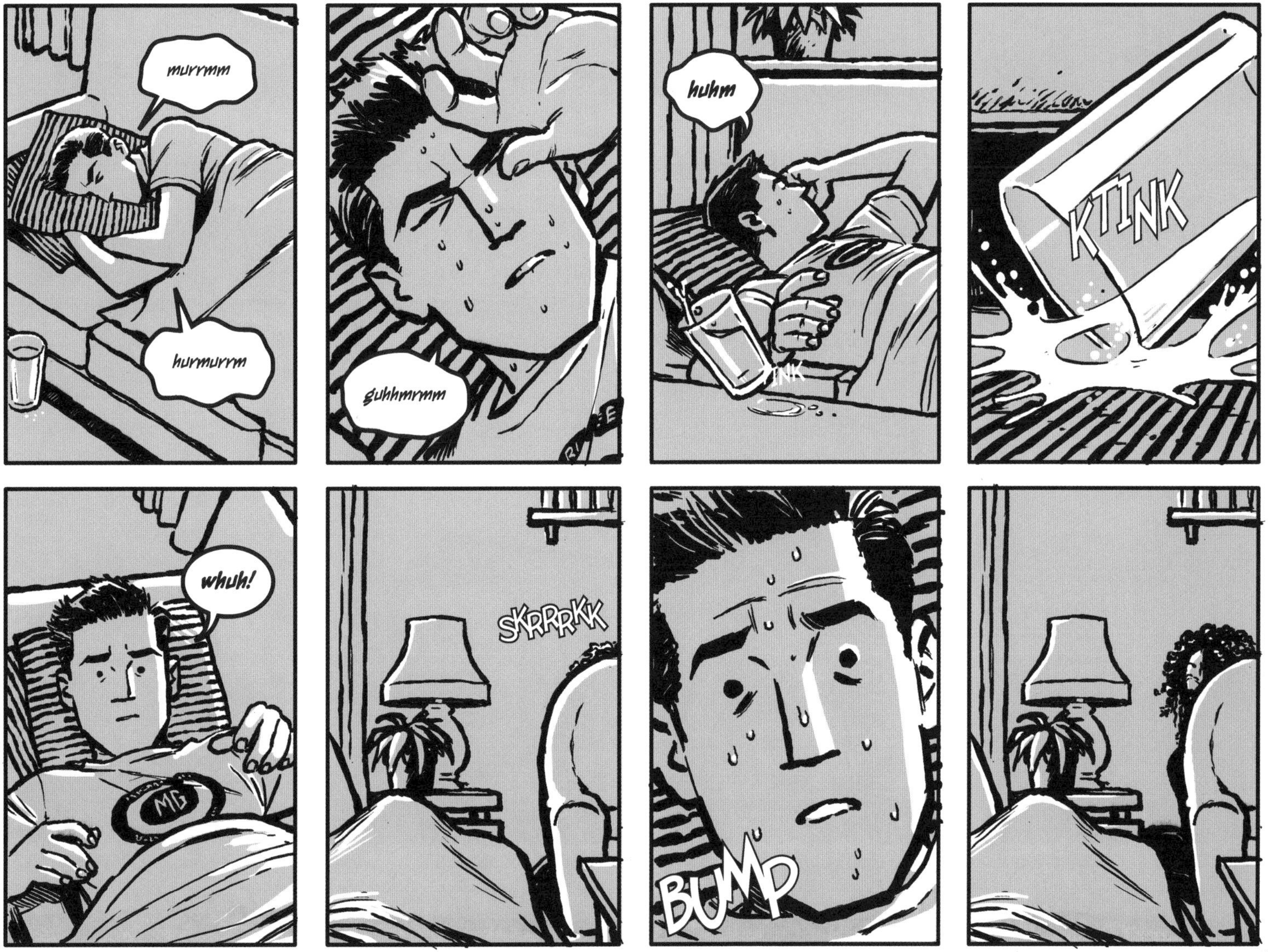
murrmm
hurmurrm
guhhmrmm
huhm
TINK
KTINK
whuh!
SKRRRRKK
BUMP

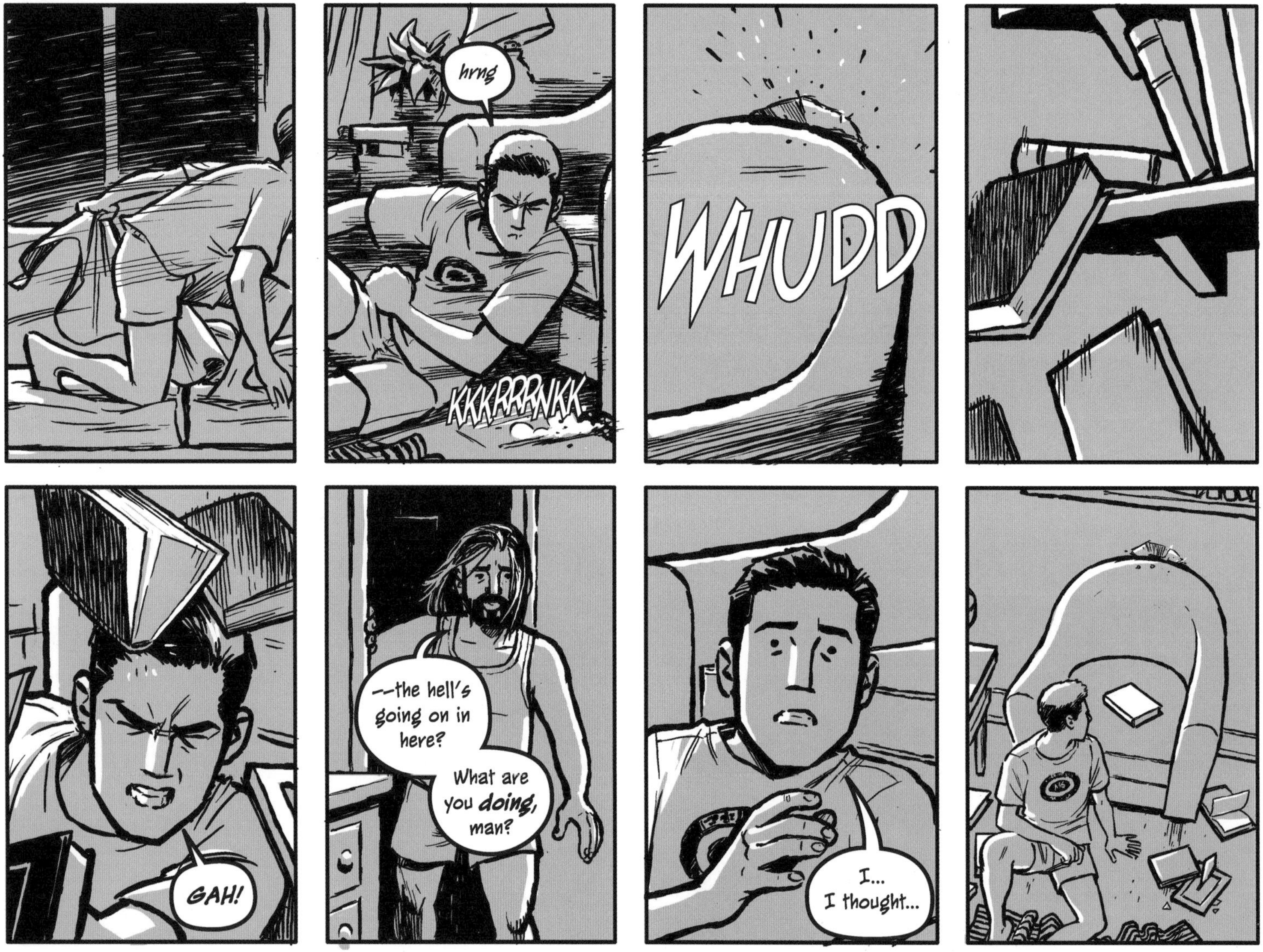
hrng
KKKRRRNKK
WHUDD
GAH!
--the hell's going on in here?
What are you **doing**, man?
I... I thought...

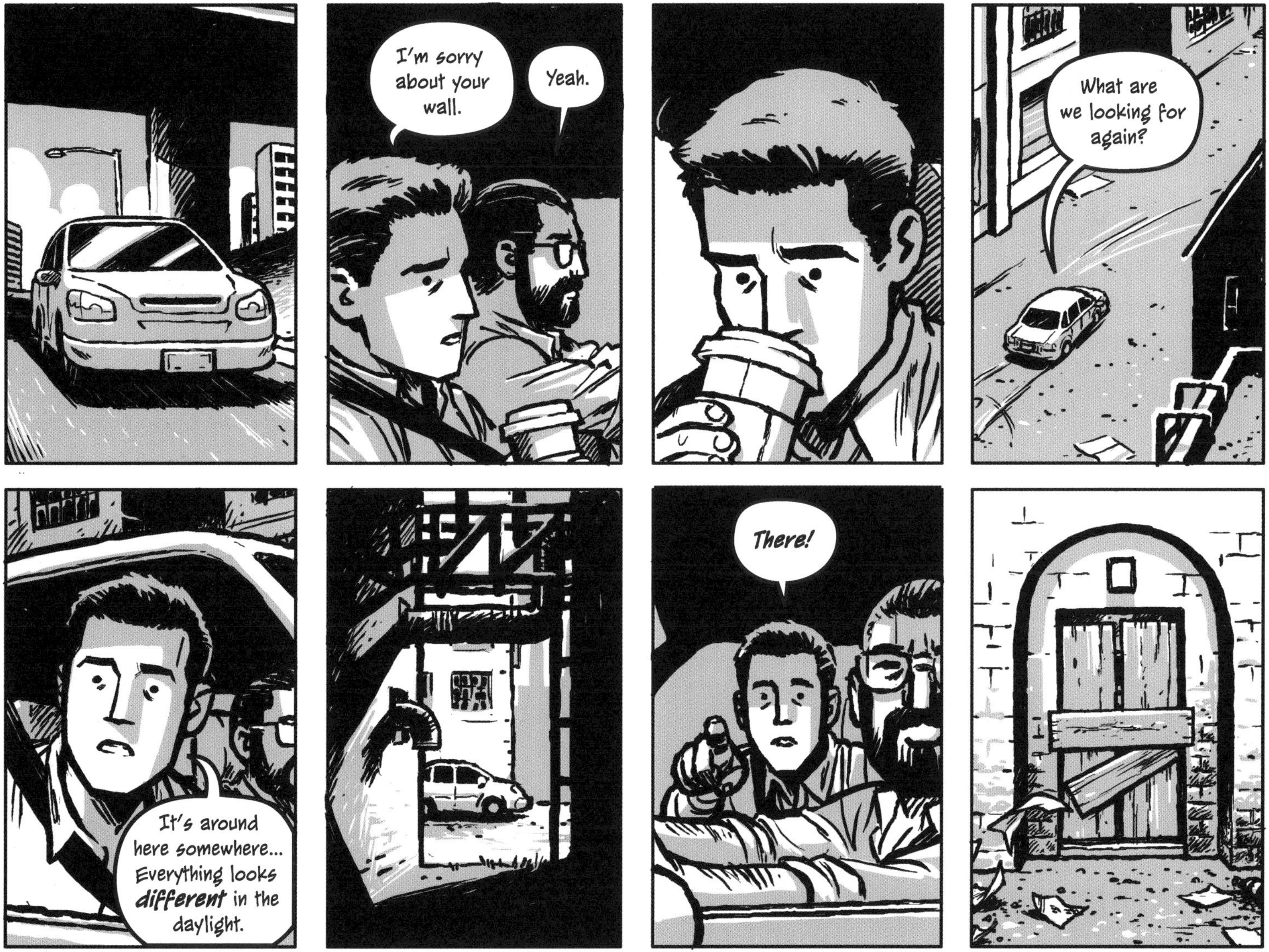
I'm sorry about your wall.
Yeah.
What are we looking for again?
It's around here somewhere... Everything looks ***different*** in the daylight.
There!

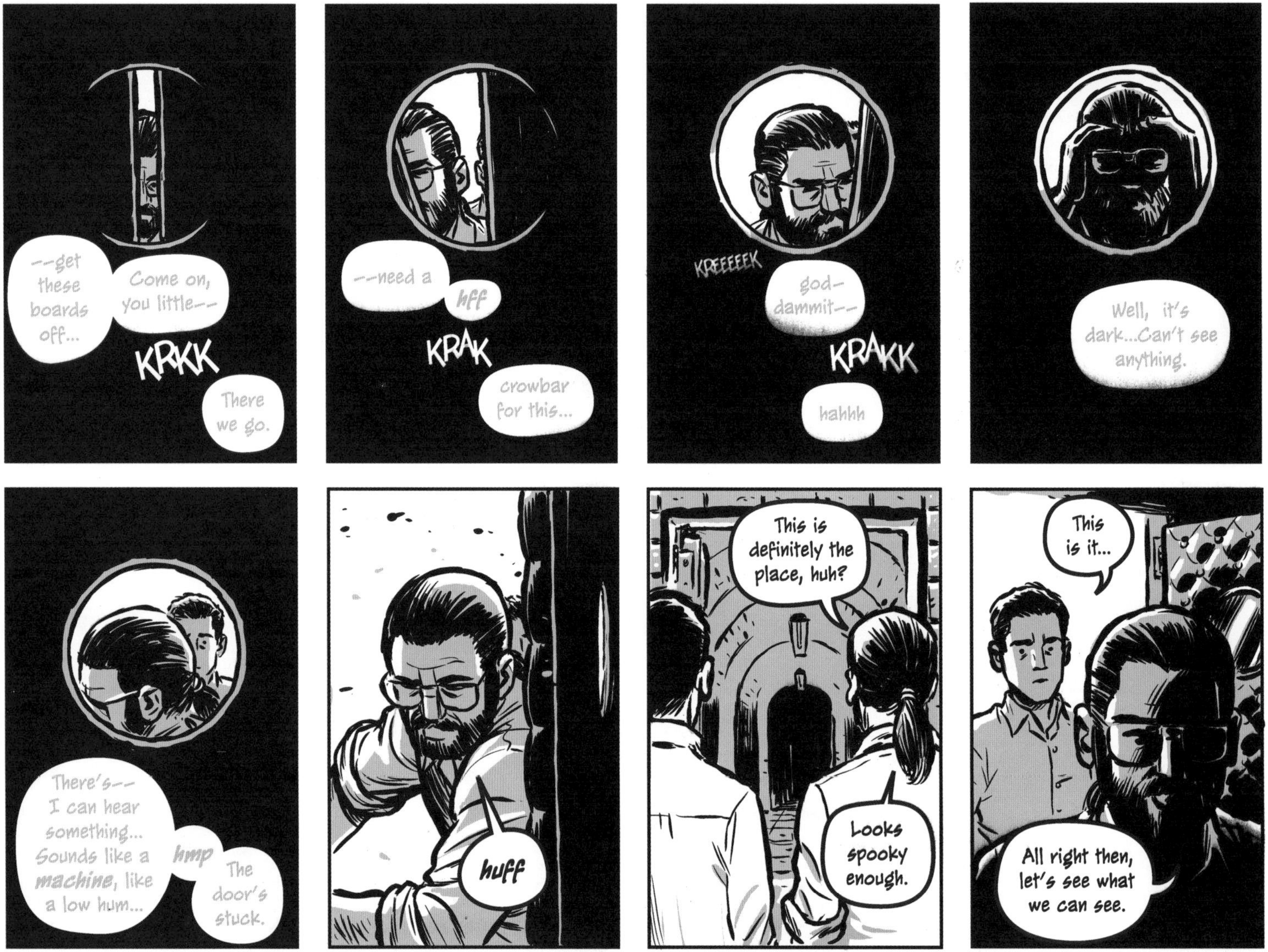
--get these boards off...
Come on, you little--
KRKK
There we go.
--need a
hff
KRAK
crowbar for this...
KREEEEEK
god-dammit--
KRAKK
hahhh
Well, it's dark...Can't see anything.
There's-- I can hear something... Sounds like a *machine*, like a low hum...
hmp
The door's stuck.
huff
This is definitely the place, huh?
Looks spooky enough.
This is it...
All right then, let's see what we can see.

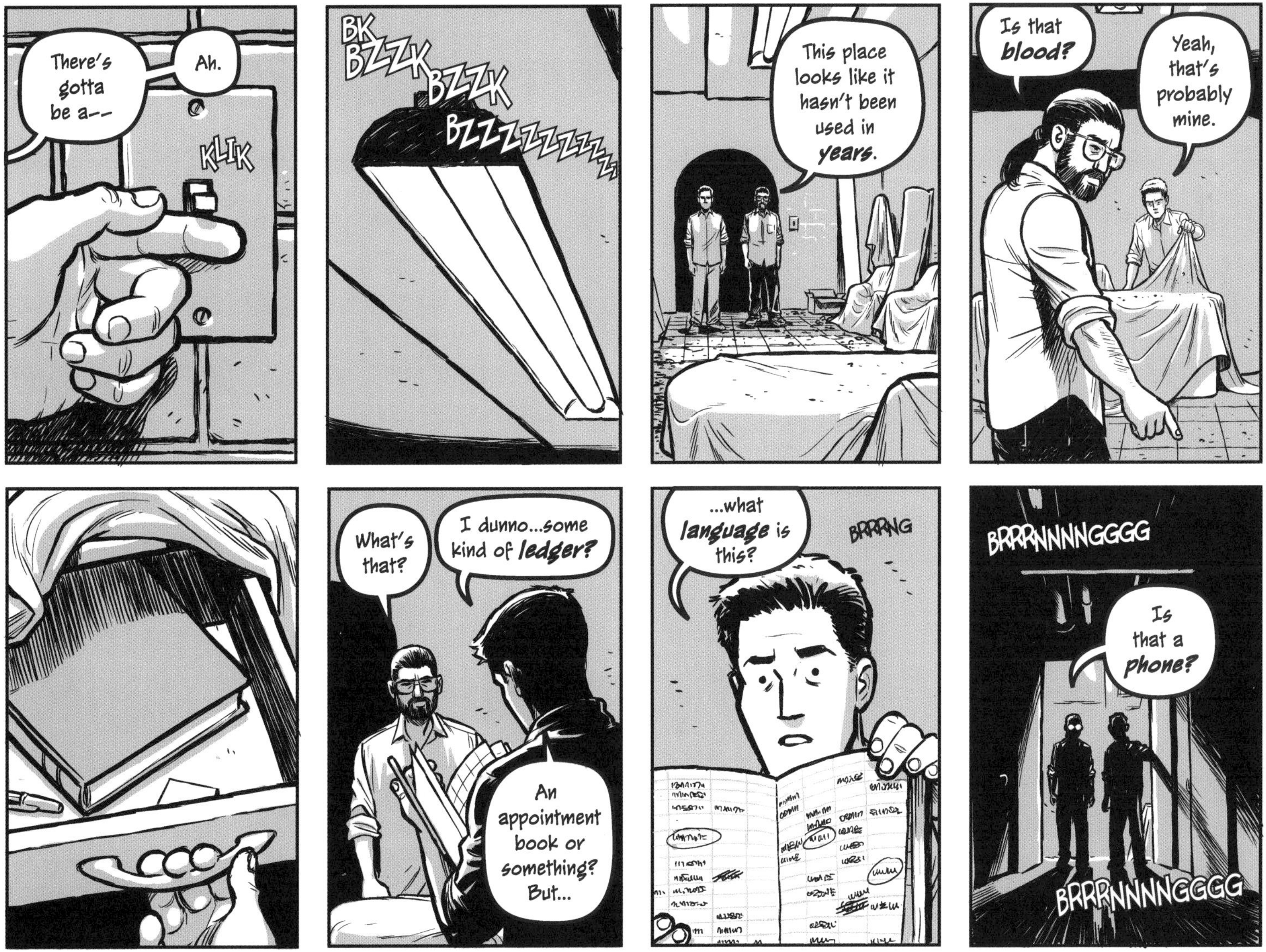
There's gotta be a--
Ah.
KLIK
BK BZZK BZZK BZZZZZZZZZ
This place looks like it hasn't been used in *years*.
Is that *blood?*
Yeah, that's probably mine.
What's that?
I dunno...some kind of *ledger?*
An appointment book or something? But...
...what *language* is this?
BRRRNG
BRRRNNNNGGGG
Is that a *phone?*
BRRRNNNNGGGG

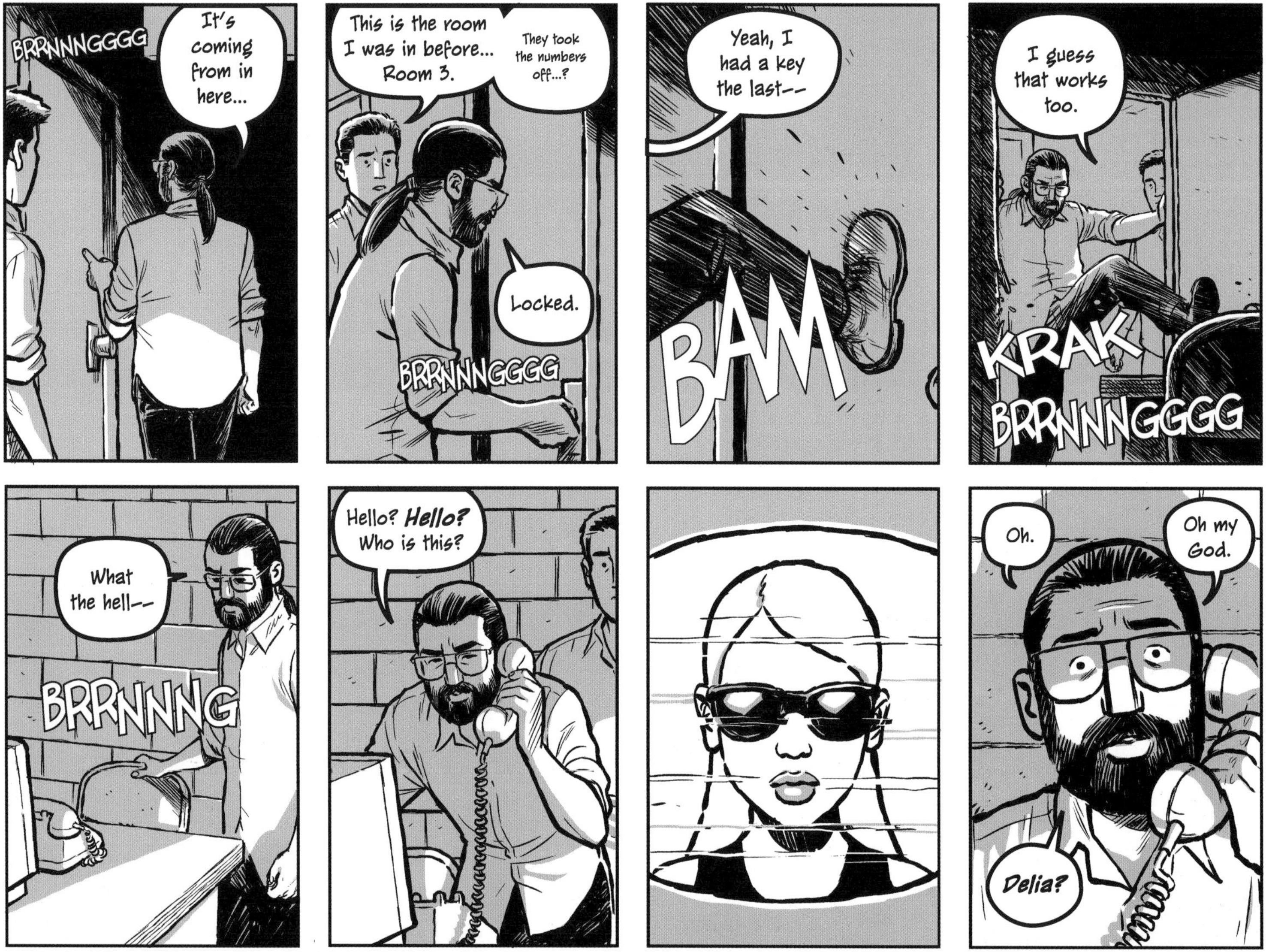
BRRNNNGGGG
It's coming from in here...
This is the room I was in before... Room 3.
They took the numbers off...?
Locked.
BRRNNNGGGG
Yeah, I had a key the last--
BAM
I guess that works too.
KRAK
BRRNNNGGGG
What the hell--
BRRNNNG
Hello? ***Hello?*** Who is this?
Oh.
Oh my God.
Delia?

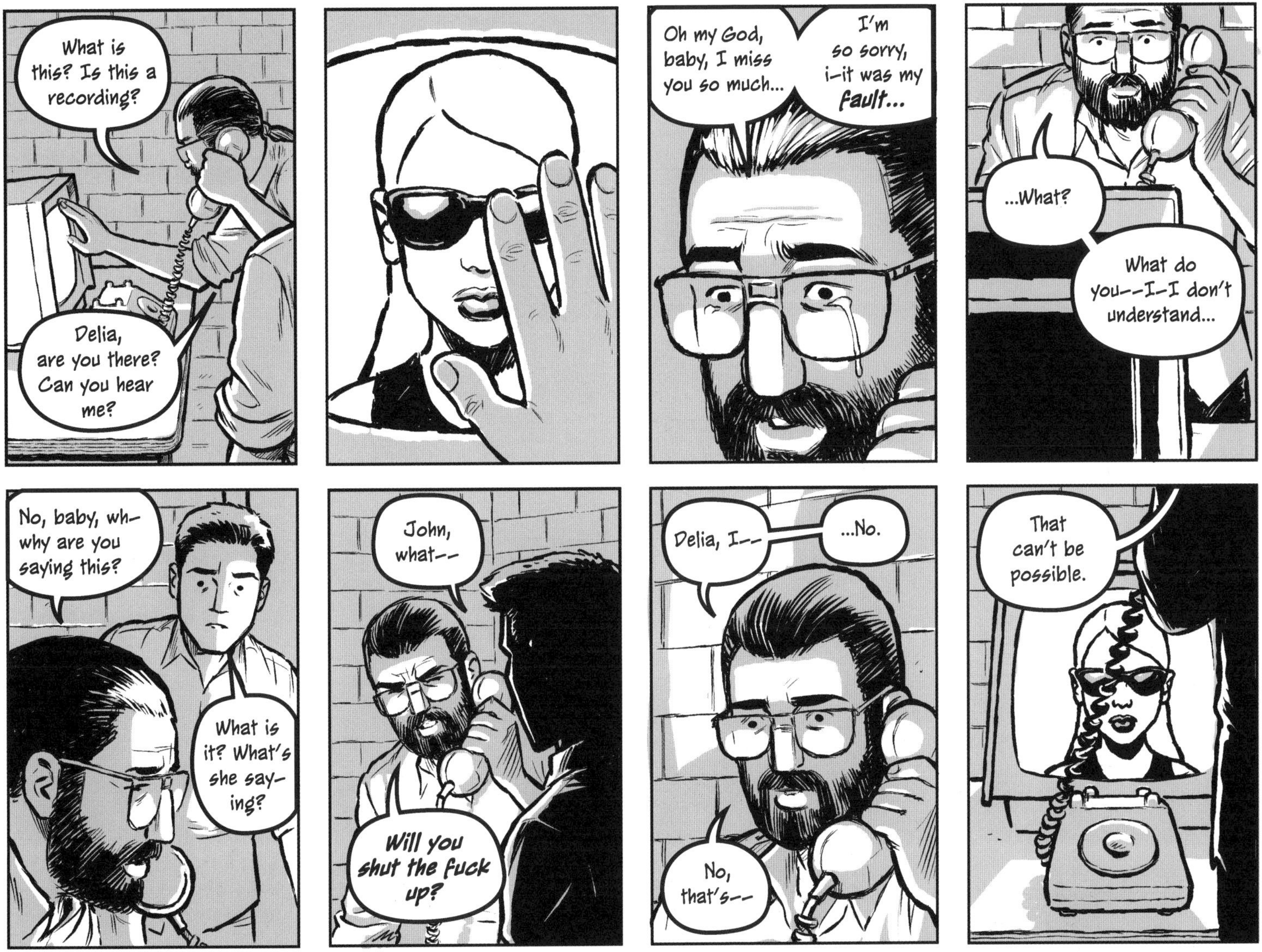

What is this? Is this a recording?
Delia, are you there? Can you hear me?
Oh my God, baby, I miss you so much...
I'm so sorry, i-it was my *fault...*
...What?
What do you--I-I don't understand...
No, baby, wh-why are you saying this?
What is it? What's she say-ing?
John, what--
Will you shut the fuck up?
Delia, I--
...No.
No, that's--
That can't be possible.

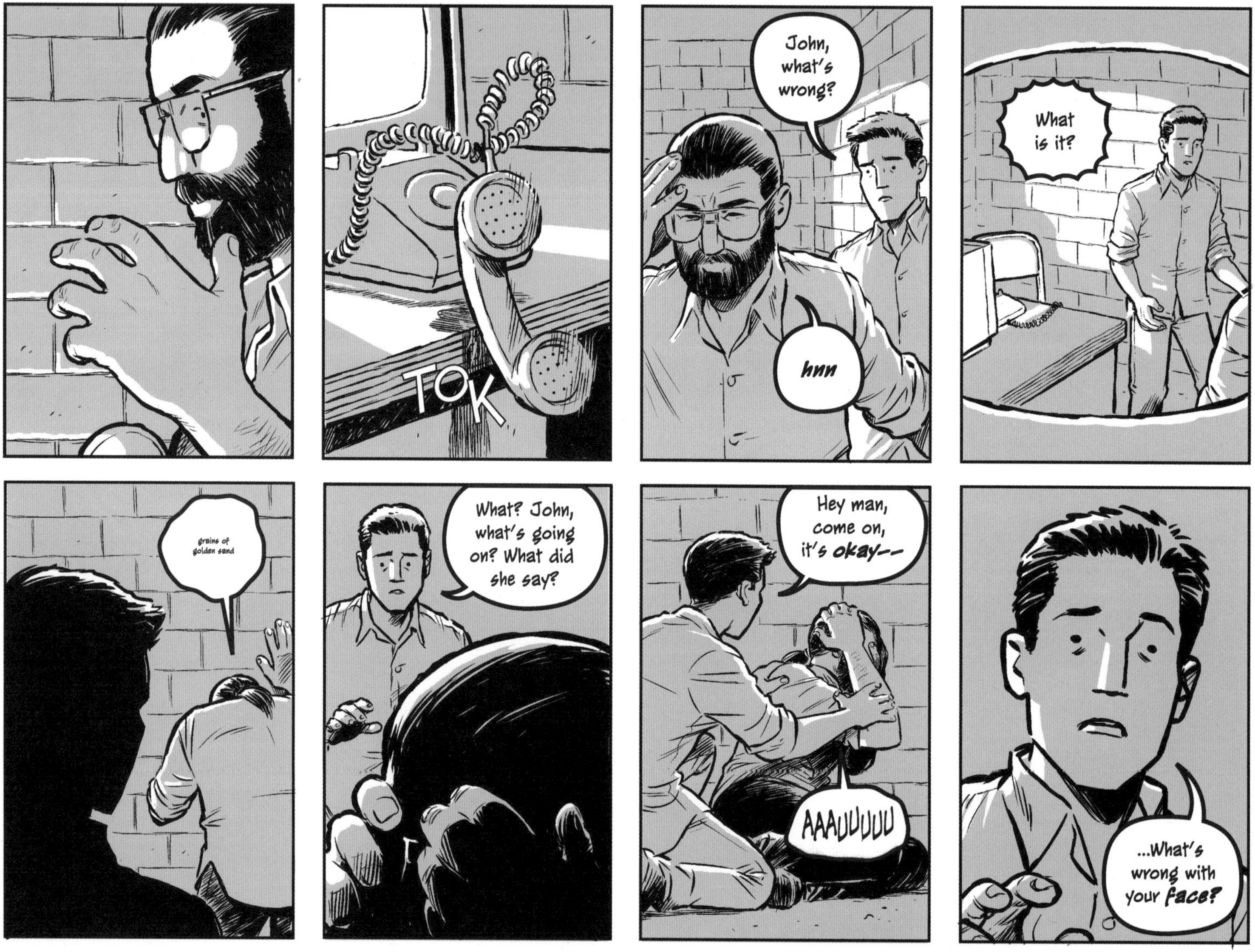
TOK
John, what's wrong?
hnn
What is it?
grains of golden sand
What? John, what's going on? What did she say?
Hey man, come on, it's okay--
AAAUUUUU
...What's wrong with your face?

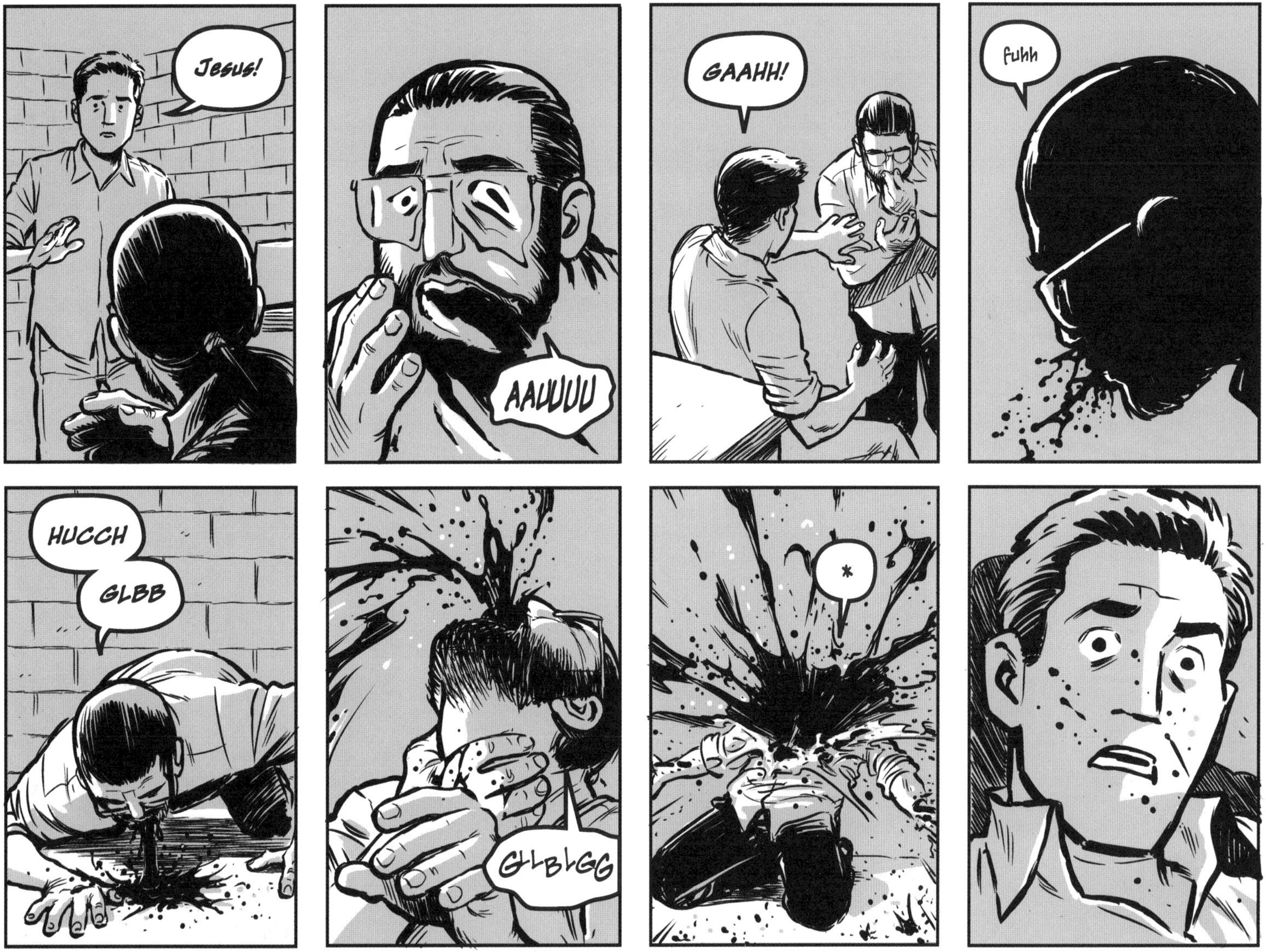
Jesus!
AAUUUU
GAAHH!
fuhh
HUCCH
GLBB
GLBLGG
*

Shortly after college, I took a job at a small publisher.

The work consisted of checking accuracy of content in their line of "general interest" magazines.

REVIEW

Our annual wine guide

LIFESTYLE

10 SURE FIRE

HAIR & BEAUTY

It was boring, but undemanding, and I reasoned that it would allow me the time to explore other creative pursuits.

I mostly spent my extra time surfing the Internet.

The editor who hired me seemed to visit my cubicle often, for a variety of insignificant reasons.

96

I'm telling you, man, she **totally** wants you.

X-Mas Party! D 20

W—what? No... I thought she was **married**?

Nah, she's divorced, or separated, or something.

Alex!

You have been here for **hours** and you haven't even wished me a mer— a **merry Christmas**.

Oh, uh... I—I'm sorry, **Liz**, I—

Come on then.

I need to see you in **my office**.

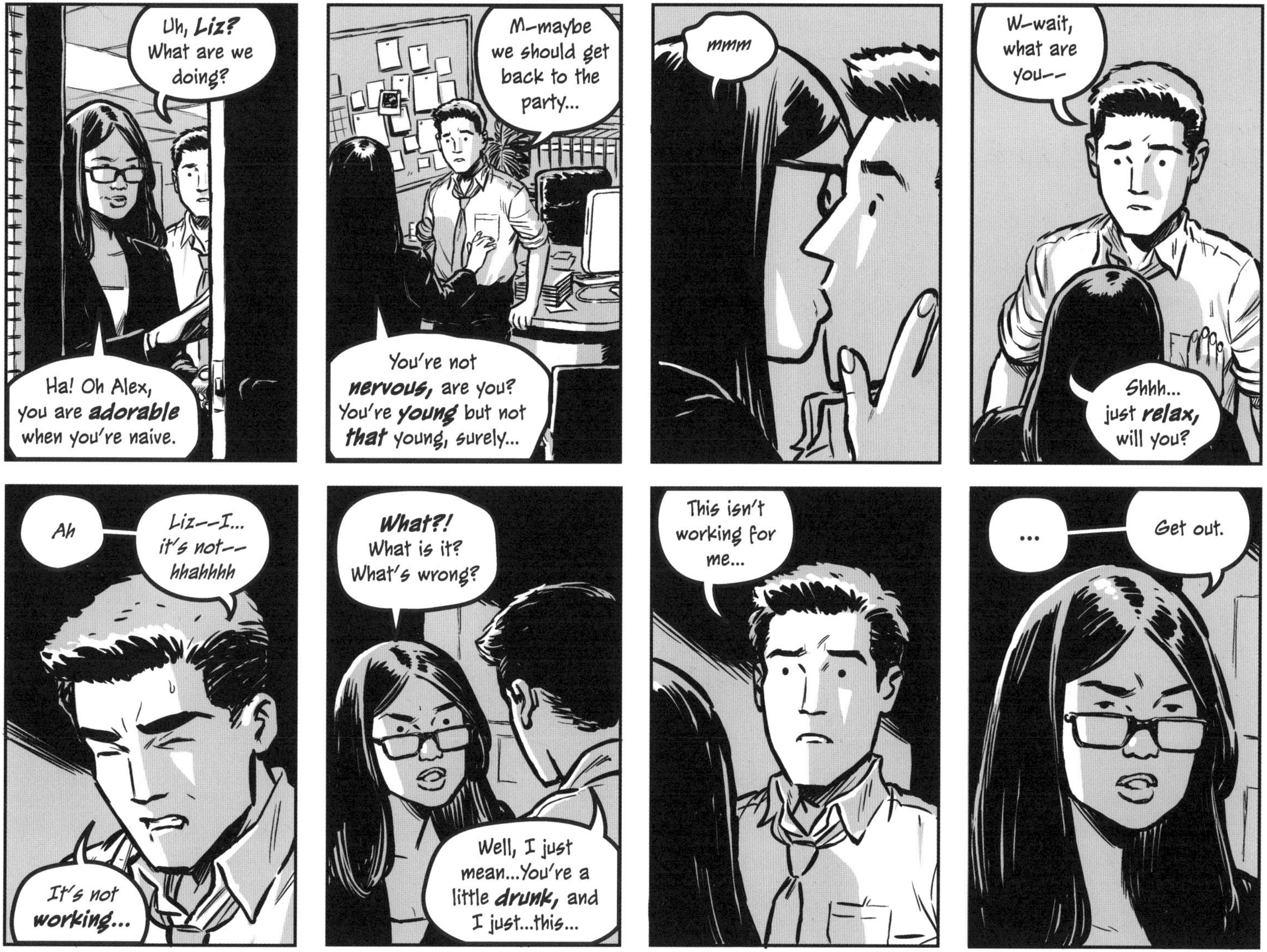
Uh, Liz? What are we doing?
Ha! Oh Alex, you are adorable when you're naive.
M-maybe we should get back to the party...
You're not nervous, are you? You're young but not that young, surely...
mmm
W-wait, what are you--
Shhh... just relax, will you?
Ah
Liz--I... it's not-- hhahhhh
It's not working...
What?! What is it? What's wrong?
Well, I just mean...You're a little drunk, and I just...this...
This isn't working for me...
...
Get out.

97

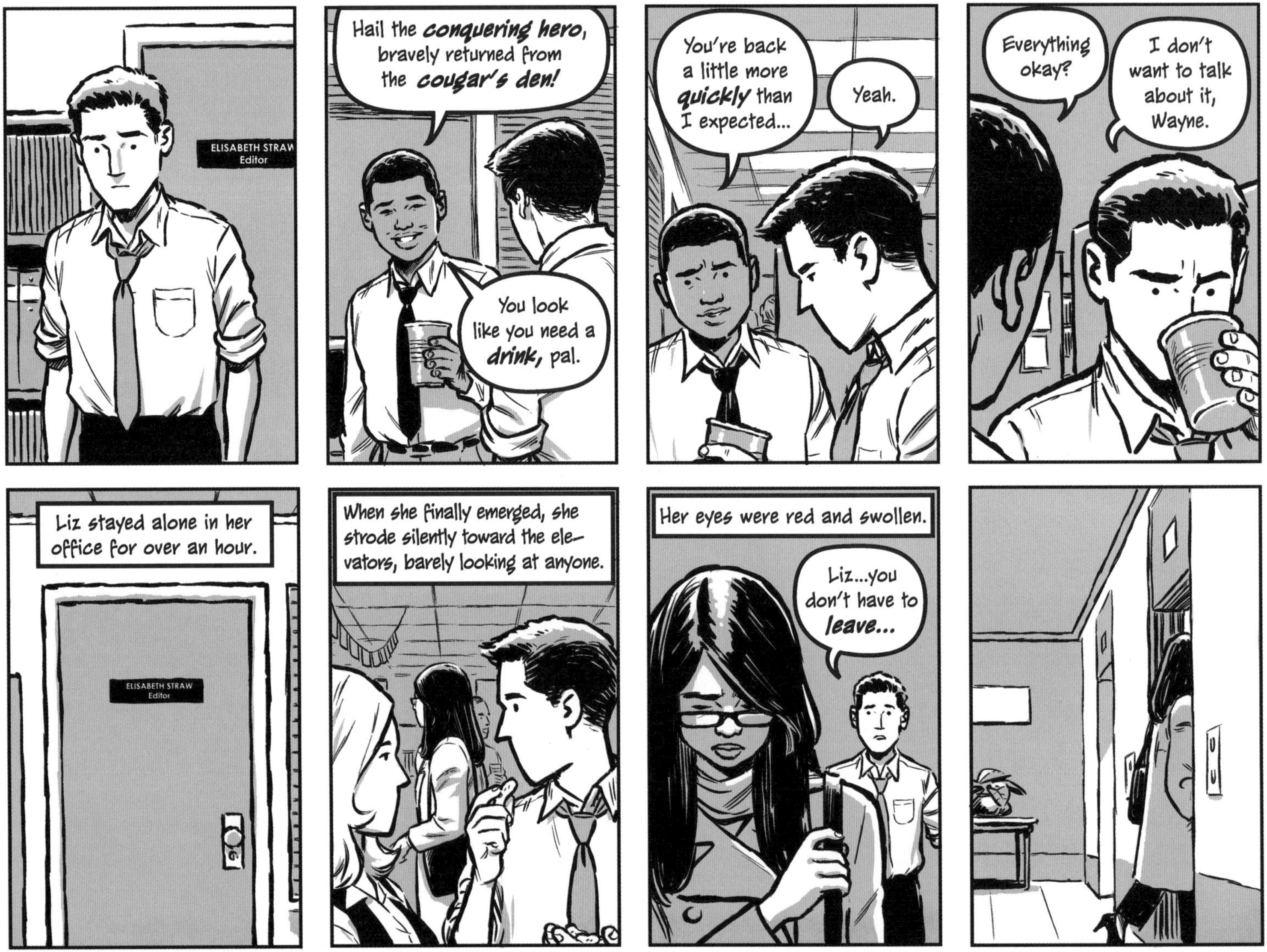
ELISABETH STRAW Editor
Hail the **conquering hero**, bravely returned from the **cougar's den!**
You look like you need a **drink**, pal.
You're back a little more **quickly** than I expected...
Yeah.
Everything okay?
I don't want to talk about it, Wayne.
Liz stayed alone in her office for over an hour.
ELISABETH STRAW Editor
When she finally emerged, she strode silently toward the elevators, barely looking at anyone.
Her eyes were red and swollen.
Liz...you don't have to **leave...**

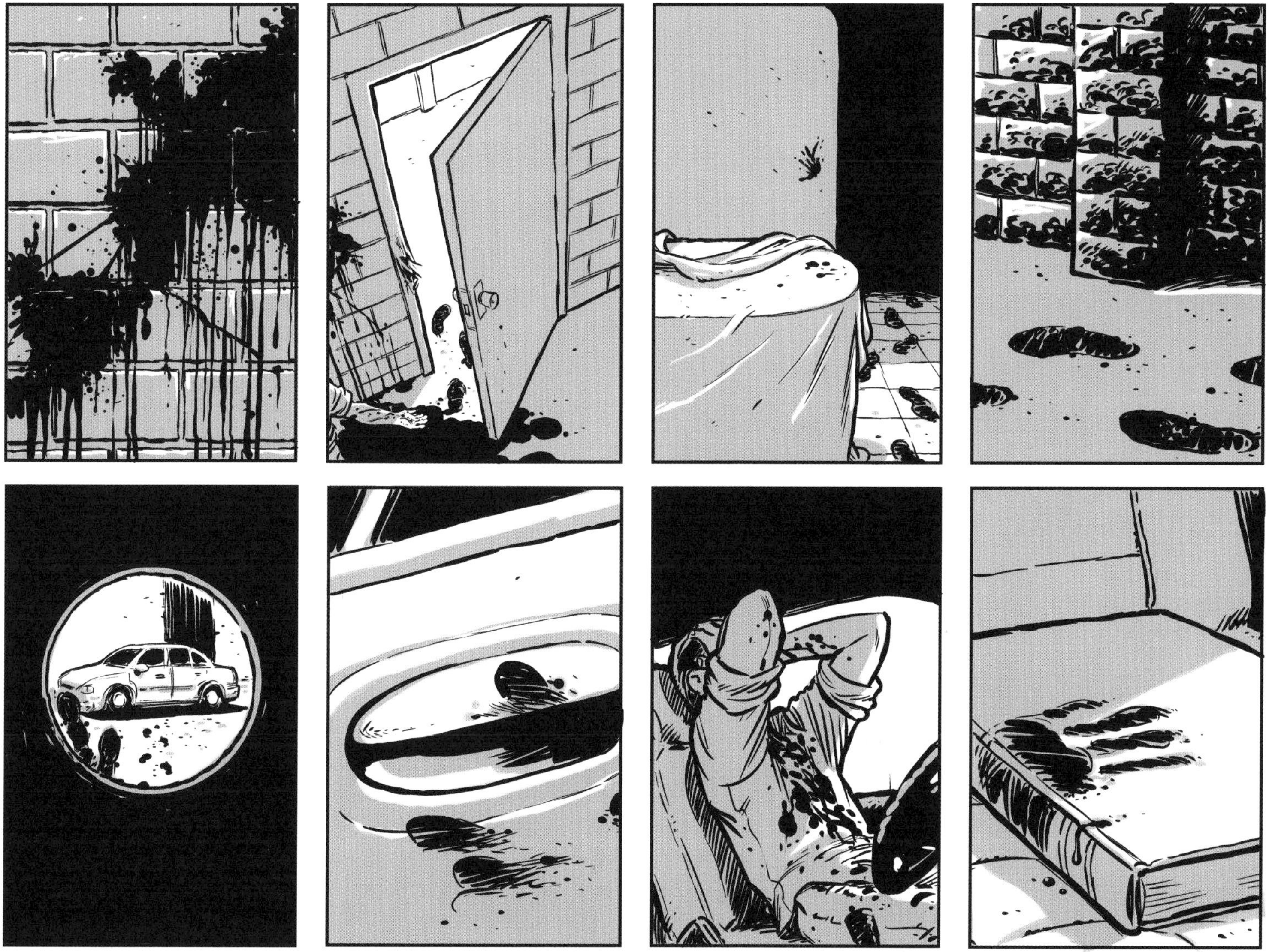

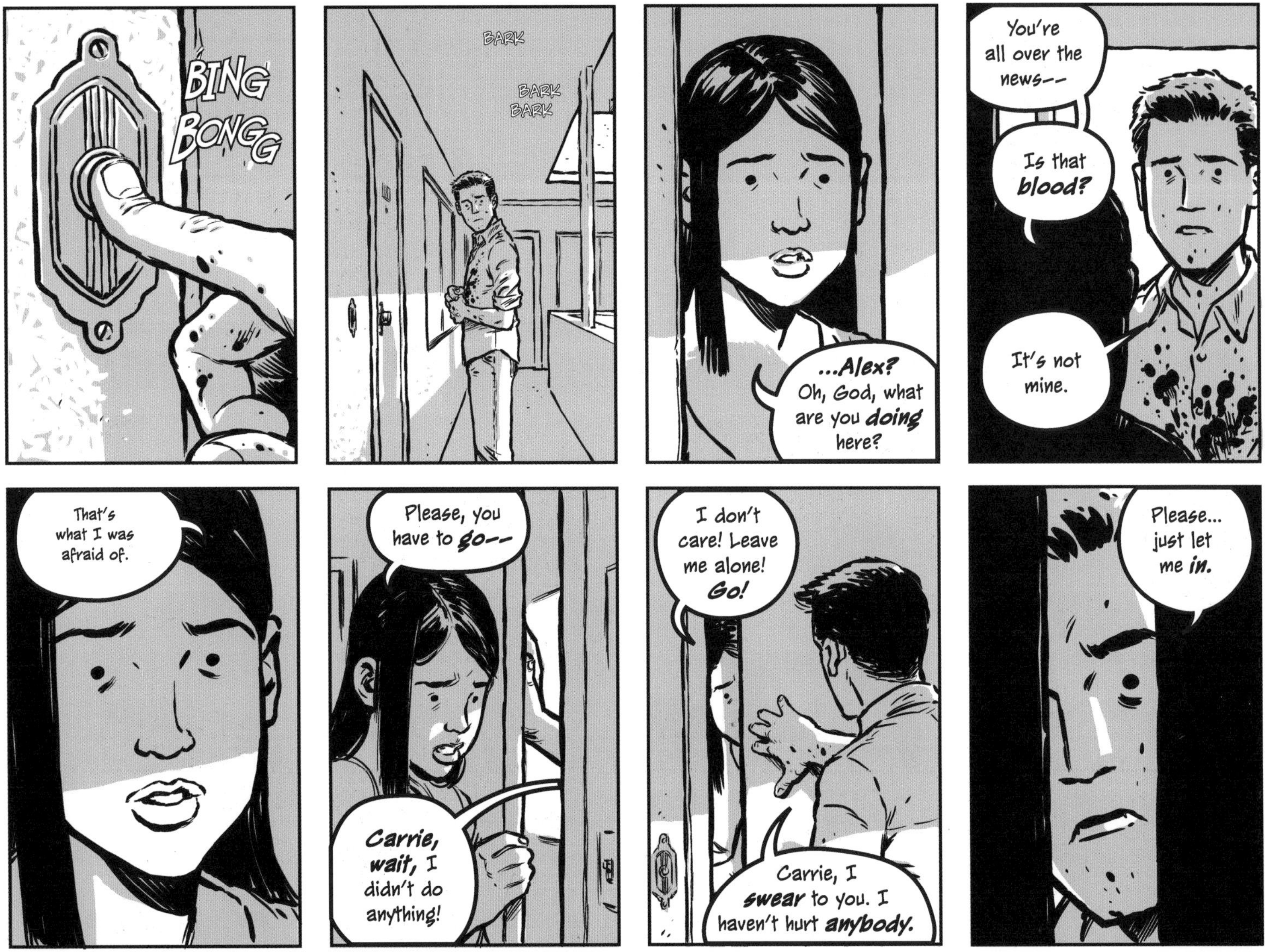
BING
BONGG
BARK
BARK
BARK
...Alex? Oh, God, what are you doing here?
You're all over the news--
Is that blood?
It's not mine.
That's what I was afraid of.
Please, you have to go--
Carrie, wait, I didn't do anything!
I don't care! Leave me alone! Go!
Carrie, I swear to you. I haven't hurt anybody.
Please... just let me in.

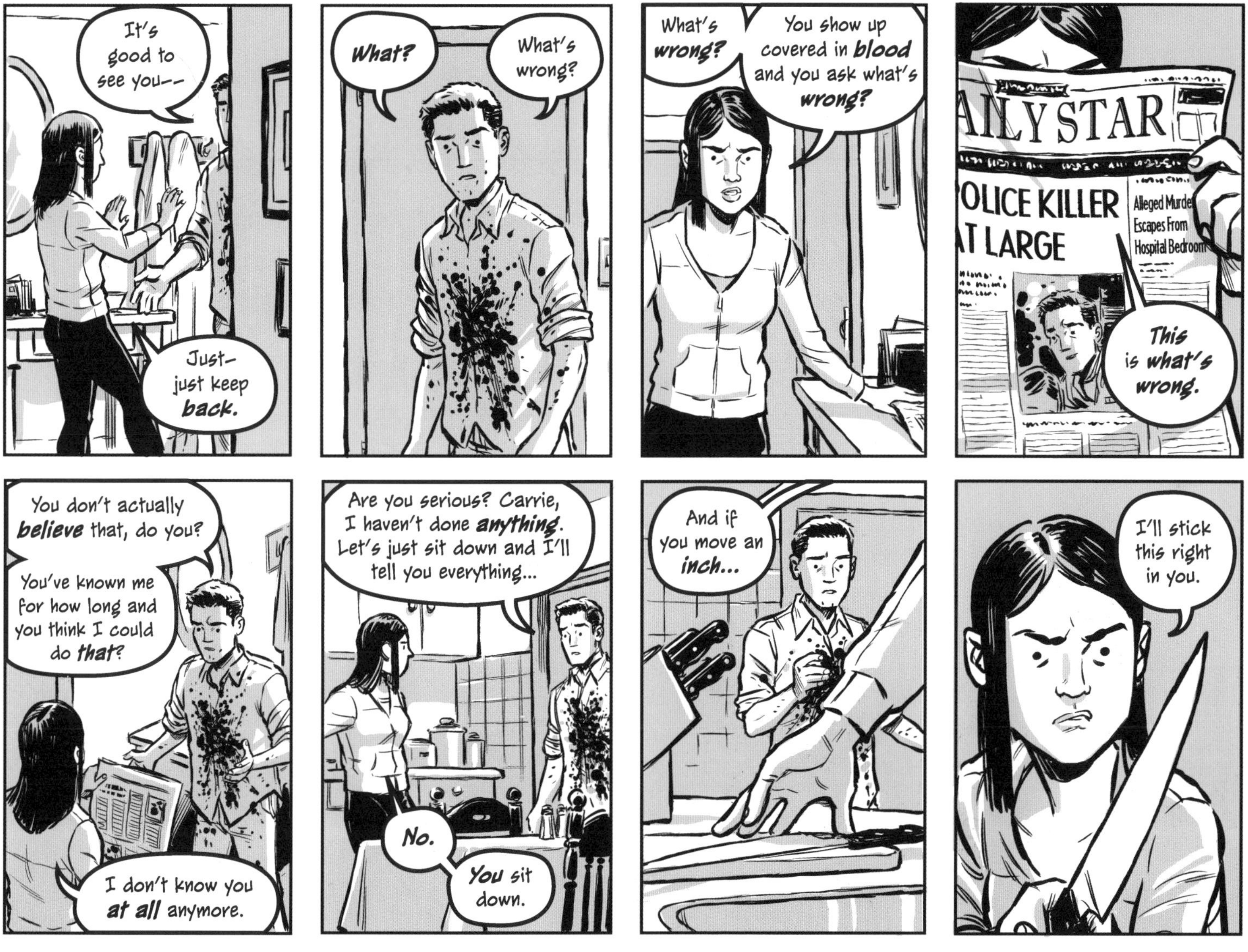
It's good to see you--
Just-just keep back.
What?
What's wrong?
What's wrong?
You show up covered in blood and you ask what's wrong?
AILY STAR
POLICE KILLER AT LARGE
Alleged Murde Escapes From Hospital Bedroom
This is what's wrong.
You don't actually believe that, do you?
You've known me for how long and you think I could do that?
I don't know you at all anymore.
Are you serious? Carrie, I haven't done anything. Let's just sit down and I'll tell you everything...
No.
You sit down.
And if you move an inch...
I'll stick this right in you.

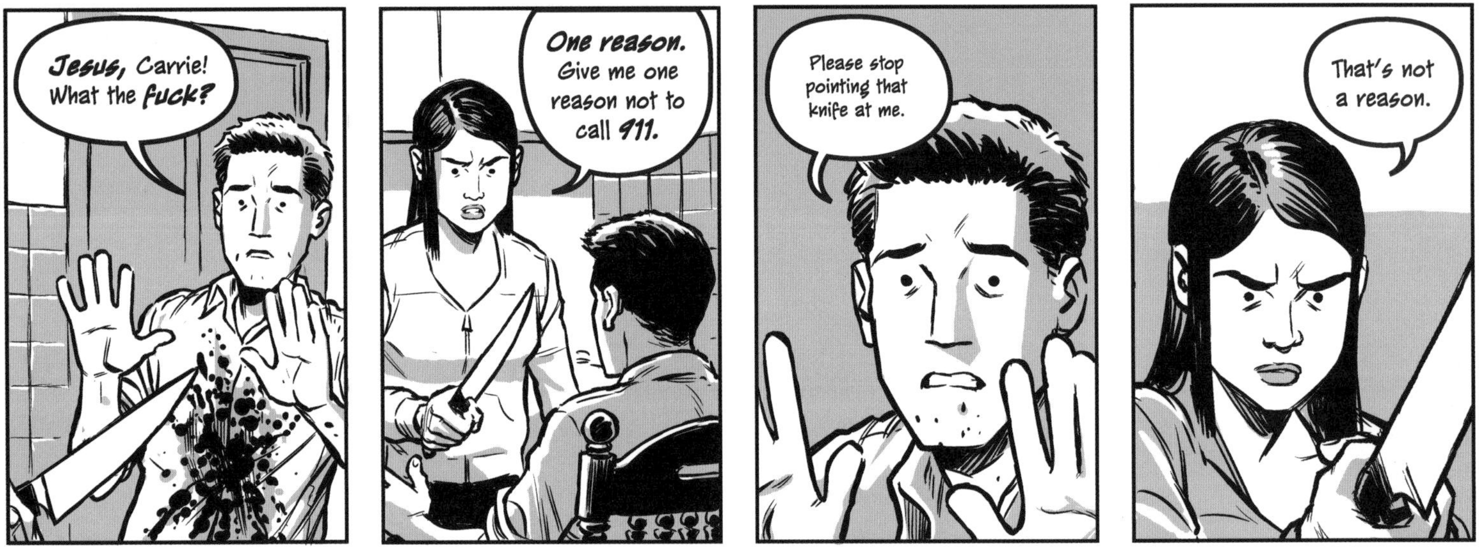

Jesus, Carrie! What the fuck?
One reason. Give me one reason not to call 911.
Please stop pointing that knife at me.
That's not a reason.

102

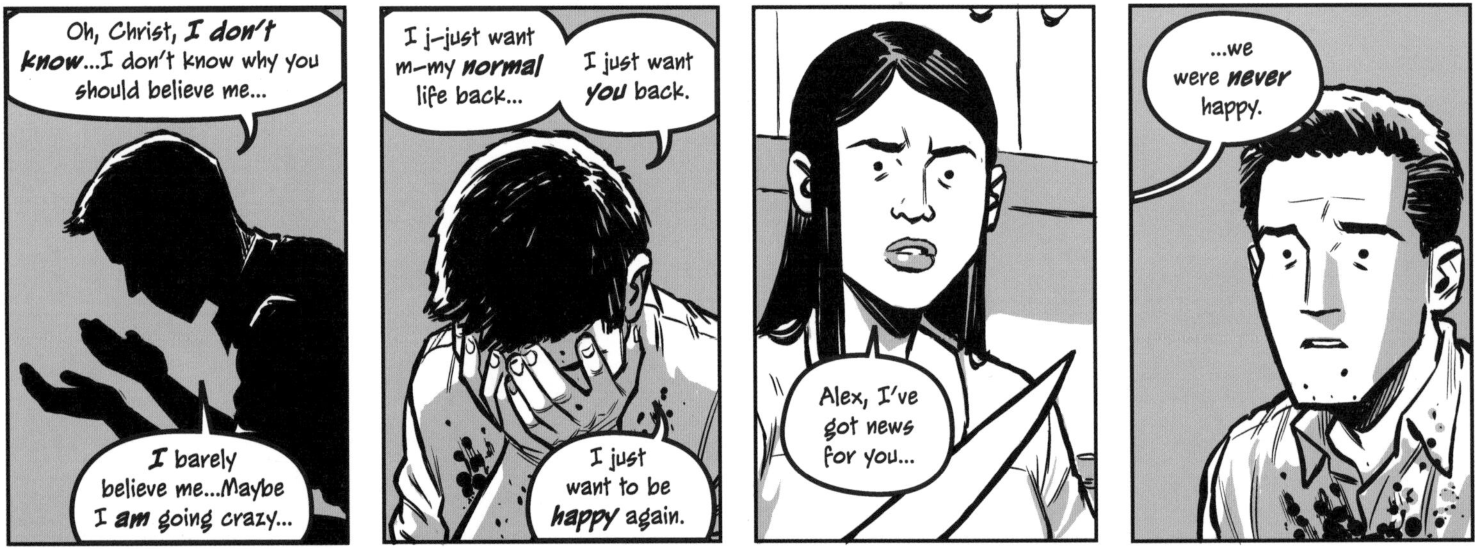

Oh, Christ, I don't know...I don't know why you should believe me...
I barely believe me...Maybe I am going crazy...
I j-just want m-my normal life back...
I just want you back.
I just want to be happy again.
Alex, I've got news for you...
...we were never happy.

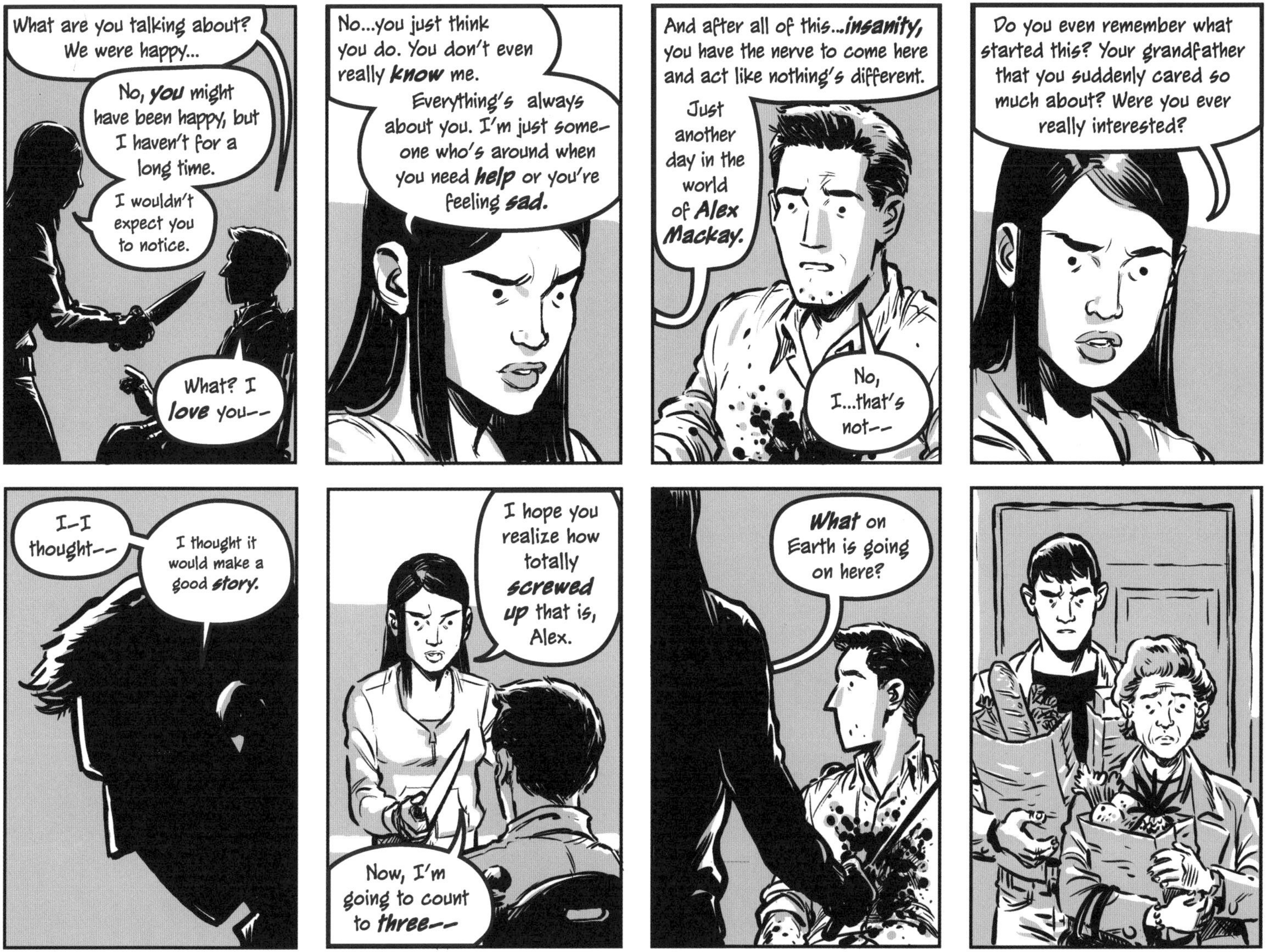
What are you talking about? We were happy...
No, *you* might have been happy, but I haven't for a long time.
I wouldn't expect you to notice.
What? I *love* you--
No...you just think you do. You don't even really *know* me.
Everything's always about you. I'm just someone who's around when you need *help* or you're feeling *sad.*
And after all of this...*insanity,* you have the nerve to come here and act like nothing's different.
Just another day in the world of *Alex Mackay.*
No, I...that's not--
Do you even remember what started this? Your grandfather that you suddenly cared so much about? Were you ever really interested?
I-I thought--
I thought it would make a good *story.*
I hope you realize how totally *screwed up* that is, Alex.
Now, I'm going to count to *three--*
What on Earth is going on here?

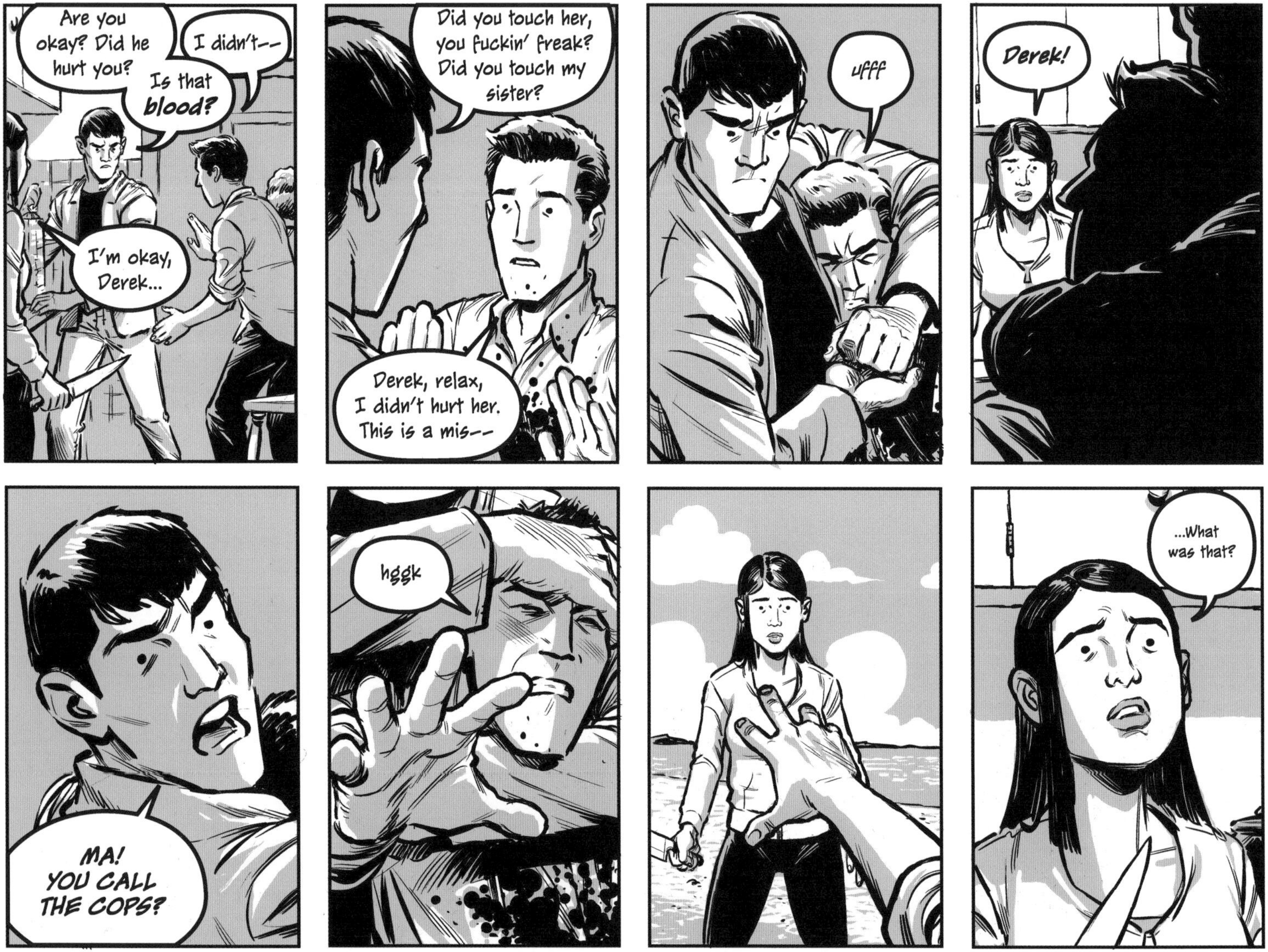
Are you okay? Did he hurt you?
I didn't--
Is that blood?
I'm okay, Derek...
Did you touch her, you fuckin' freak? Did you touch my sister?
Derek, relax, I didn't hurt her. This is a mis--
ufff
Derek!
MA! YOU CALL THE COPS?
hggk
...What was that?

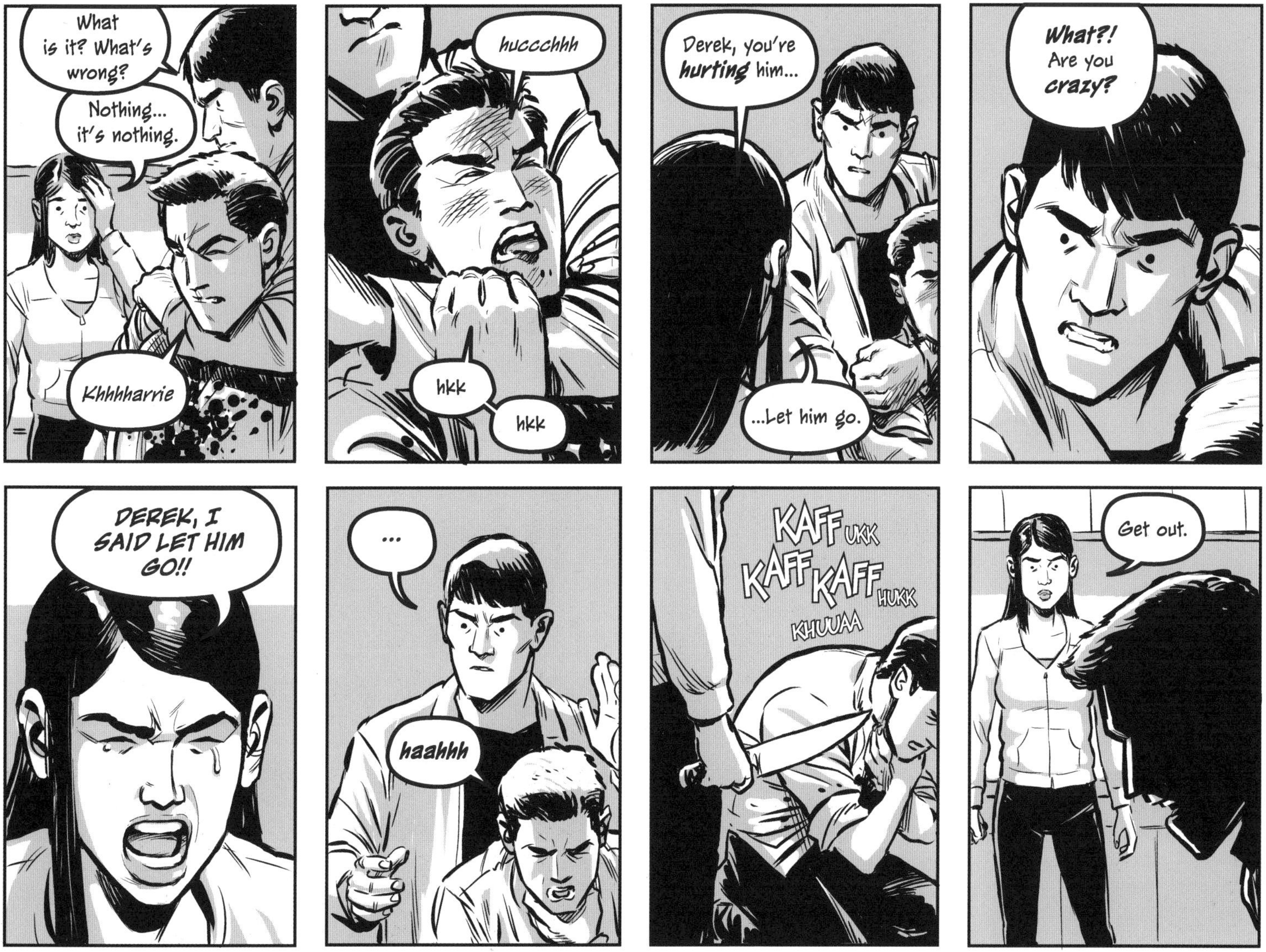
What is it? What's wrong?
Nothing... it's nothing.
Khhhharrie
huccchhh
hkk
hkk
Derek, you're hurting him...
...Let him go.
What?! Are you crazy?
DEREK, I SAID LET HIM GO!!
...
haahhh
KAFF UKK
KAFF KAFF HUKK
KHUUAA
Get out.

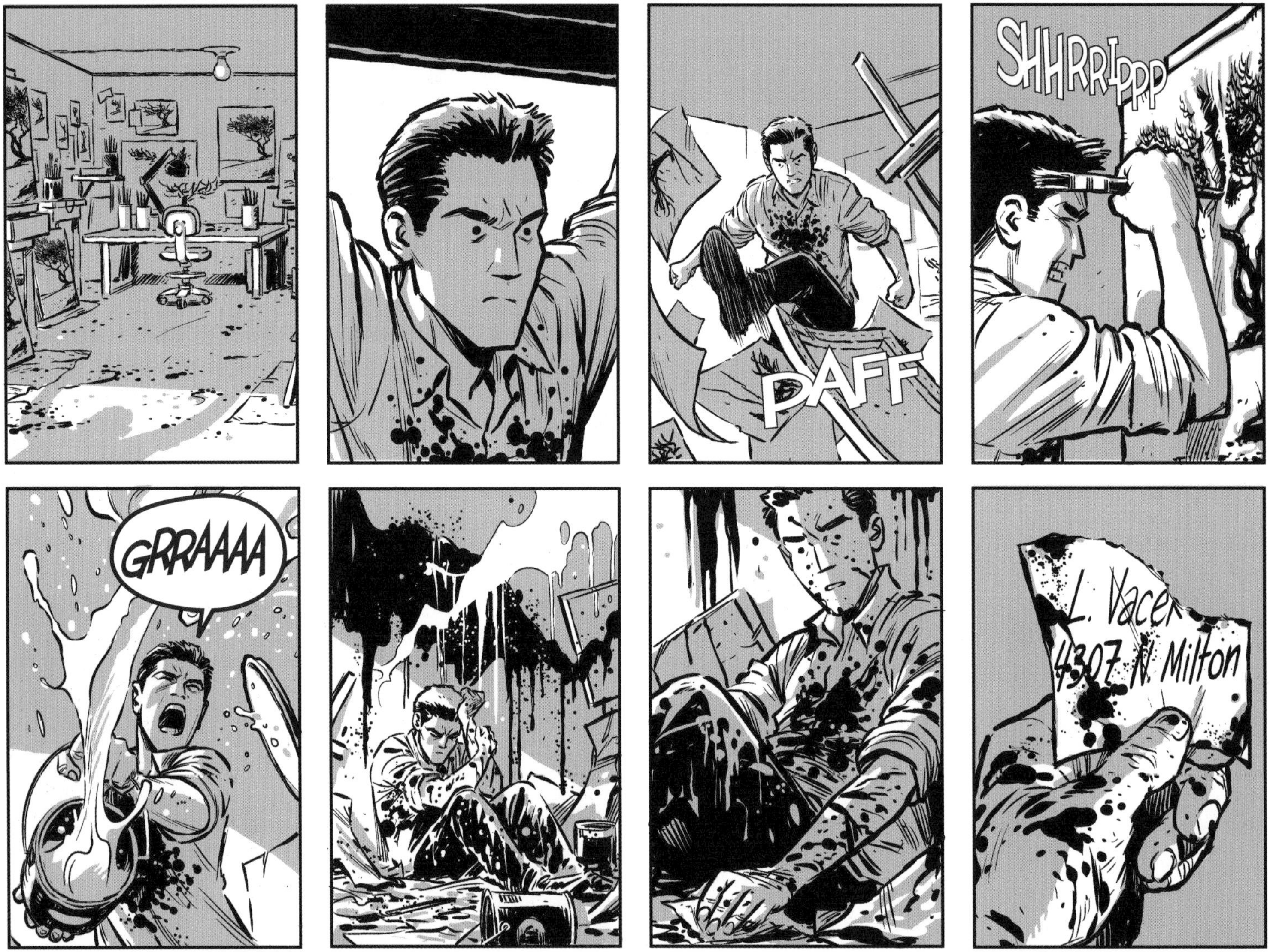
SHHRRIPPP
PAFF
GRRAAAA
L. Vacek
4307 N. Milton

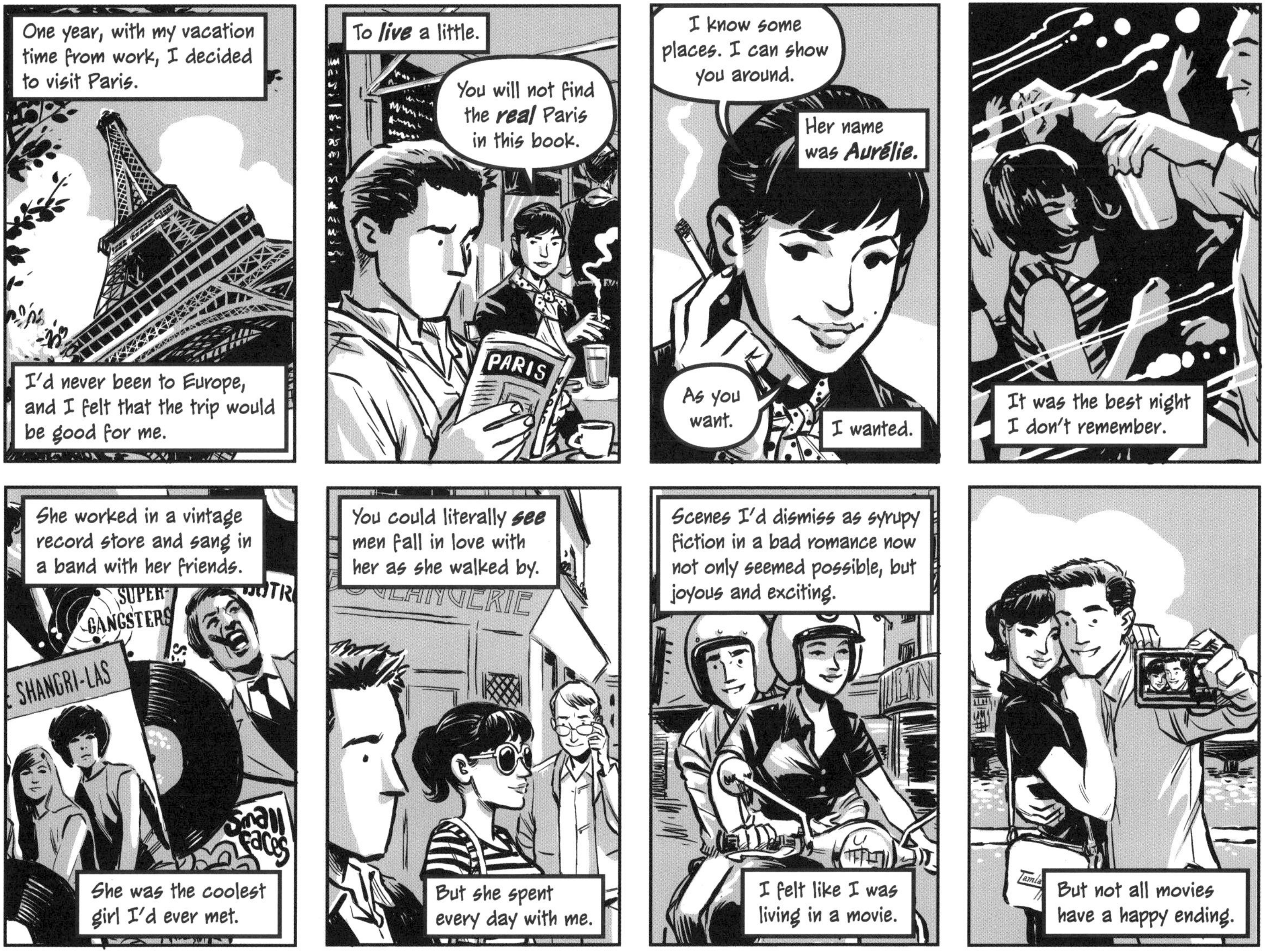
One year, with my vacation time from work, I decided to visit Paris.
I'd never been to Europe, and I felt that the trip would be good for me.
To *live* a little.
You will not find the ***real*** Paris in this book.
PARIS
I know some places. I can show you around.
Her name was ***Aurélie.***
As you want.
I wanted.
It was the best night I don't remember.
She worked in a vintage record store and sang in a band with her friends.
SUPER-
GANGSTERS
SHANGRI-LAS
Small Faces
She was the coolest girl I'd ever met.
You could literally ***see*** men fall in love with her as she walked by.
But she spent every day with me.
Scenes I'd dismiss as syrupy fiction in a bad romance now not only seemed possible, but joyous and exciting.
I felt like I was living in a movie.
But not all movies have a happy ending.

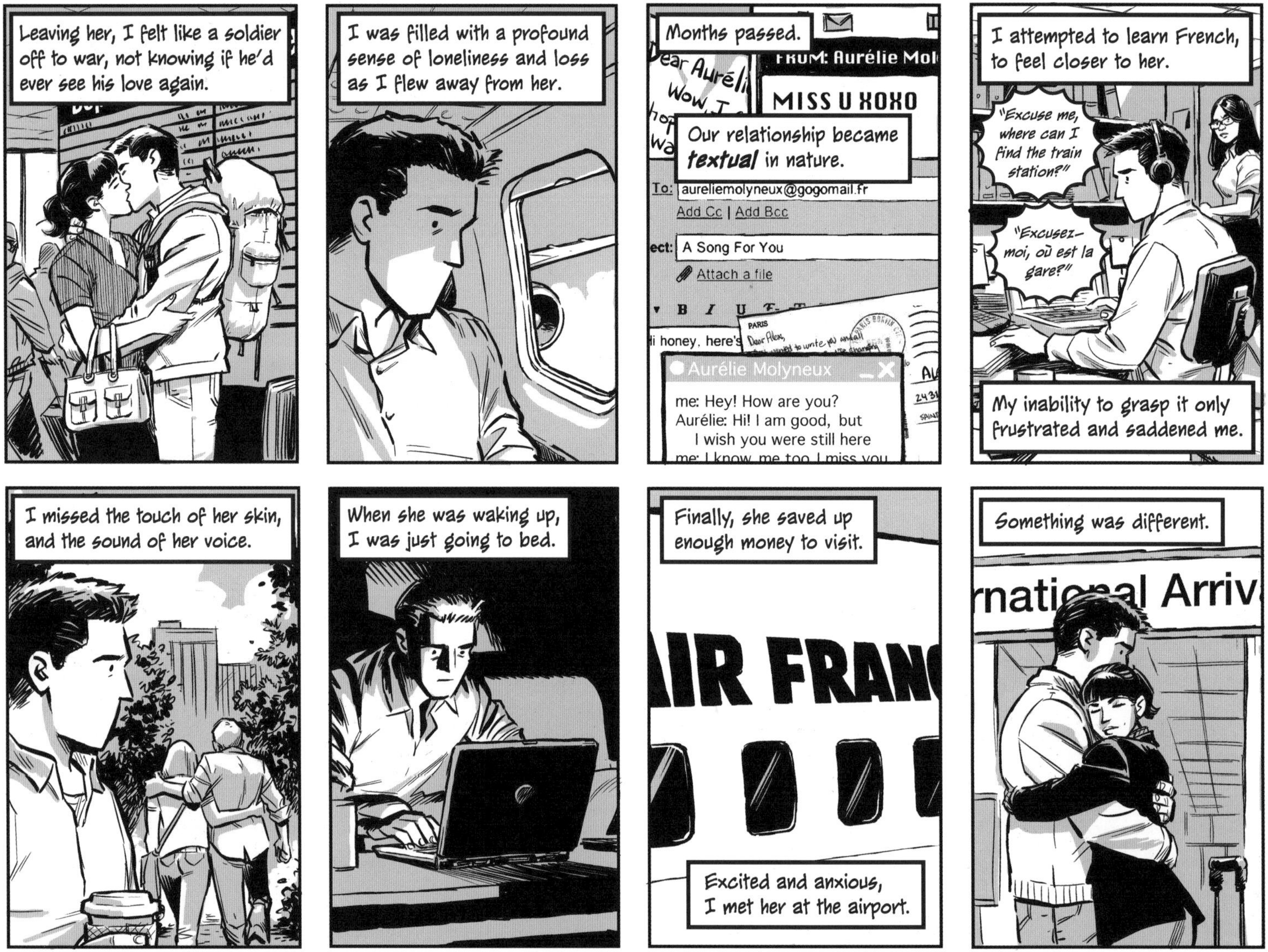
Leaving her, I felt like a soldier off to war, not knowing if he'd ever see his love again.
I was filled with a profound sense of loneliness and loss as I flew away from her.
Months passed.
FROM: Aurélie Mol
MISS U XOXO
Our relationship became *textual* in nature.
To: aureliemolyneux@gogomail.fr
Add Cc | Add Bcc
A Song For You
Attach a file
i honey, here's
PARIS
Dear Alex,
Aurélie Molyneux
me: Hey! How are you?
Aurélie: Hi! I am good, but I wish you were still here
I attempted to learn French, to feel closer to her.
"Excuse me, where can I find the train station?"
"Excusez-moi, où est la gare?"
My inability to grasp it only frustrated and saddened me.
I missed the touch of her skin, and the sound of her voice.
When she was waking up, I was just going to bed.
Finally, she saved up enough money to visit.
AIR FRANC
Excited and anxious, I met her at the airport.
Something was different.
rnational Arriv

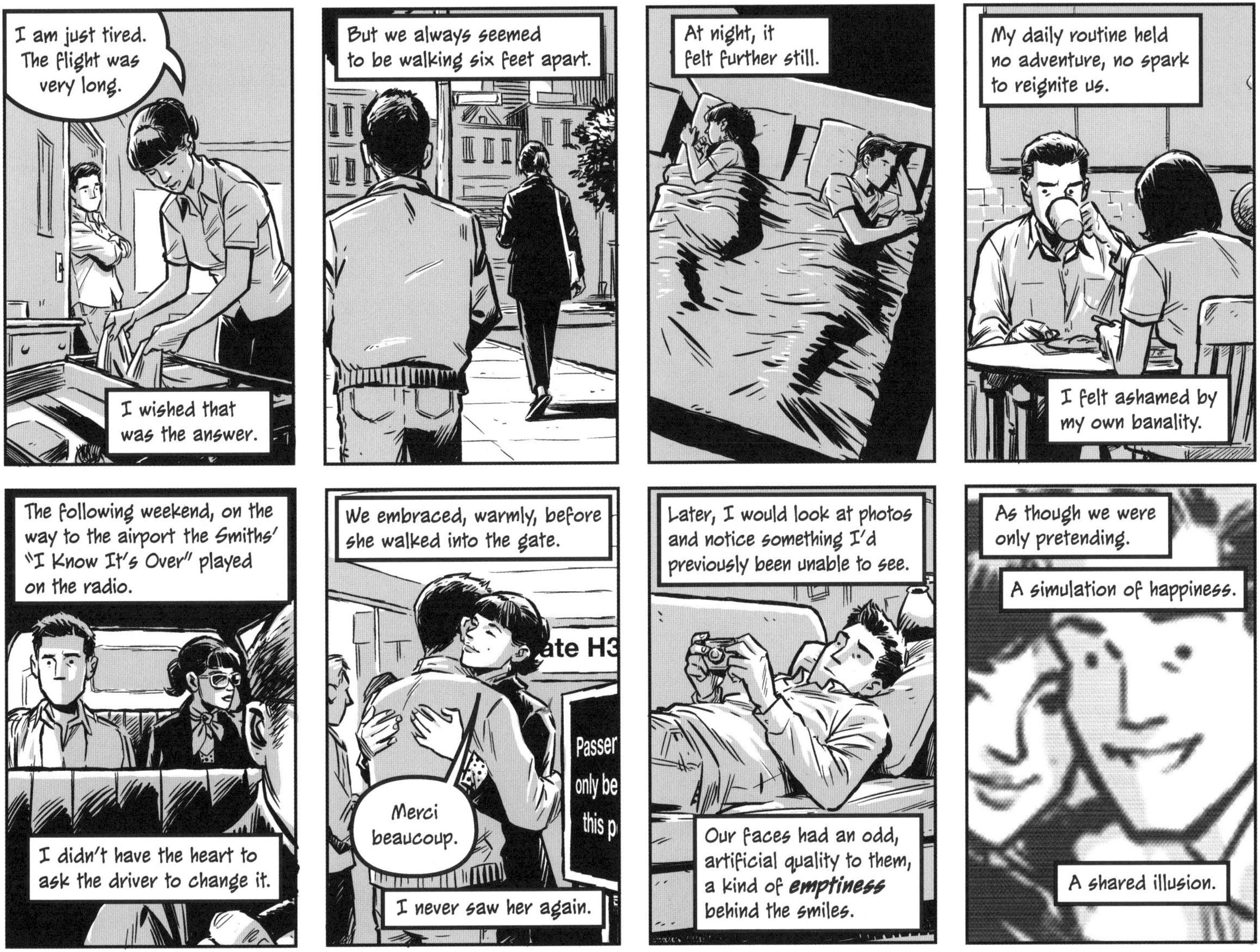

I am just tired. The flight was very long.
I wished that was the answer.
But we always seemed to be walking six feet apart.
At night, it felt further still.
My daily routine held no adventure, no spark to reignite us.
I felt ashamed by my own banality.
The following weekend, on the way to the airport the Smiths' "I Know It's Over" played on the radio.
I didn't have the heart to ask the driver to change it.
We embraced, warmly, before she walked into the gate.
ate H3
Passer
only be
this p
Merci beaucoup.
I never saw her again.
Later, I would look at photos and notice something I'd previously been unable to see.
Our faces had an odd, artificial quality to them, a kind of ***emptiness*** behind the smiles.
As though we were only pretending.
A simulation of happiness.
A shared illusion.

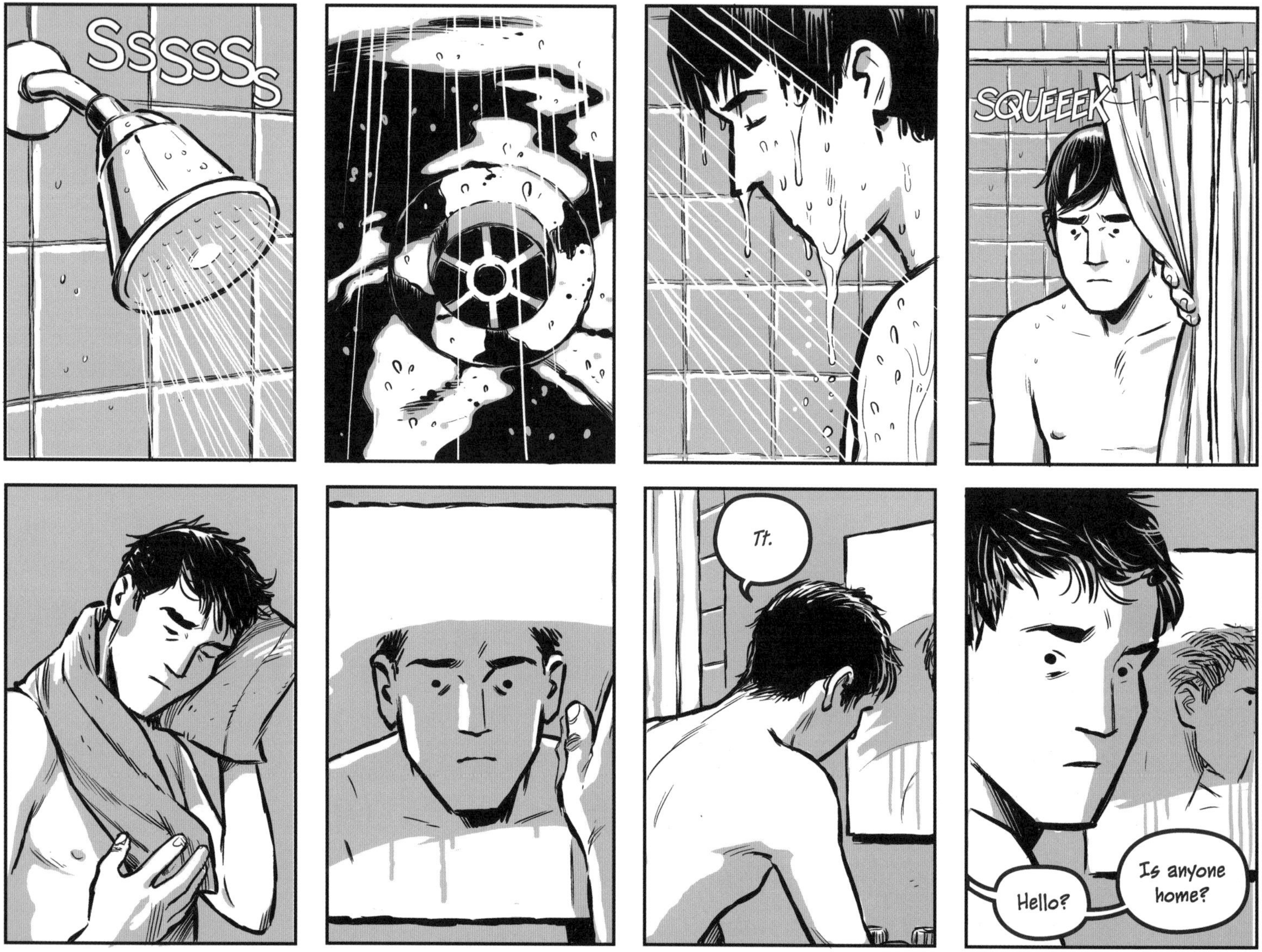
SSSSSs
SQUEEEK
Tt.
Hello?
Is anyone home?

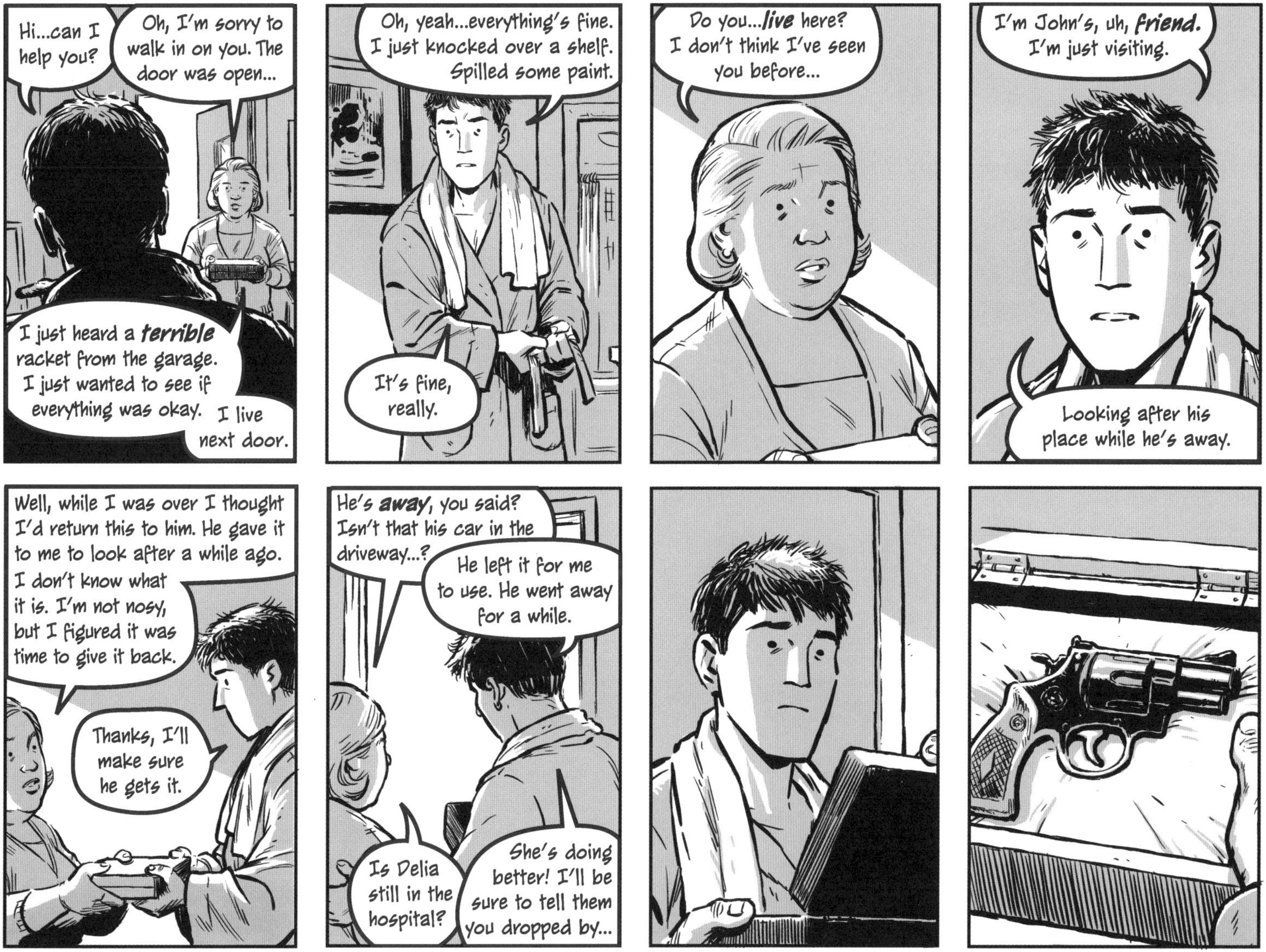

Hi...can I help you?
Oh, I'm sorry to walk in on you. The door was open...
I just heard a terrible racket from the garage. I just wanted to see if everything was okay.
I live next door.
Oh, yeah...everything's fine. I just knocked over a shelf. Spilled some paint.
It's fine, really.
Do you...live here? I don't think I've seen you before...
I'm John's, uh, friend. I'm just visiting.
Looking after his place while he's away.
Well, while I was over I thought I'd return this to him. He gave it to me to look after a while ago.
I don't know what it is. I'm not nosy, but I figured it was time to give it back.
Thanks, I'll make sure he gets it.
He's away, you said? Isn't that his car in the driveway...?
He left it for me to use. He went away for a while.
Is Delia still in the hospital?
She's doing better! I'll be sure to tell them you dropped by...

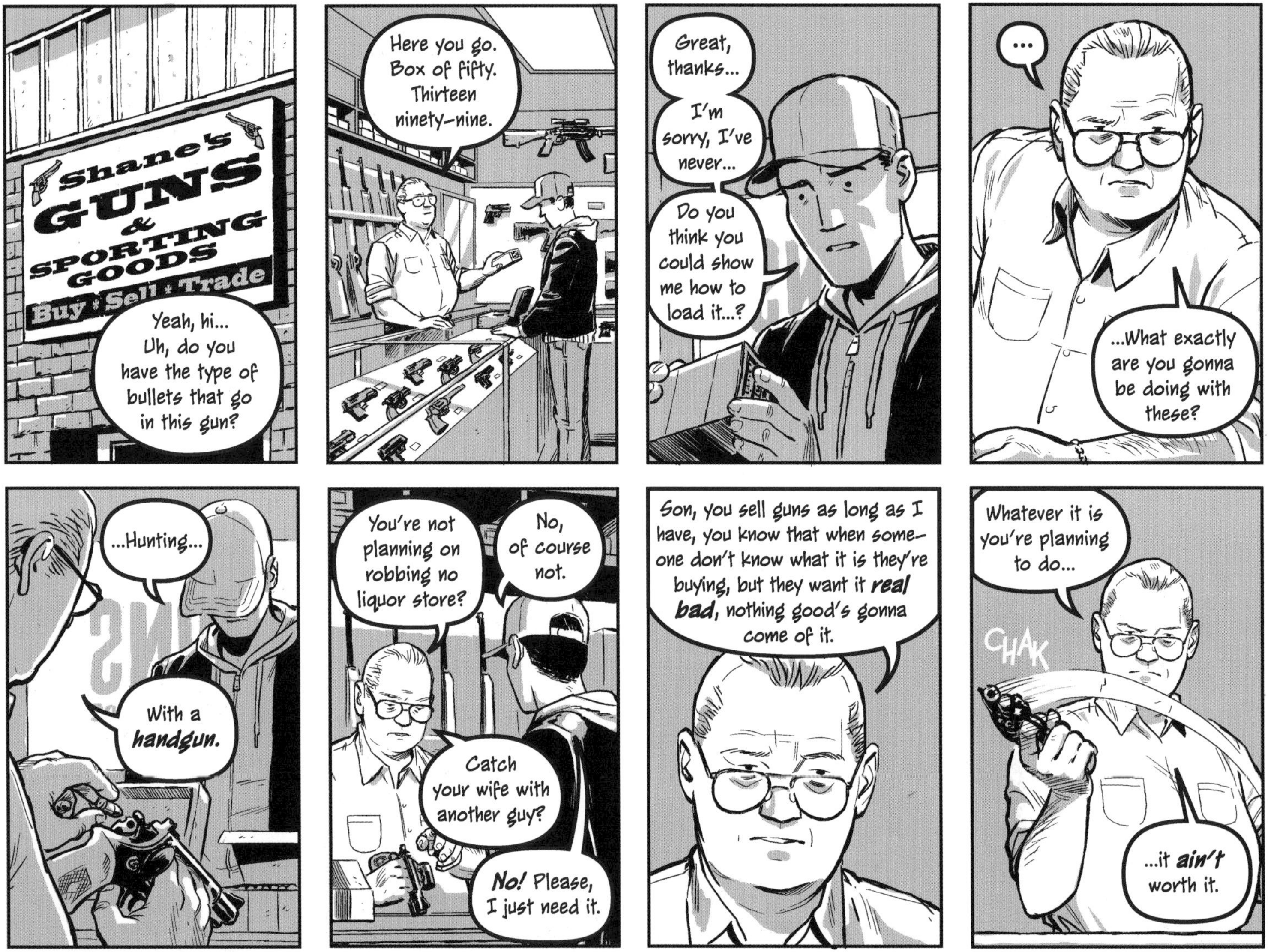
Shane's GUNS & SPORTING GOODS
Buy * Sell * Trade
Yeah, hi... Uh, do you have the type of bullets that go in this gun?
Here you go. Box of fifty. Thirteen ninety-nine.
Great, thanks...
I'm sorry, I've never...
Do you think you could show me how to load it...?
...
...What exactly are you gonna be doing with these?
...Hunting...
With a **handgun.**
You're not planning on robbing no liquor store?
No, of course not.
Catch your wife with another guy?
No! Please, I just need it.
Son, you sell guns as long as I have, you know that when some-one don't know what it is they're buying, but they want it ***real bad***, nothing good's gonna come of it.
Whatever it is you're planning to do...
CHAK
...it ***ain't*** worth it.

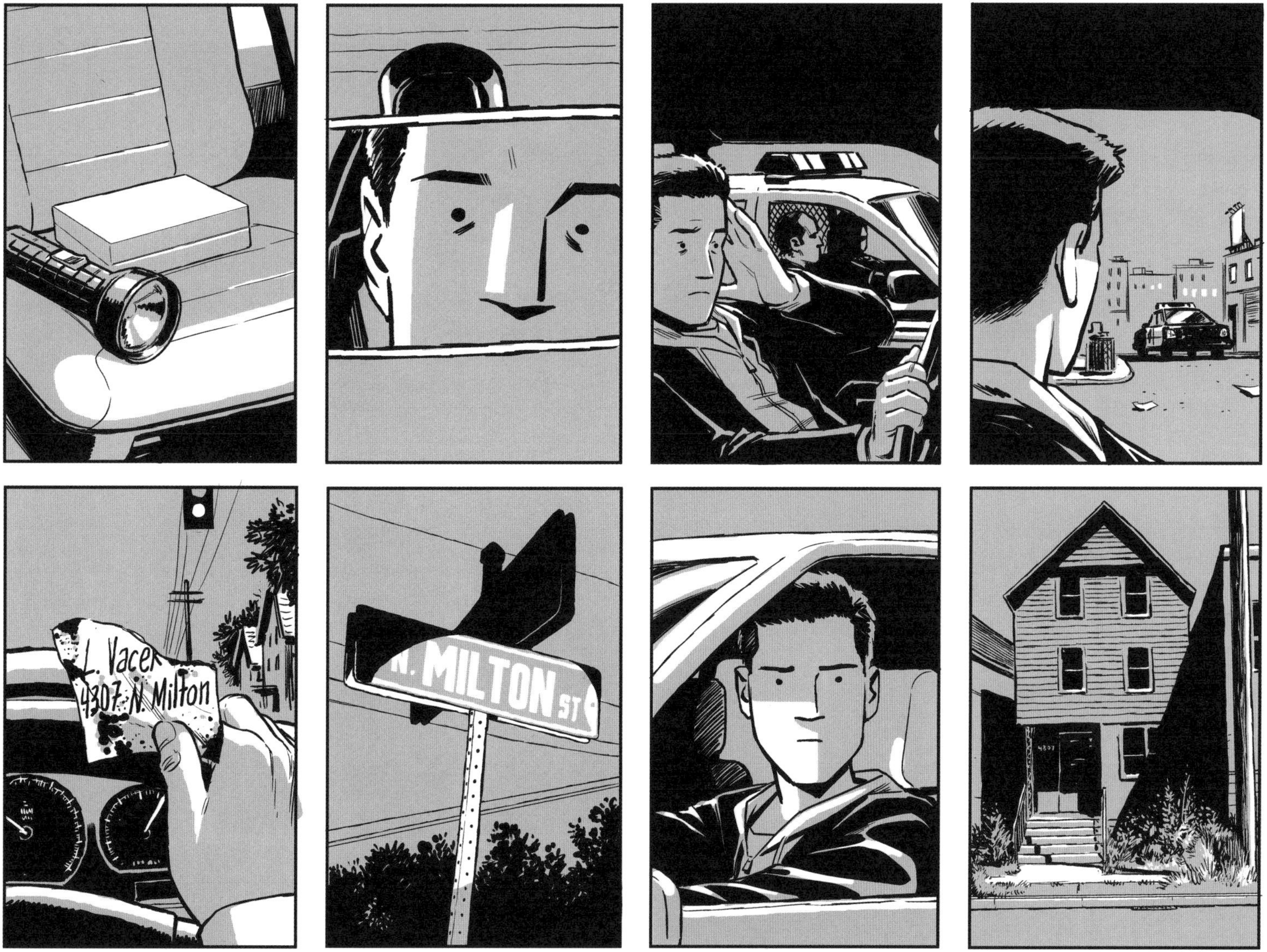
L. Vacek
4307 N. Milton
N. MILTON ST

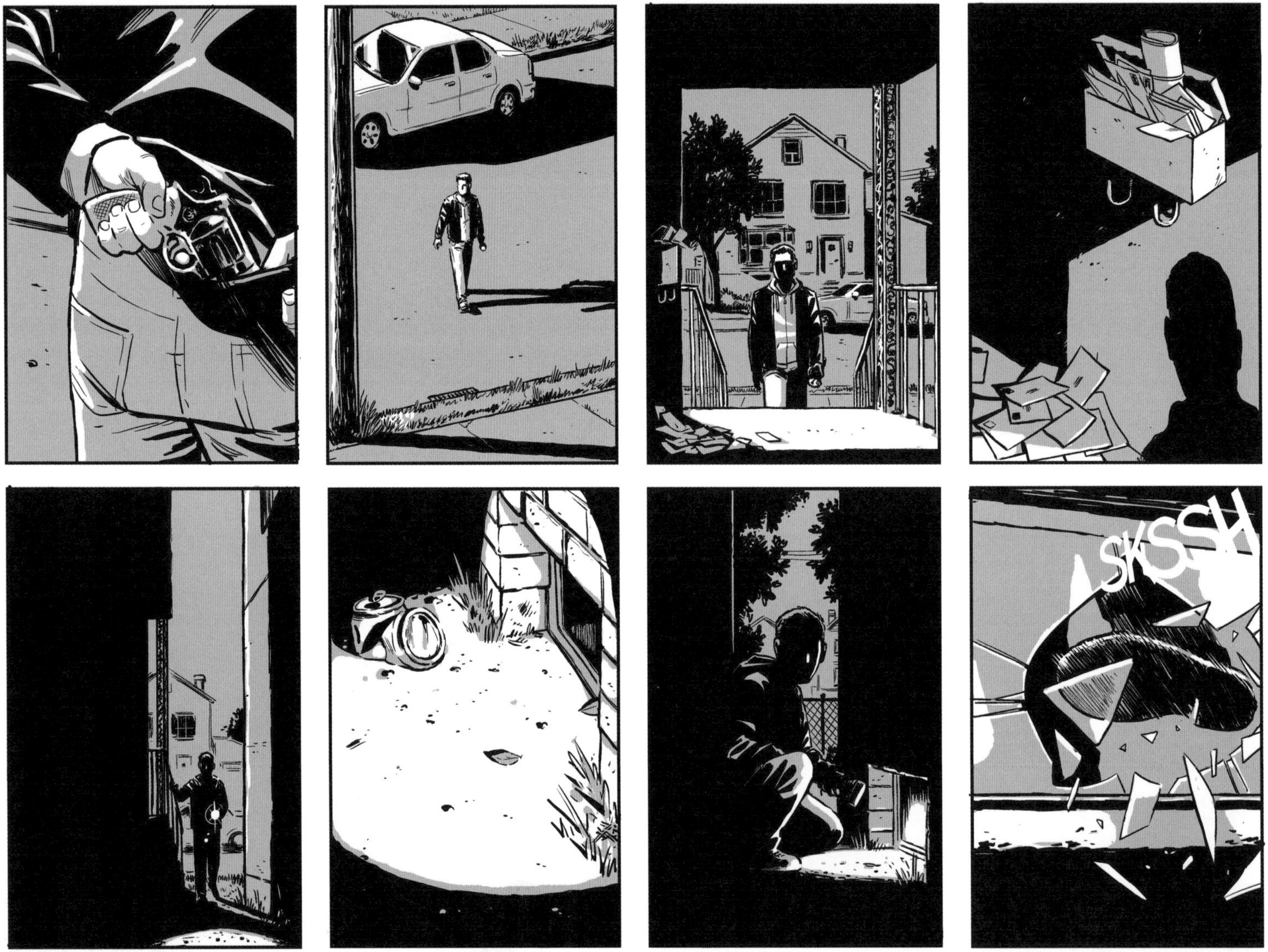
SKSSH

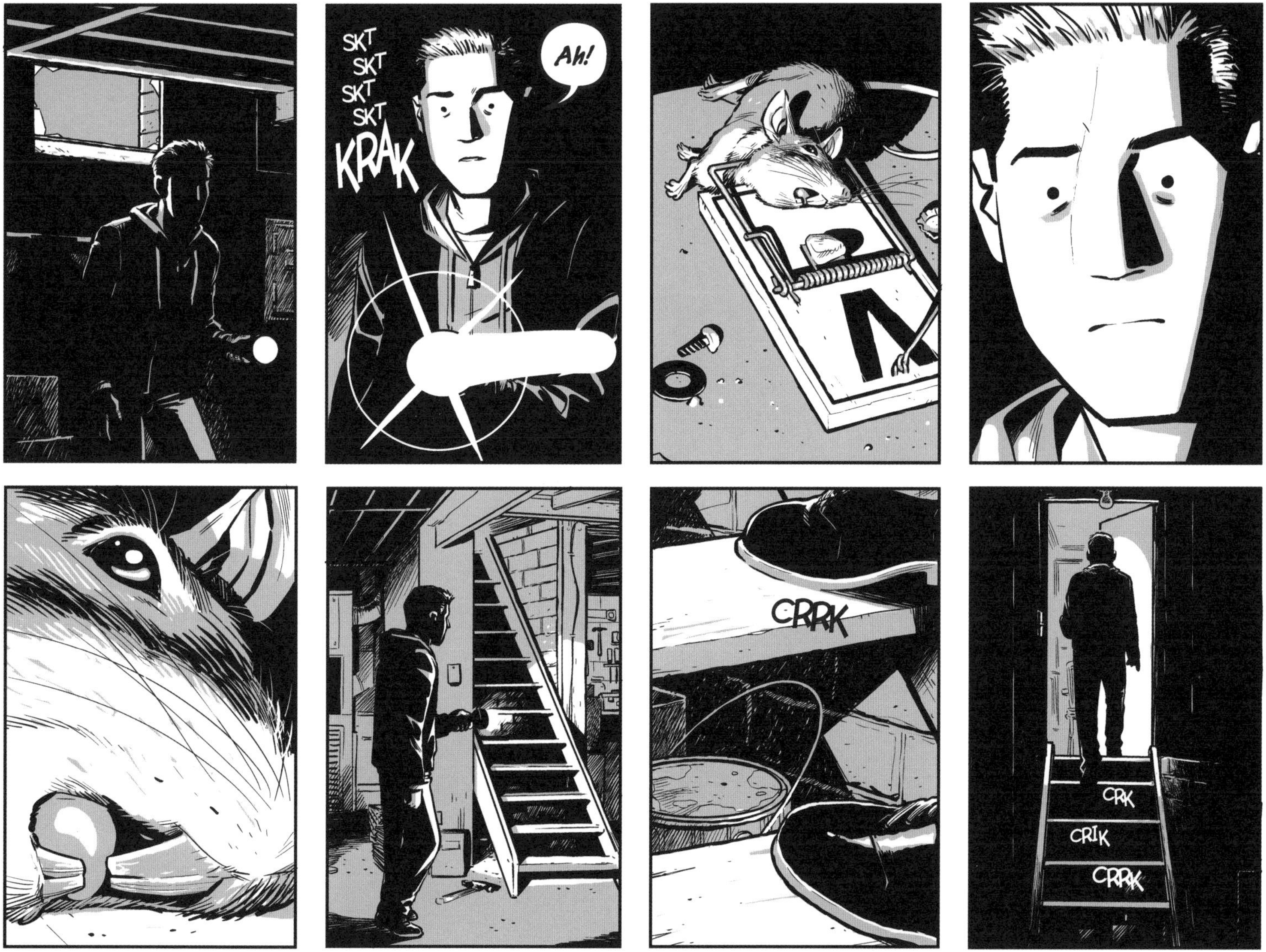
SKT SKT SKT SKT
KRAK
Ah!
CRRK
CRK
CRIK
CRRK

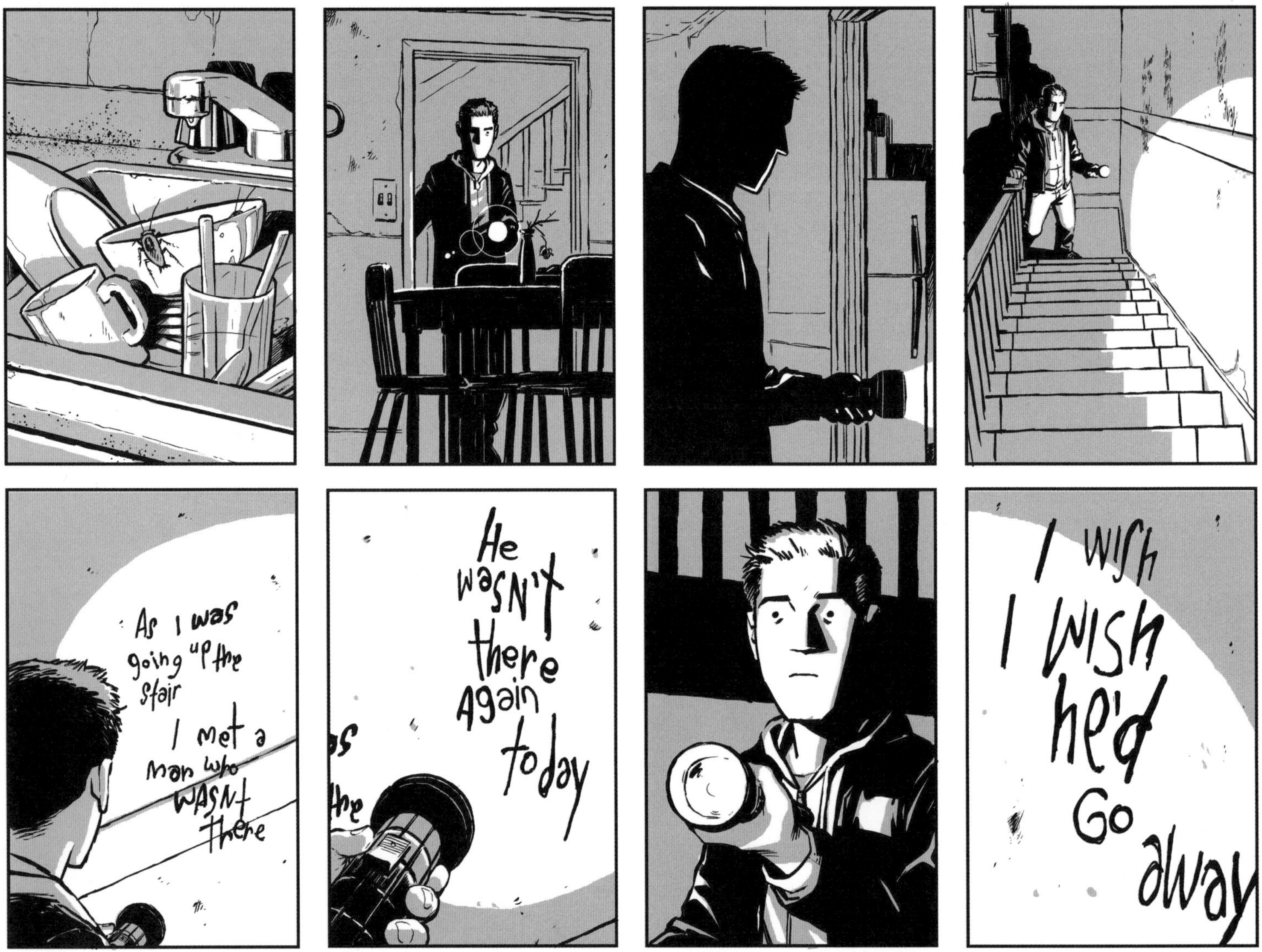
Go away
As I was going up the stair
I met a man who WASNt there
He wasn't there again today
I wish
I wish he'd Go away

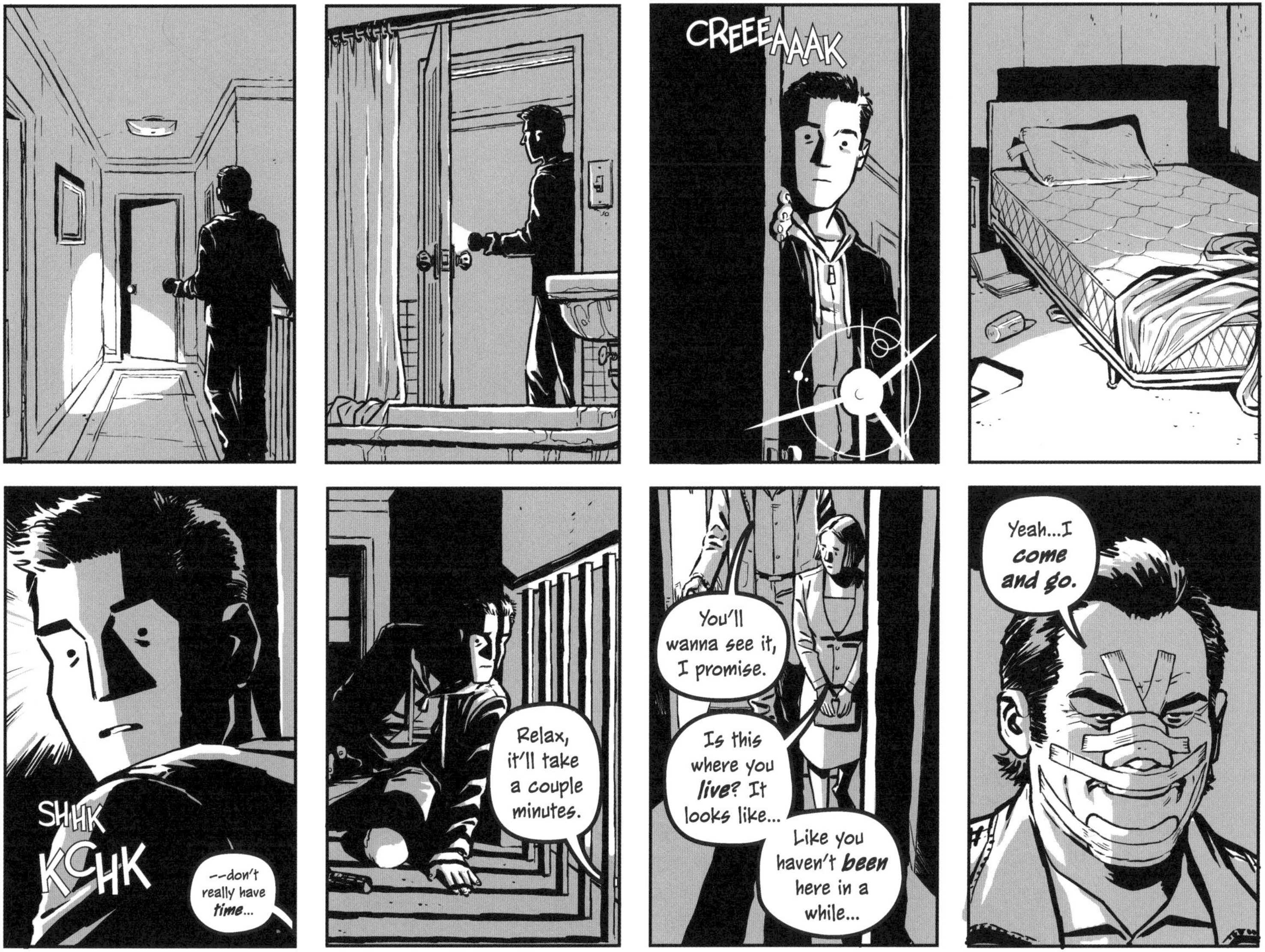
CREEEAAAK
SHHK
KCHK
--don't really have *time*...
Relax, it'll take a couple minutes.
You'll wanna see it, I promise.
Is this where you *live*? It looks like...
Like you haven't *been* here in a while...
Yeah...I *come and go*.

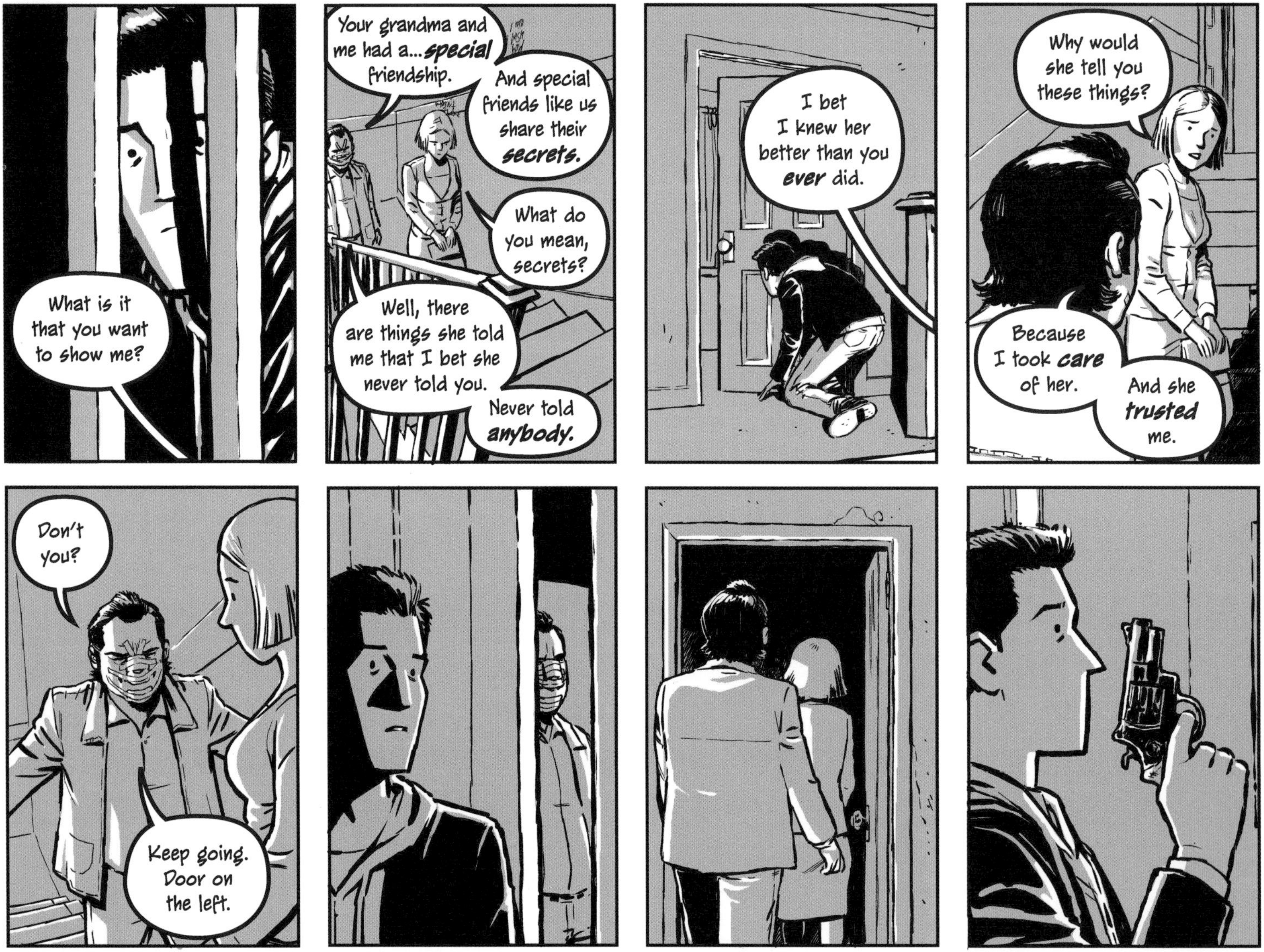

What is it that you want to show me?
Your grandma and me had a...special friendship.
And special friends like us share their secrets.
What do you mean, secrets?
Well, there are things she told me that I bet she never told you.
Never told anybody.
I bet I knew her better than you ever did.
Why would she tell you these things?
Because I took care of her.
And she trusted me.
Don't you?
Keep going. Door on the left.

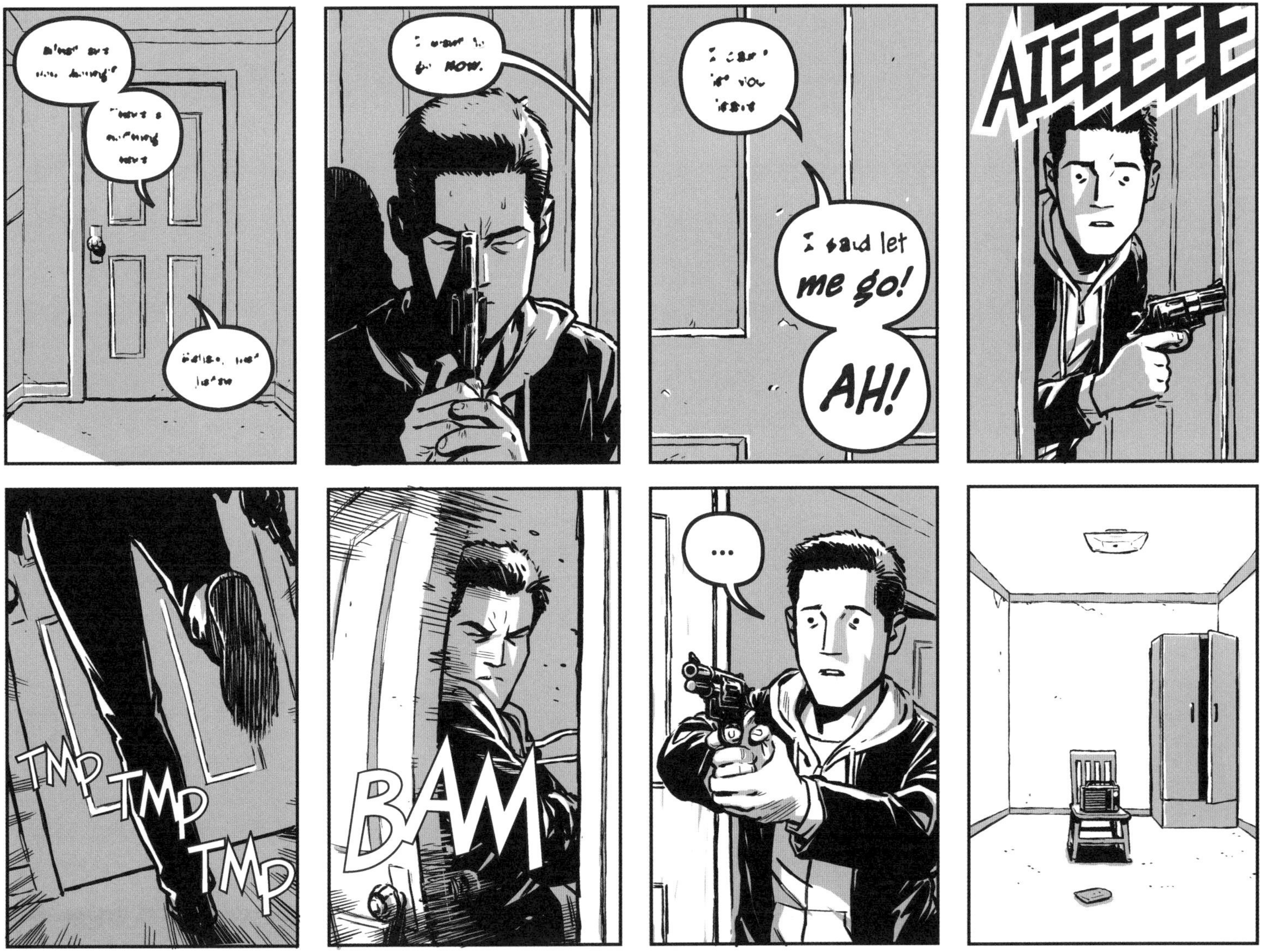
I said let me go!
AH!
AIEEEEE
TMP TMP TMP
BAM
...

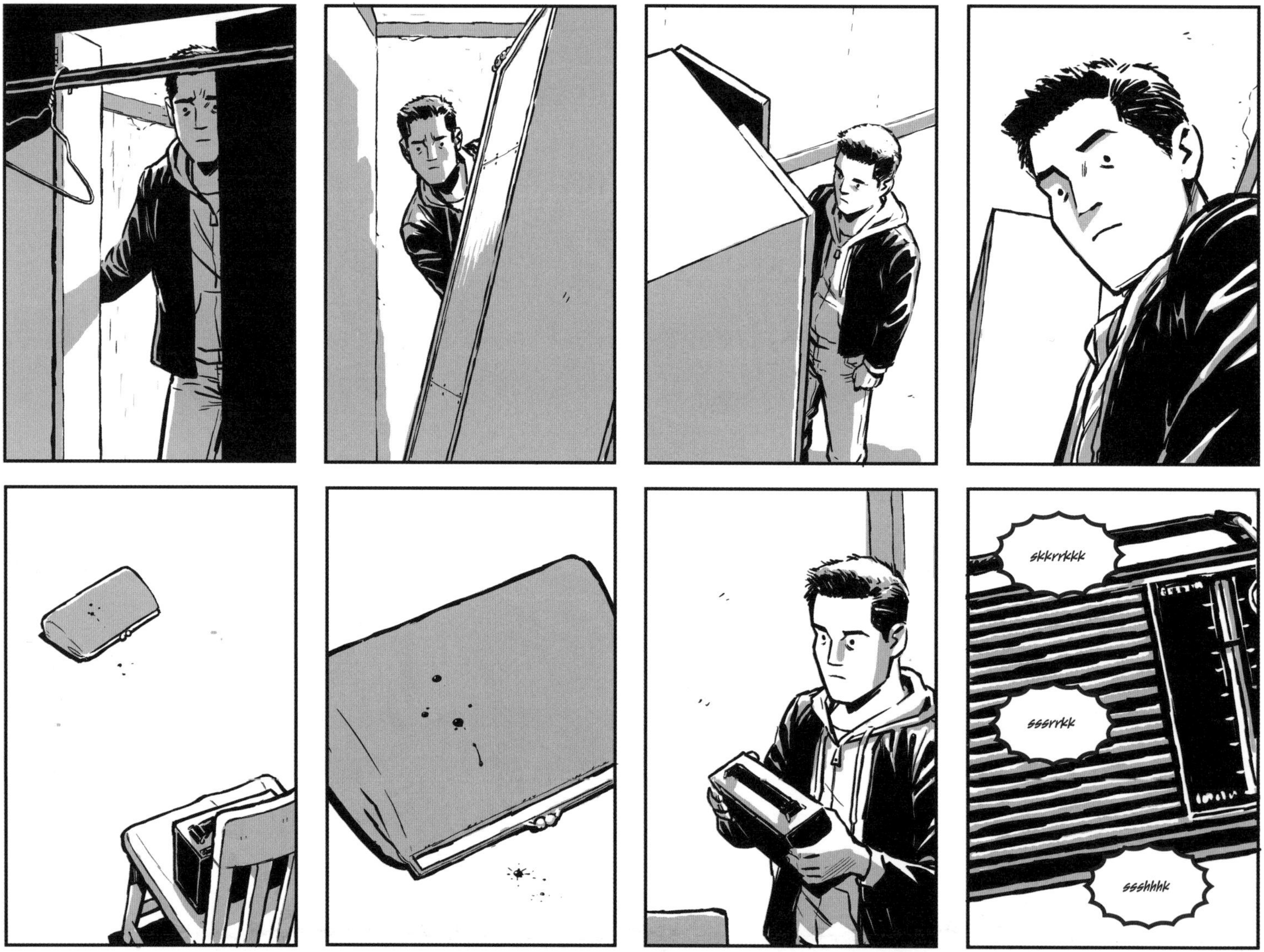
skkrrkkk
sssrrkk
ssshhhk

120

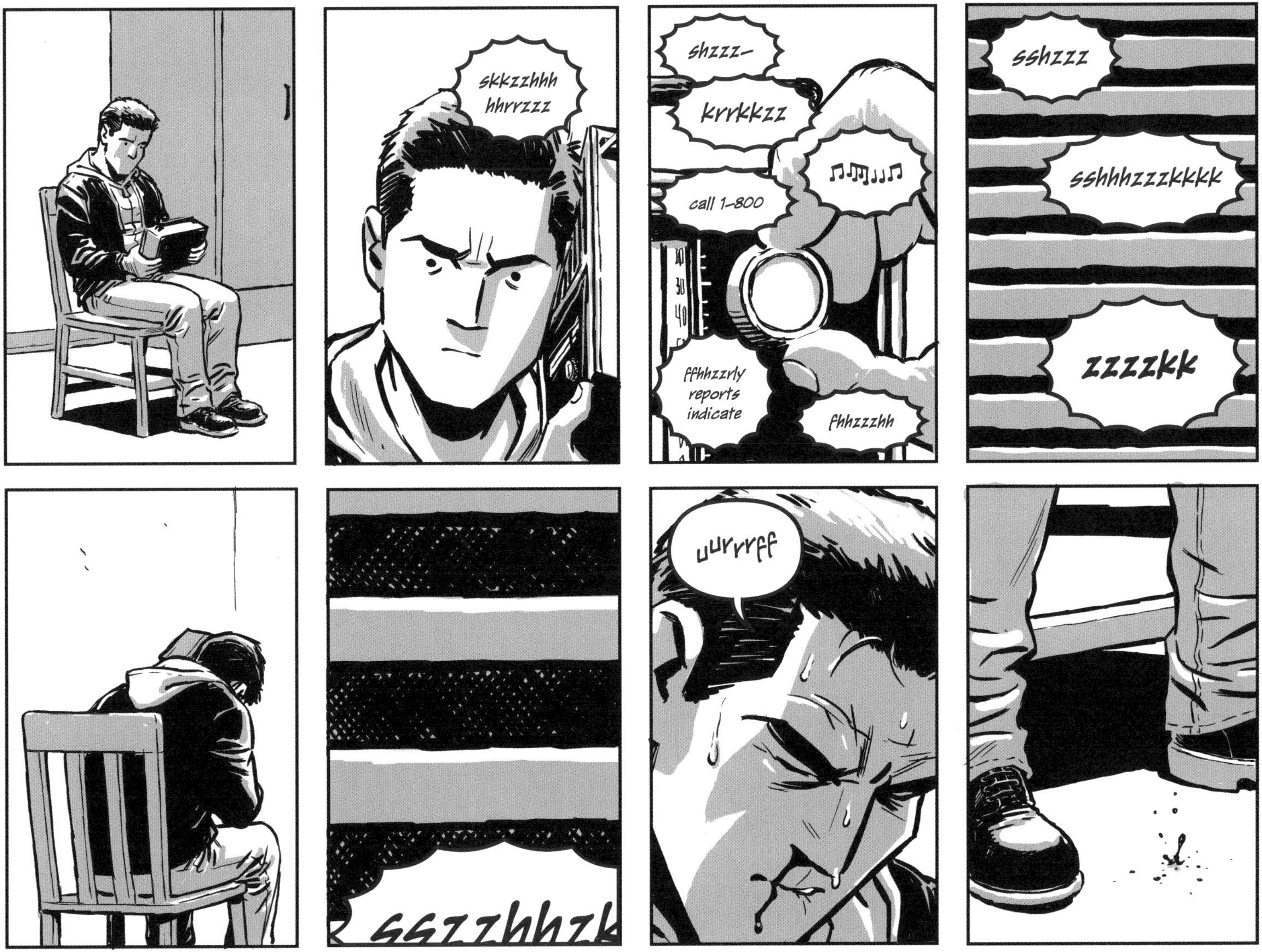
skkzzhhh hhrrzzz
shzzz-
krrkkzz
♫♬♩♩♫
call 1-800
ffhhzzrly reports indicate
fhhzzzhh
sshzzz
sshhhzzzkkkk
zzzzkk
sszzhhzk
uurrff

121

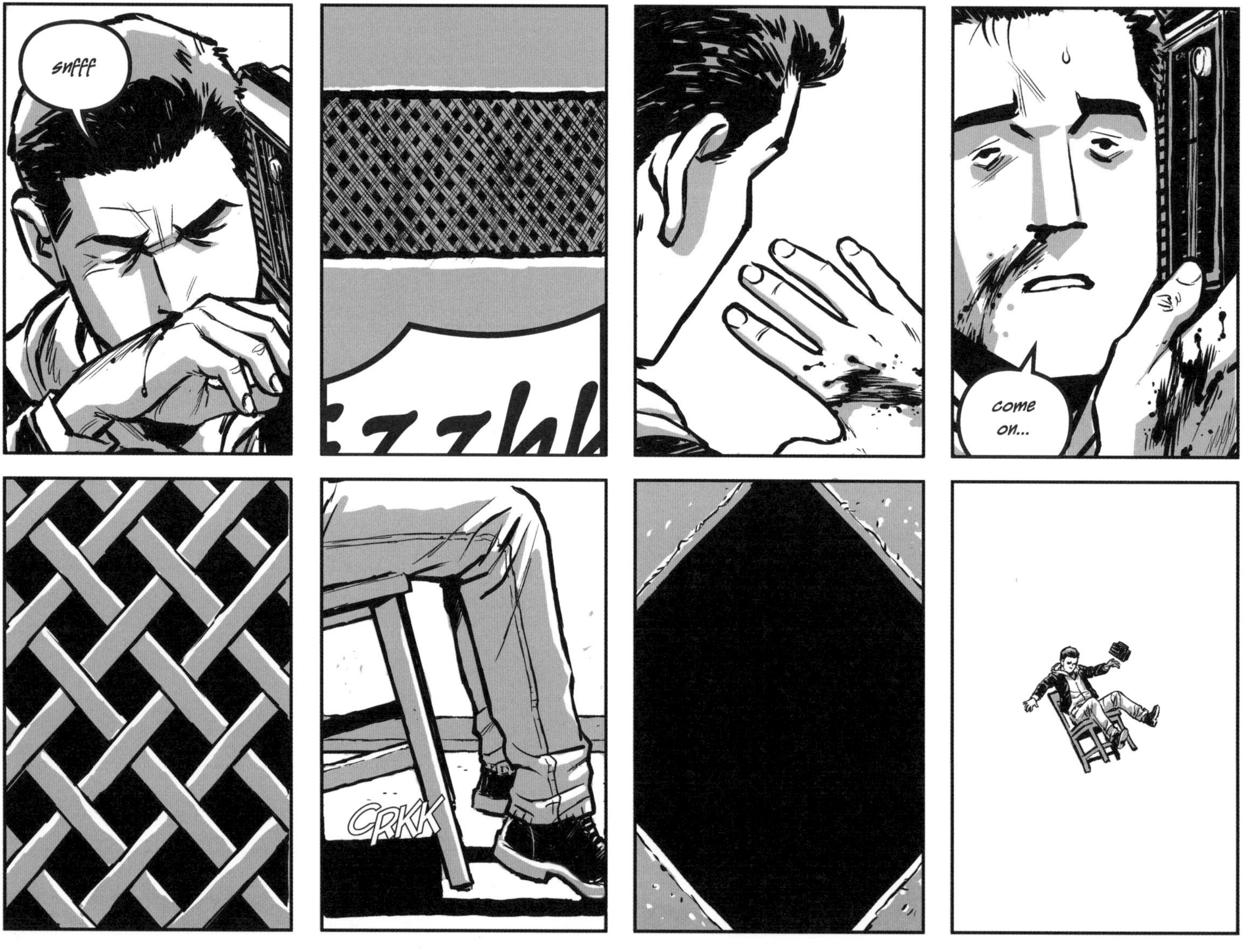
snfff
come on...
CRKK

122

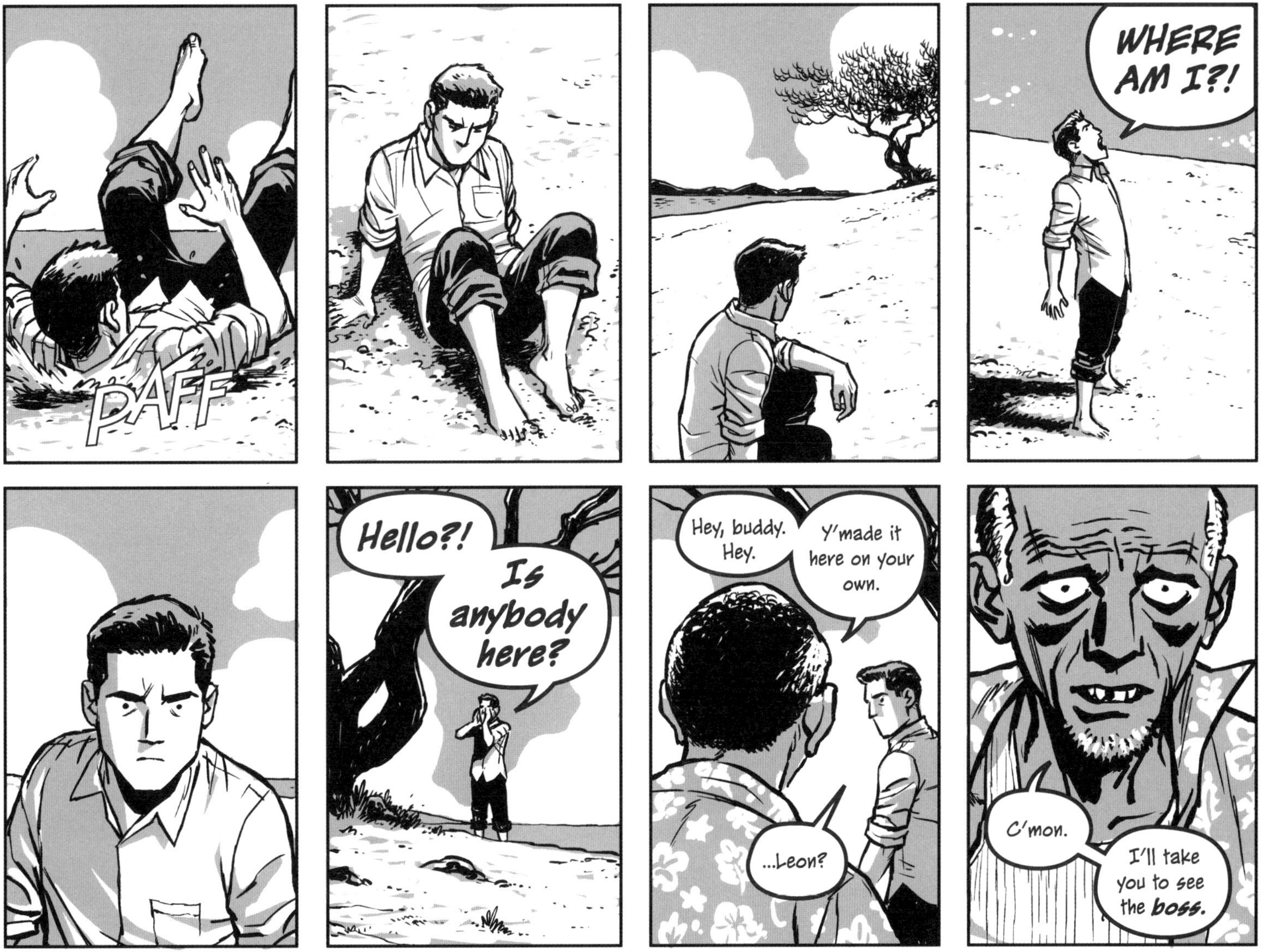
PAFF
WHERE AM I?!
Hello?!
Is anybody here?
Hey, buddy. Hey.
Y'made it here on your own.
...Leon?
C'mon.
I'll take you to see the boss.

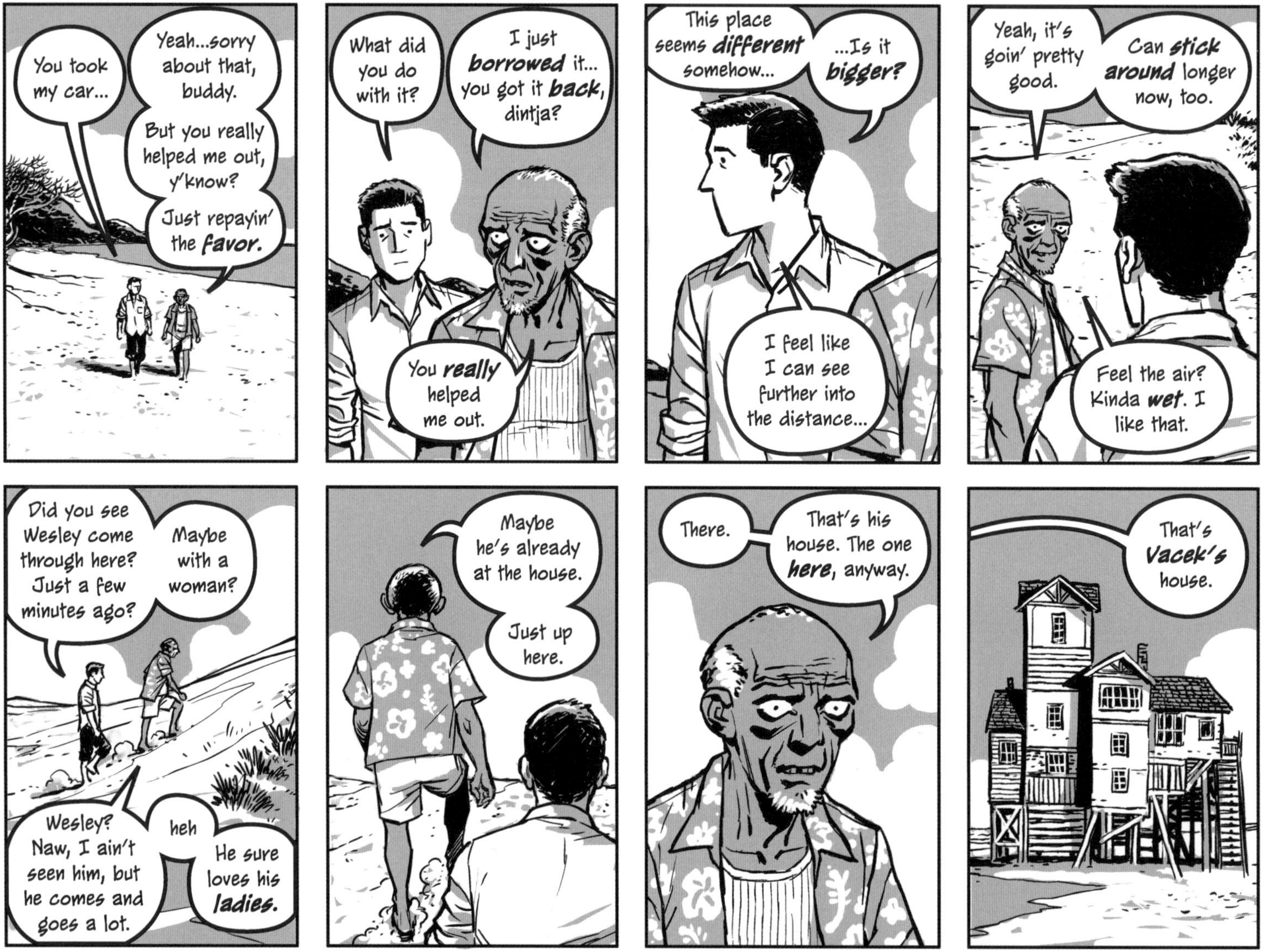
You took my car...
Yeah...sorry about that, buddy.
But you really helped me out, y'know?
Just repayin' the favor.
What did you do with it?
I just borrowed it... you got it back, dintja?
You really helped me out.
This place seems different somehow...
...Is it bigger?
I feel like I can see further into the distance...
Yeah, it's goin' pretty good.
Can stick around longer now, too.
Feel the air? Kinda wet. I like that.
Did you see Wesley come through here? Just a few minutes ago?
Maybe with a woman?
Wesley? Naw, I ain't seen him, but he comes and goes a lot.
heh
He sure loves his ladies.
Maybe he's already at the house.
Just up here.
There.
That's his house. The one here, anyway.
That's Vacek's house.

C'mon, buddy!

Ah!

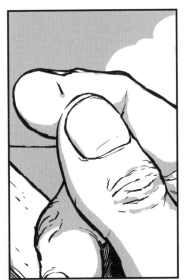

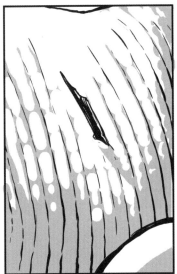

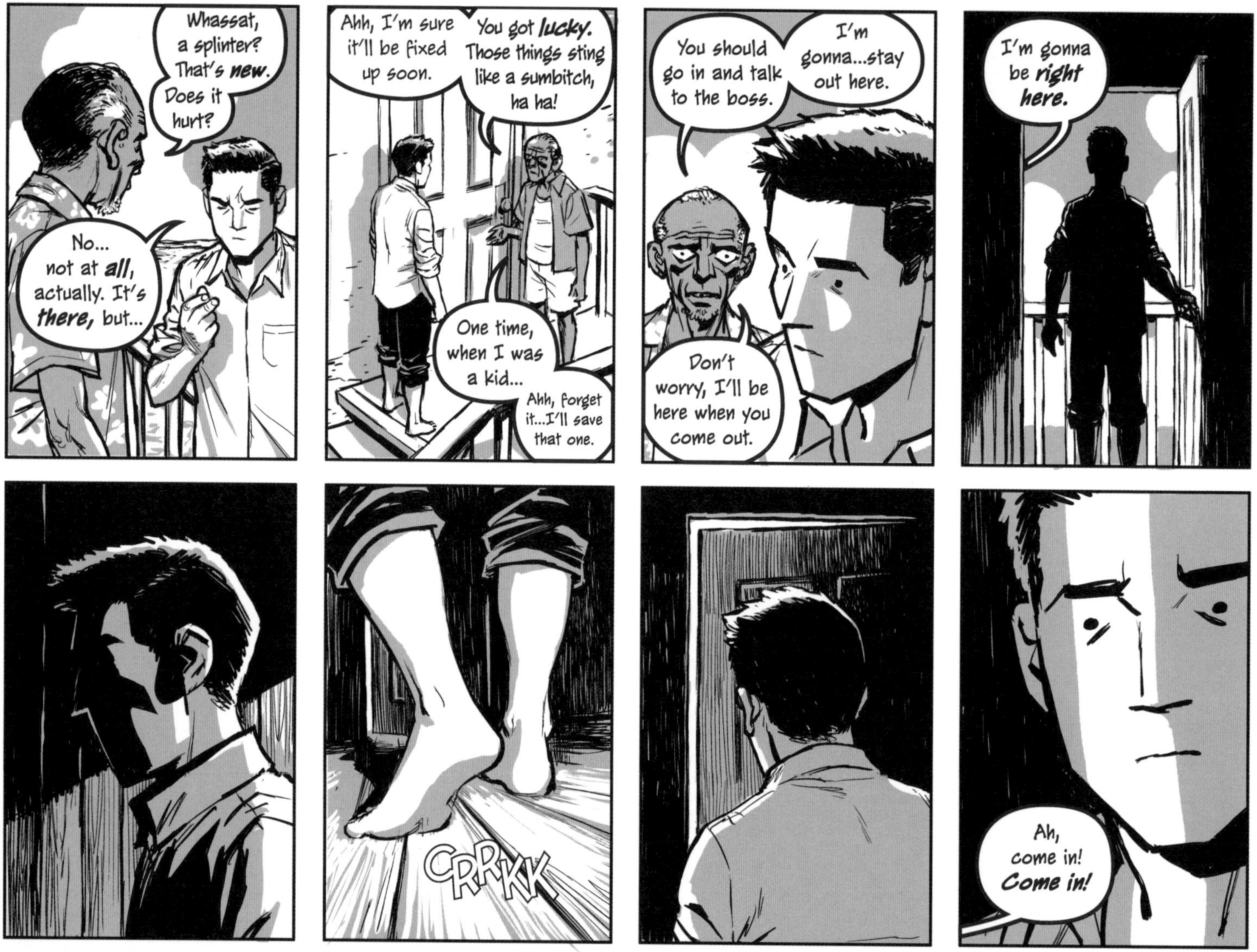
Whassat, a splinter? That's **new**. Does it hurt?
No... not at **all**, actually. It's **there,** but...
Ahh, I'm sure it'll be fixed up soon.
You got **lucky.** Those things sting like a sumbitch, ha ha!
One time, when I was a kid...
Ahh, forget it...I'll save that one.
You should go in and talk to the boss.
I'm gonna...stay out here.
Don't worry, I'll be here when you come out.
I'm gonna be **right here.**
CRRKK
Ah, come in! **Come in!**

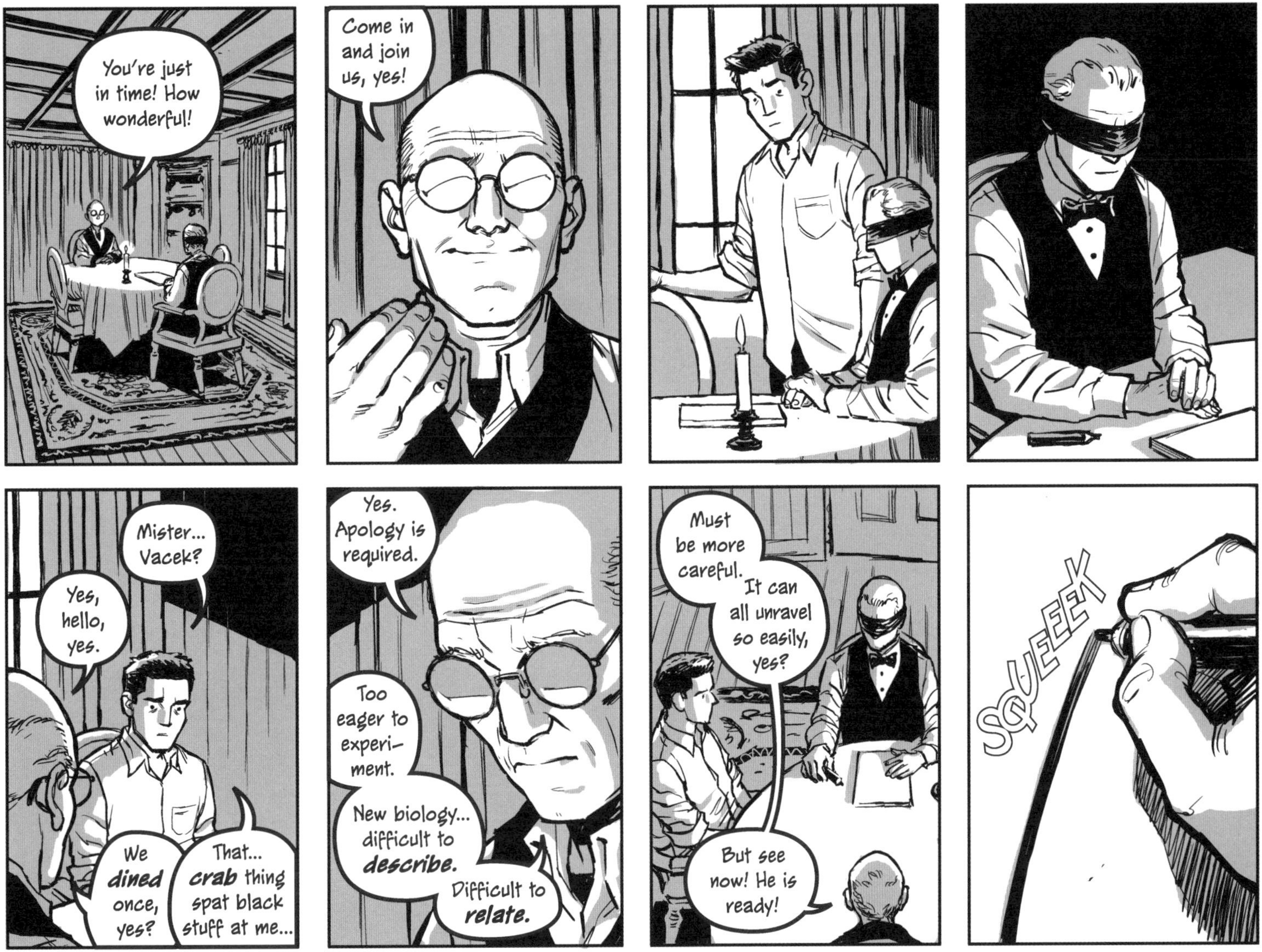
You're just in time! How wonderful!
Come in and join us, yes!
Mister... Vacek?
Yes, hello, yes.
We dined once, yes?
That... crab thing spat black stuff at me...
Yes. Apology is required.
Too eager to experi-ment.
New biology... difficult to describe.
Difficult to relate.
Must be more careful.
It can all unravel so easily, yes?
But see now! He is ready!
SQUEEEK

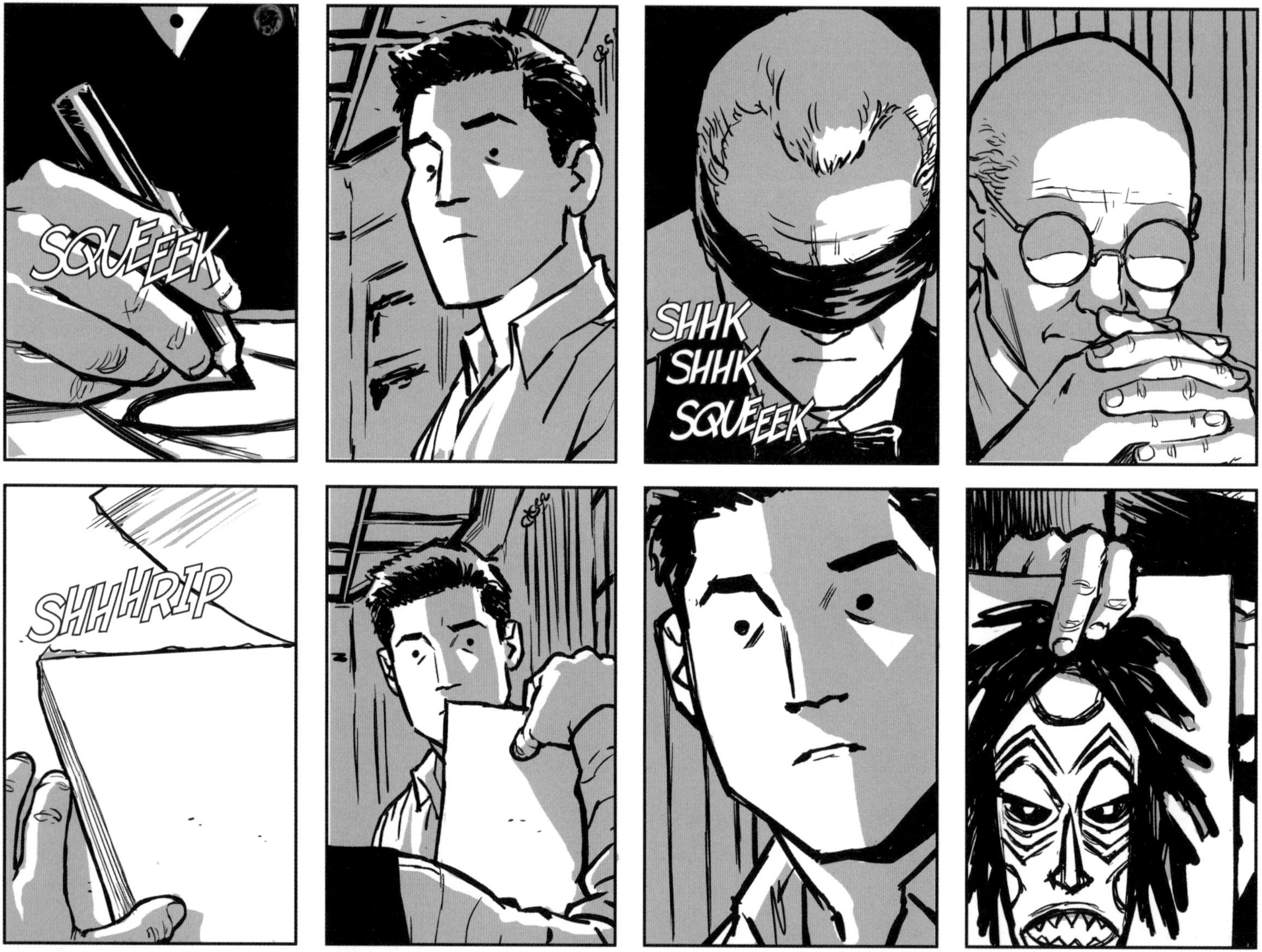
SQUEEEK
SHHK
SHHK
SQUEEEK
SHHHRIP

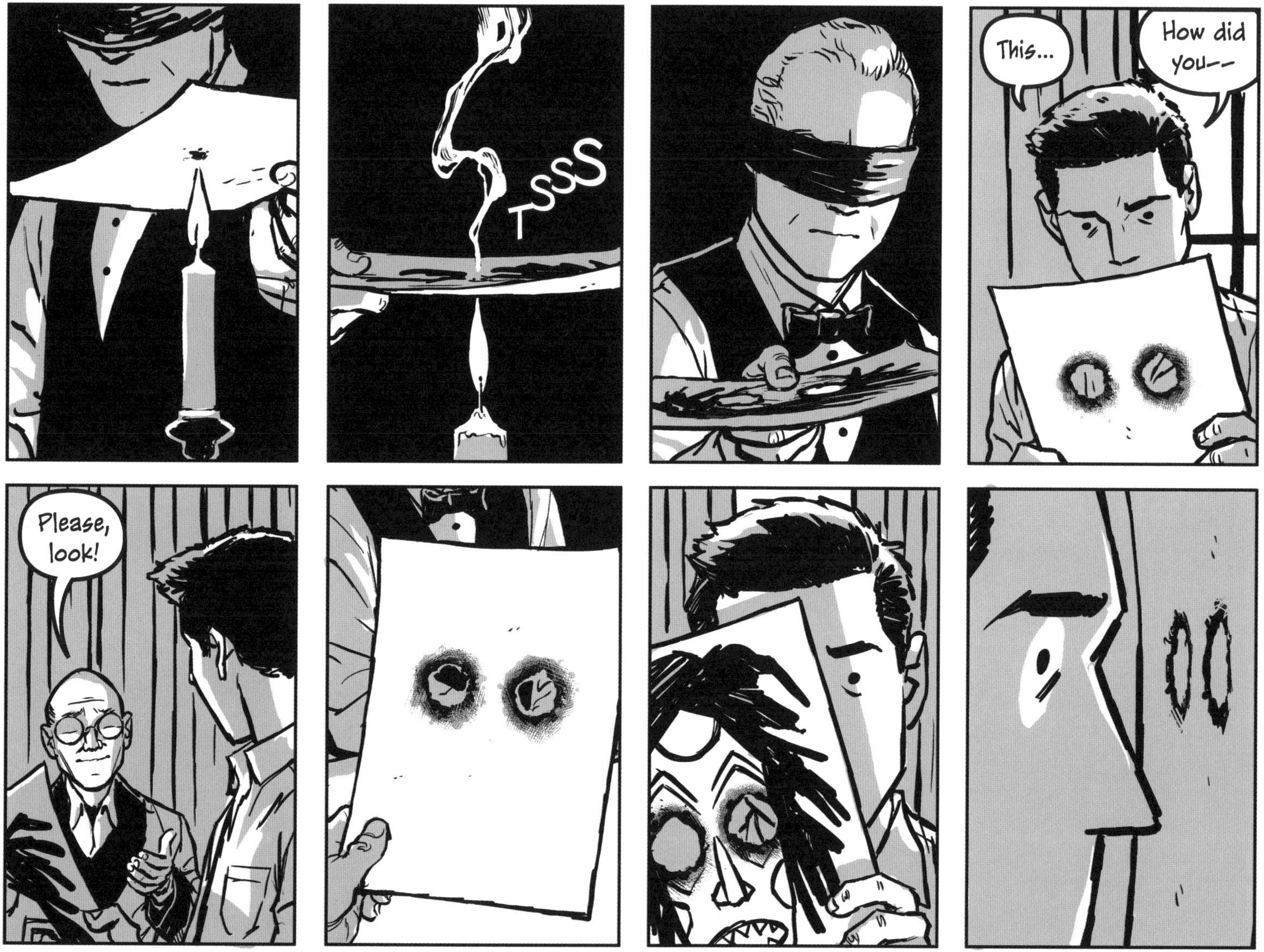
TSSS
This...
How did you--
Please, look!

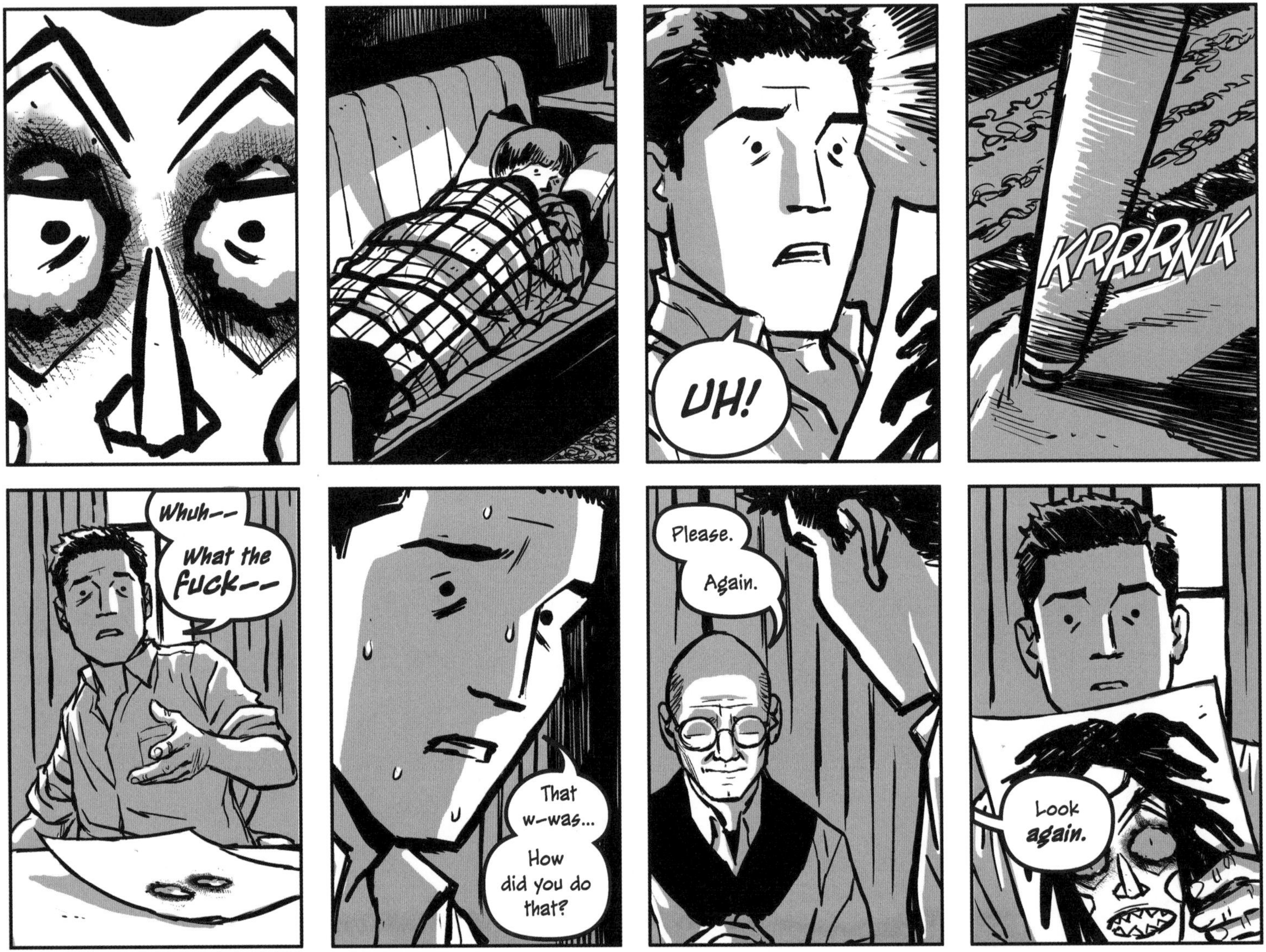
UH!
KRRRNK
Whuh--
What the fuck--
That w-was...
How did you do that?
Please.
Again.
Look again.

130

huhm

KTINK

whuh!

TMP
TMP
TMP
WHUDD

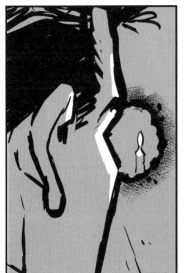

Enough for now, I think.

We have another guest.

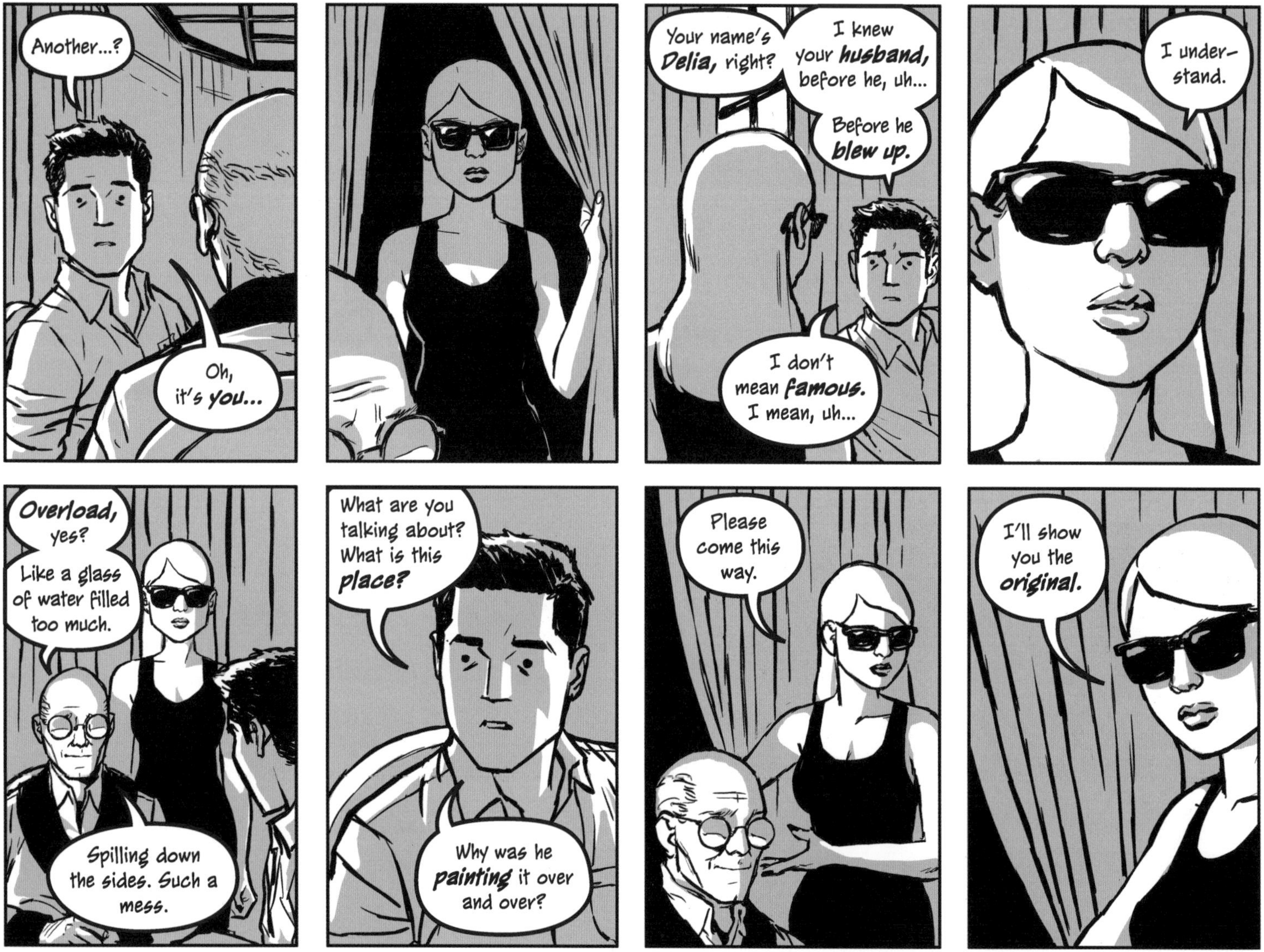
Another...?
Oh, it's *you...*
Your name's *Delia,* right?
I knew your *husband,* before he, uh...
Before he *blew up.*
I don't mean *famous.* I mean, uh...
I understand.
Overload, yes?
Like a glass of water filled too much.
Spilling down the sides. Such a mess.
What are you talking about? What is this *place?*
Why was he *painting* it over and over?
Please come this way.
I'll show you the *original.*

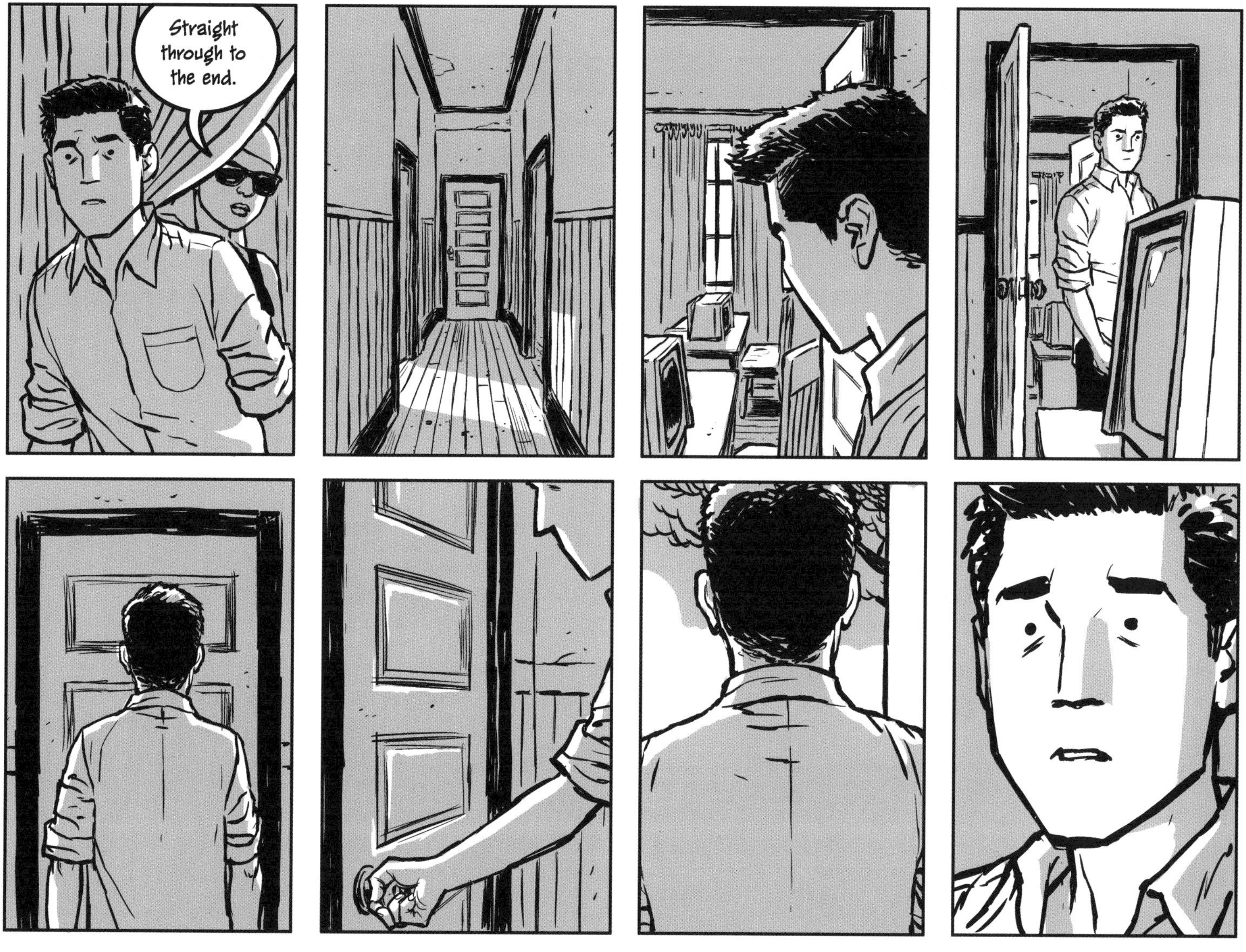
Straight through to the end.

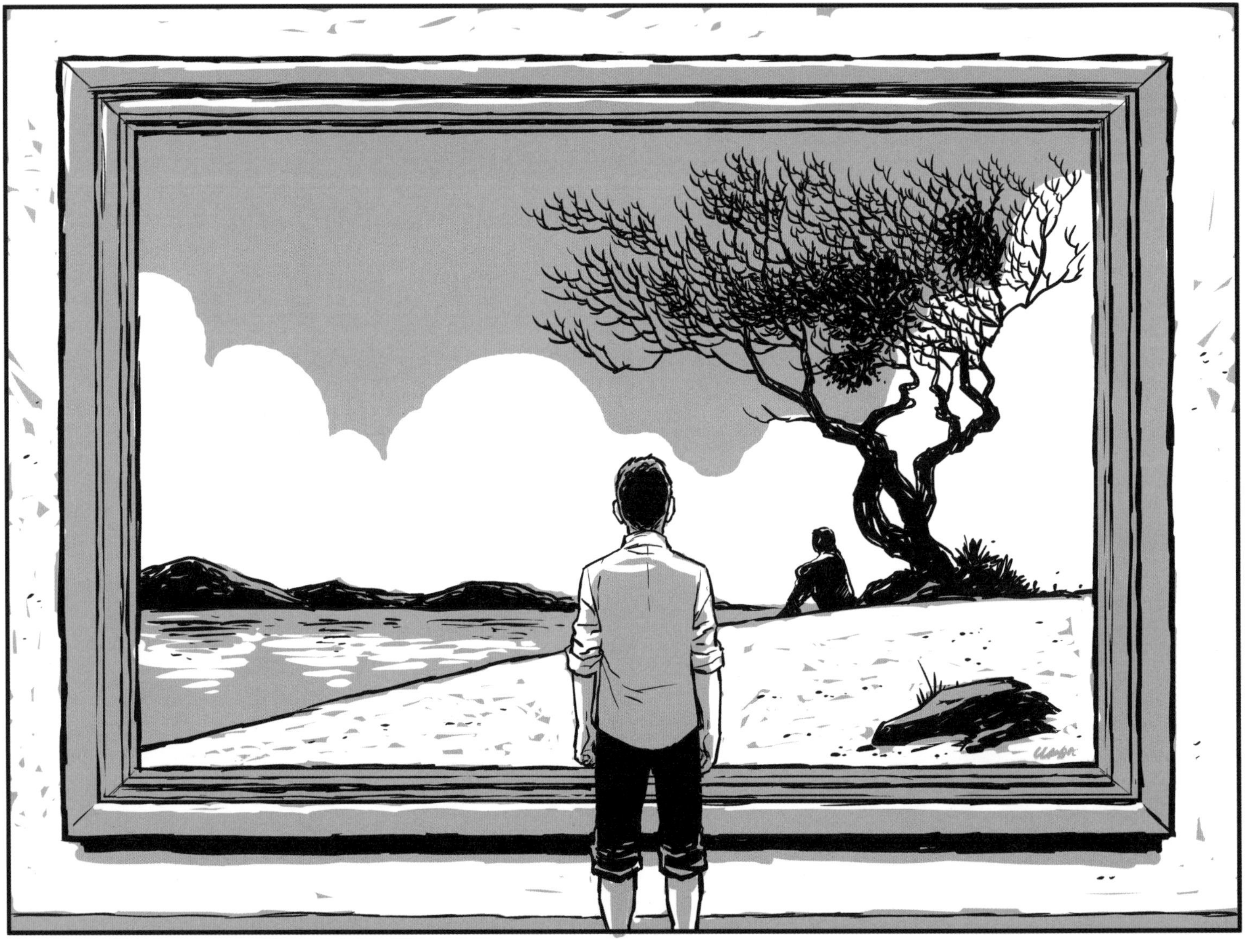

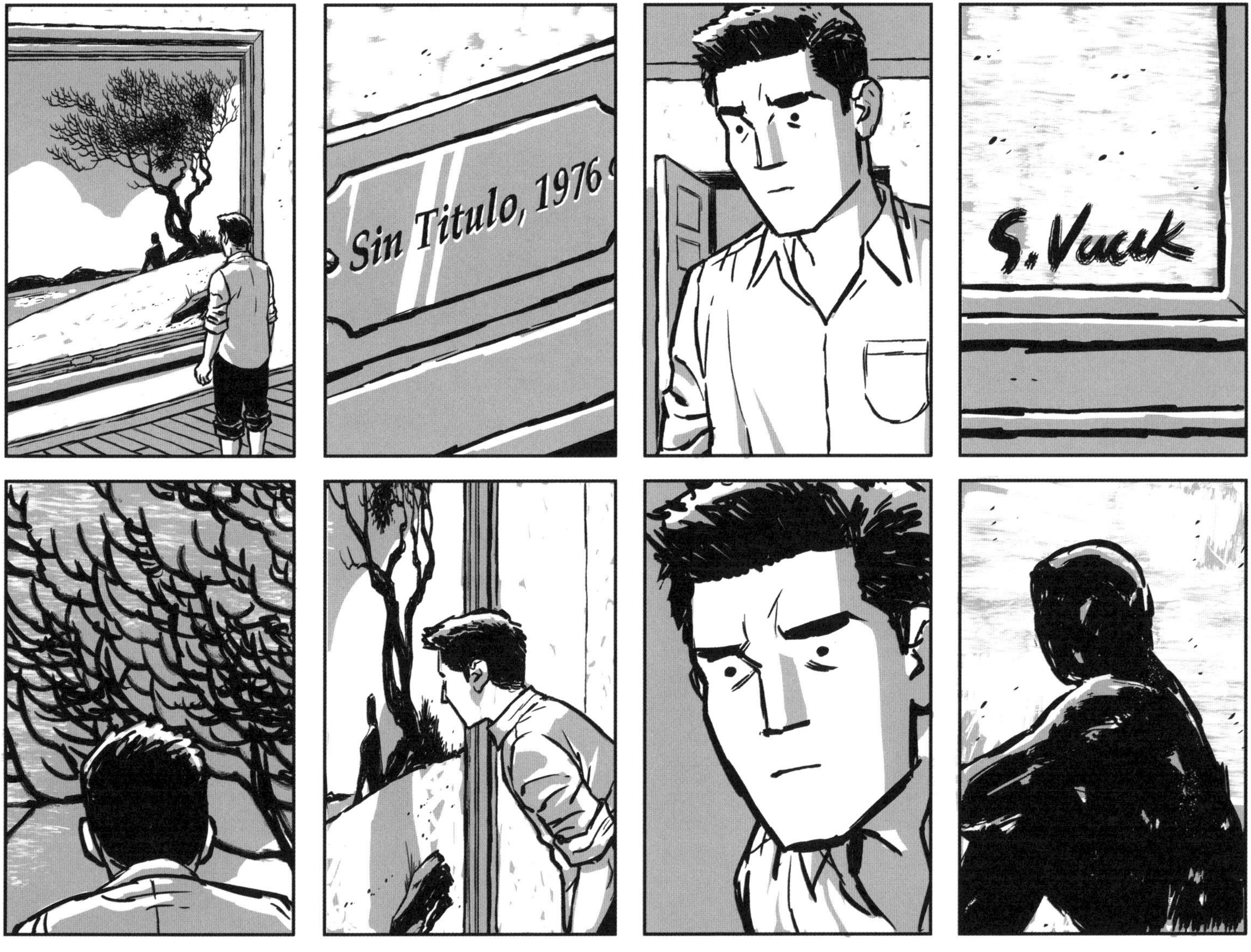
Sin Titulo, 1976

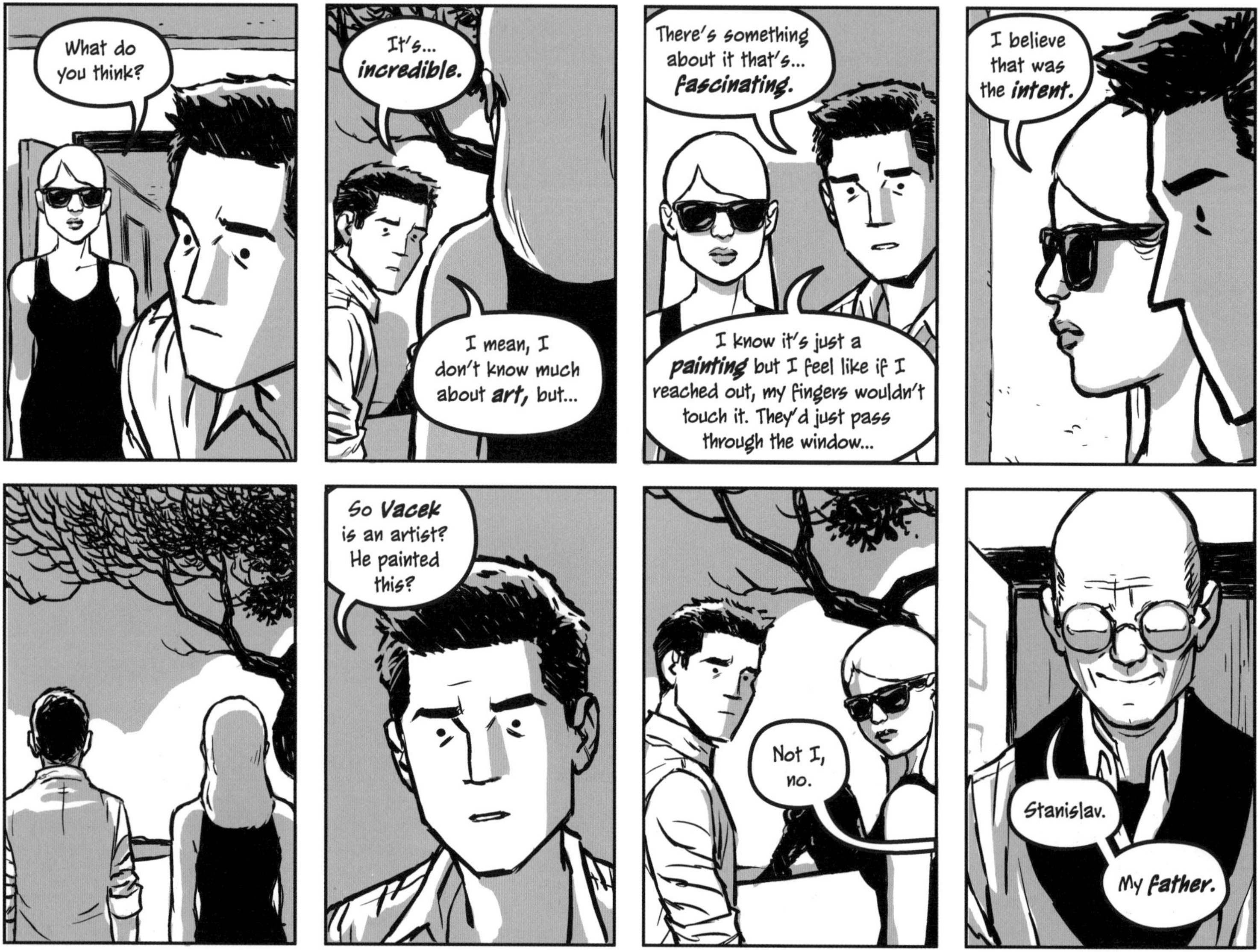
What do you think?
It's... incredible.
I mean, I don't know much about art, but...
There's something about it that's... fascinating.
I know it's just a painting but I feel like if I reached out, my fingers wouldn't touch it. They'd just pass through the window...
I believe that was the intent.
So Vacek is an artist? He painted this?
Not I, no.
Stanislav.
My father.

Consider a *bed*.

Or, rather, *three* beds.

The first is created by *God*.

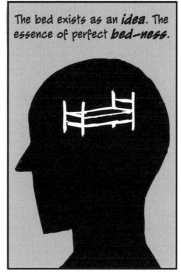

The bed exists as an *idea*. The essence of perfect *bed-ness*.

The *carpenter* gives *shape* to the idea.

But he has not made *the* bed, merely *a* bed.

Finally, the *painter* makes an *image* of a bed.

An *imitation* of an imitation.

A falsehood, a shallow replica of only its *appearance*.

The true artist would be concerned with *creating* reality, not imitation of it.

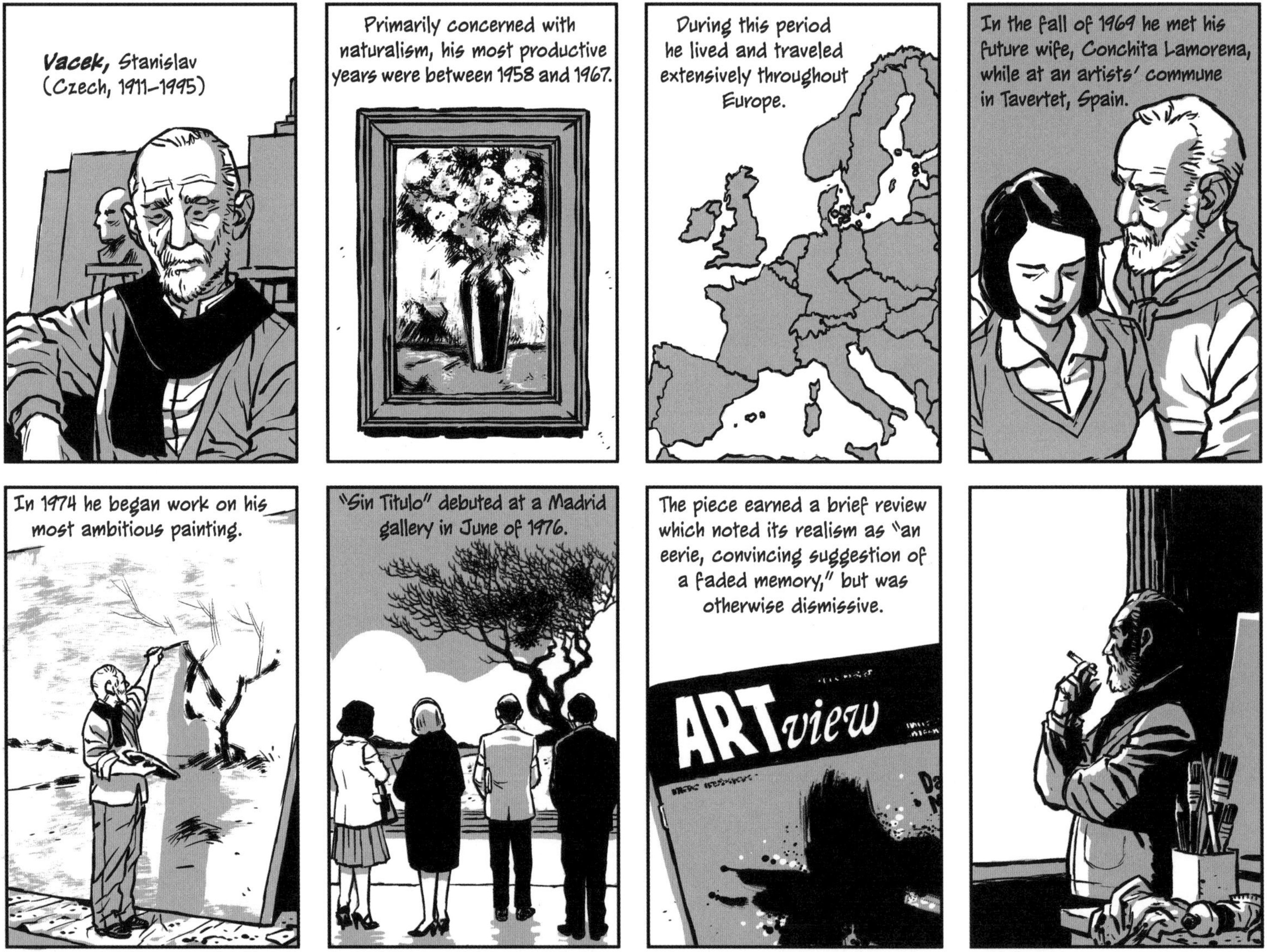
Vacek, Stanislav
(Czech, 1911–1995)
Primarily concerned with naturalism, his most productive years were between 1958 and 1967.
During this period he lived and traveled extensively throughout Europe.
In the fall of 1969 he met his future wife, Conchita Lamorena, while at an artists' commune in Tavertet, Spain.
In 1974 he began work on his most ambitious painting.
"Sin Titulo" debuted at a Madrid gallery in June of 1976.
The piece earned a brief review which noted its realism as "an eerie, convincing suggestion of a faded memory," but was otherwise dismissive.
ARTview

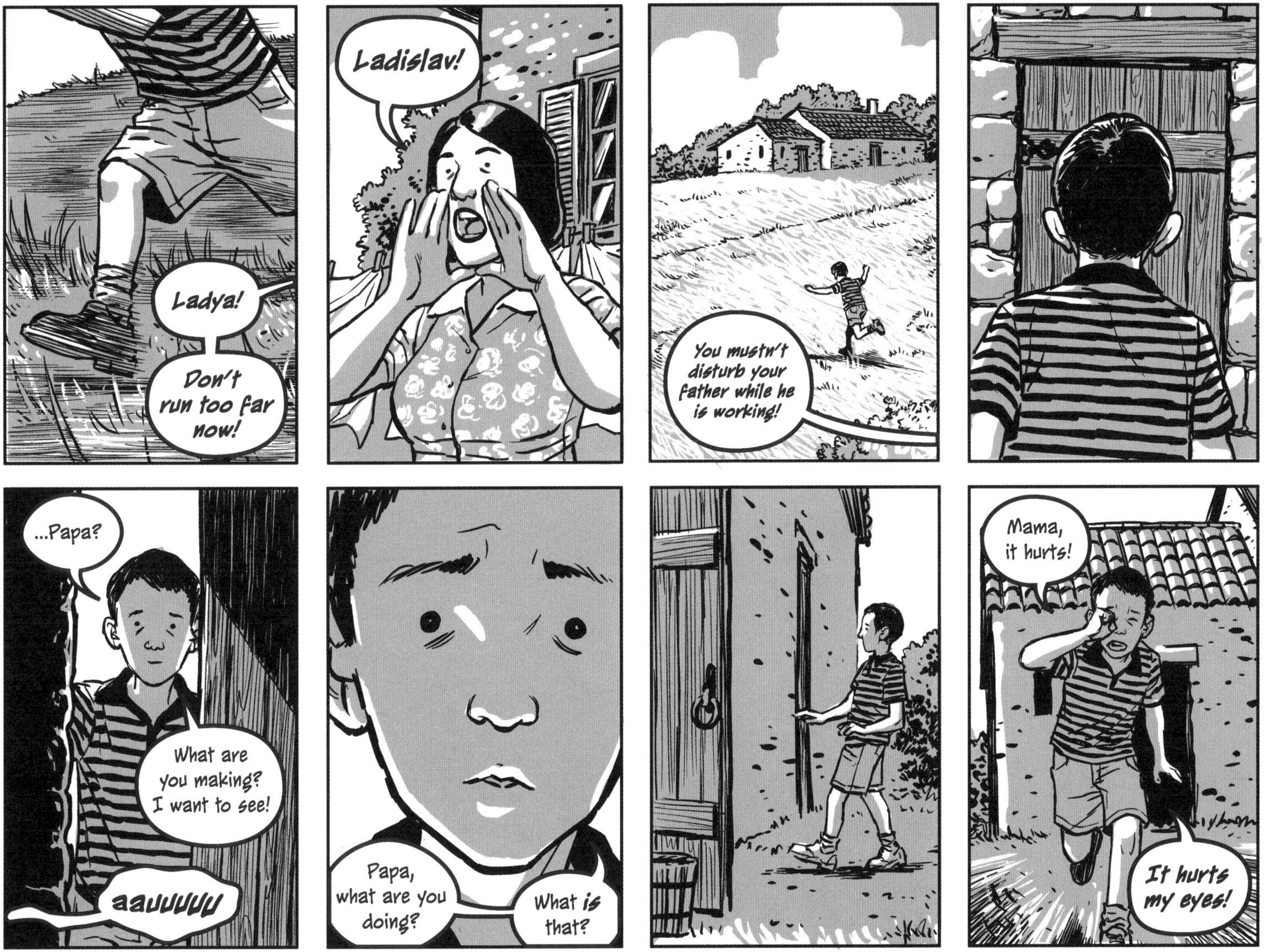
Ladya!
Don't run too far now!
Ladislav!
You mustn't disturb your father while he is working!
...Papa?
What are you making? I want to see!
aauuuuu
Papa, what are you doing?
What is that?
Mama, it hurts!
It hurts my eyes!

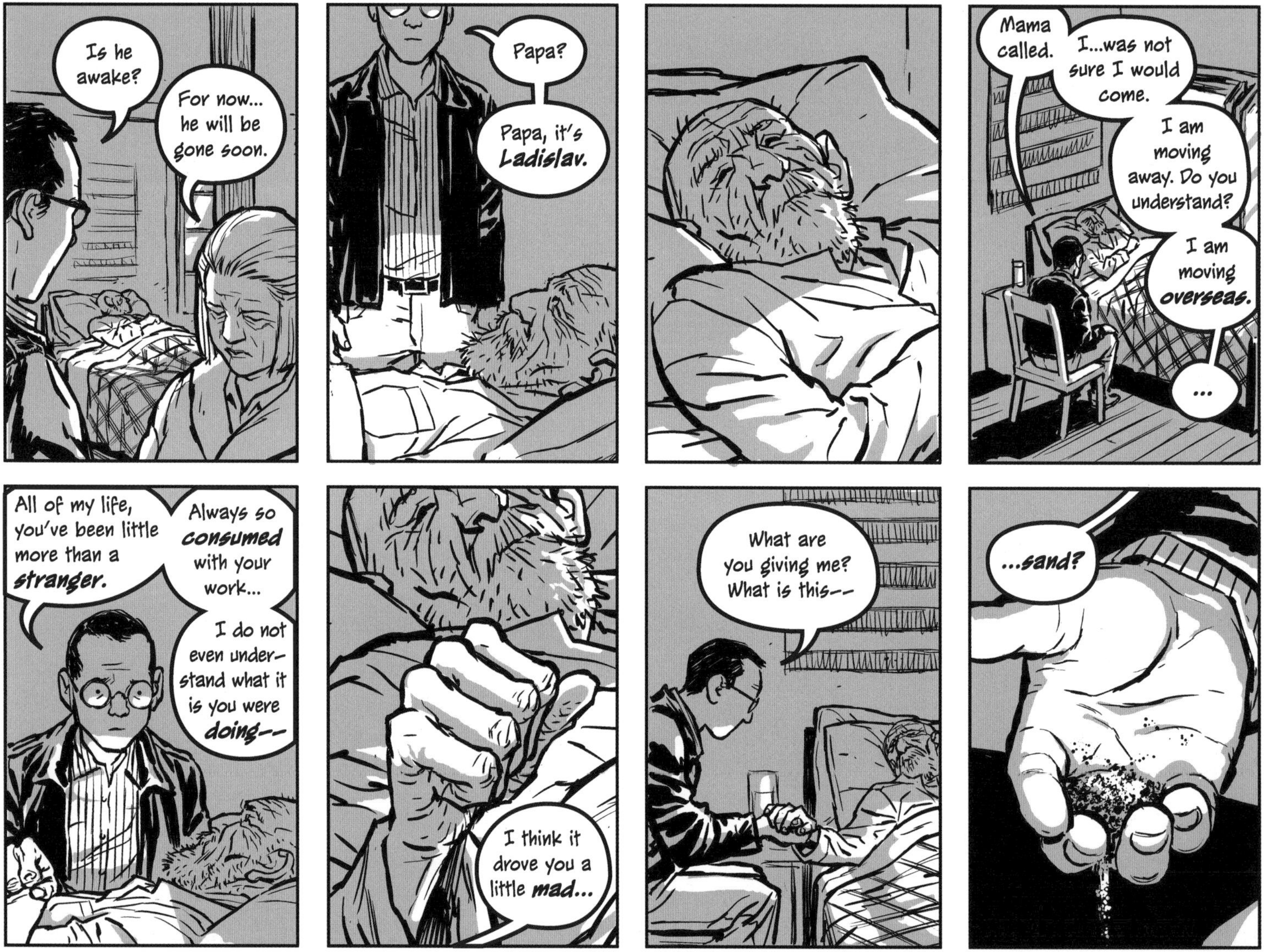
Is he awake?
For now... he will be gone soon.
Papa?
Papa, it's **Ladislav.**
Mama called.
I...was not sure I would come.
I am moving away. Do you understand?
I am moving **overseas.**
...
All of my life, you've been little more than a **stranger.**
Always so **consumed** with your work...
I do not even under-stand what it is you were **doing--**
I think it drove you a little **mad...**
What are you giving me? What is this--
...sand?

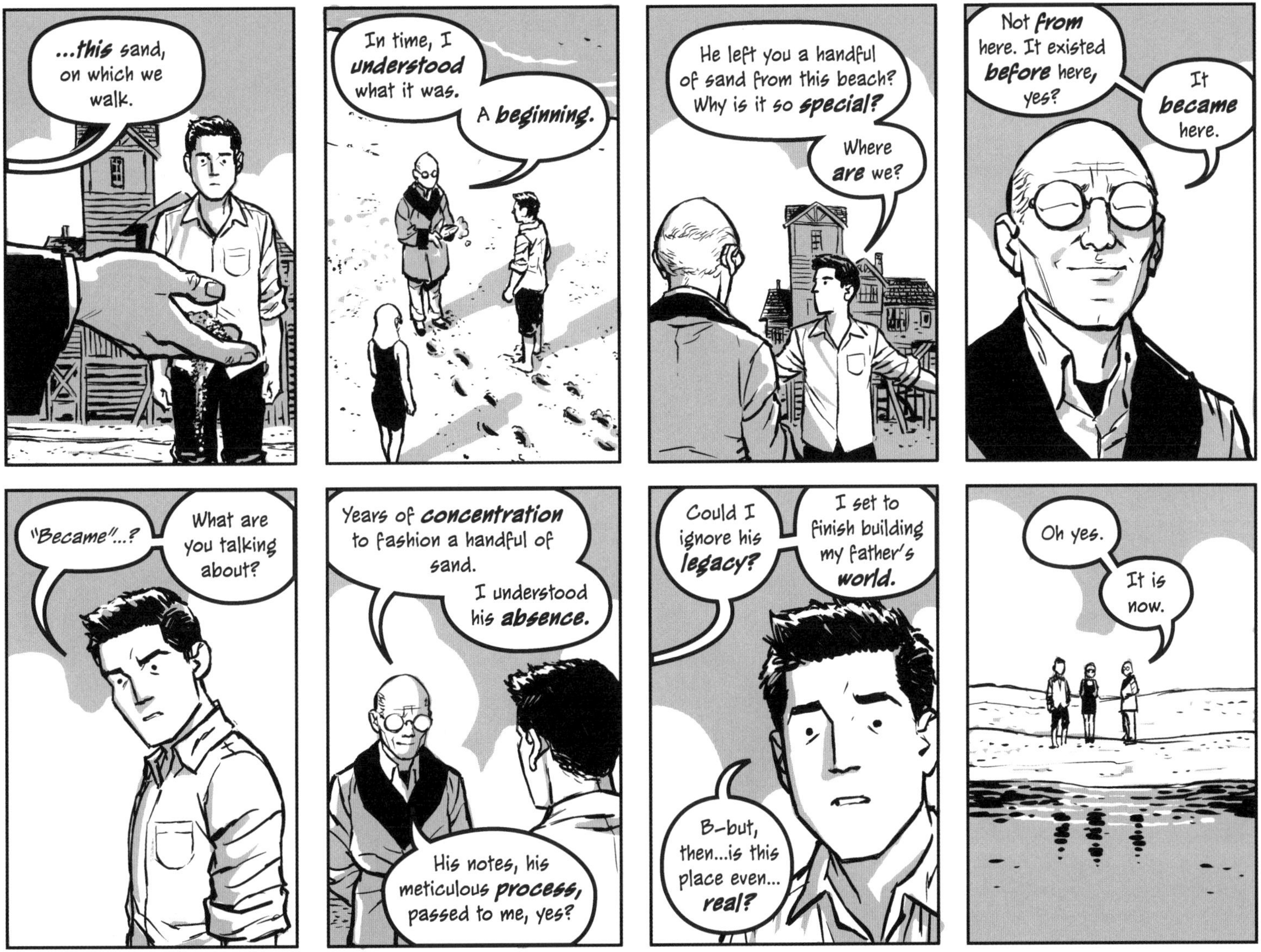
...this sand, on which we walk.
In time, I understood what it was.
A beginning.
He left you a handful of sand from this beach? Why is it so special?
Where are we?
Not from here. It existed before here, yes?
It became here.
"Became"...?
What are you talking about?
Years of concentration to fashion a handful of sand.
I understood his absence.
His notes, his meticulous process, passed to me, yes?
Could I ignore his legacy?
I set to finish building my father's world.
B-but, then...is this place even... real?
Oh yes.
It is now.

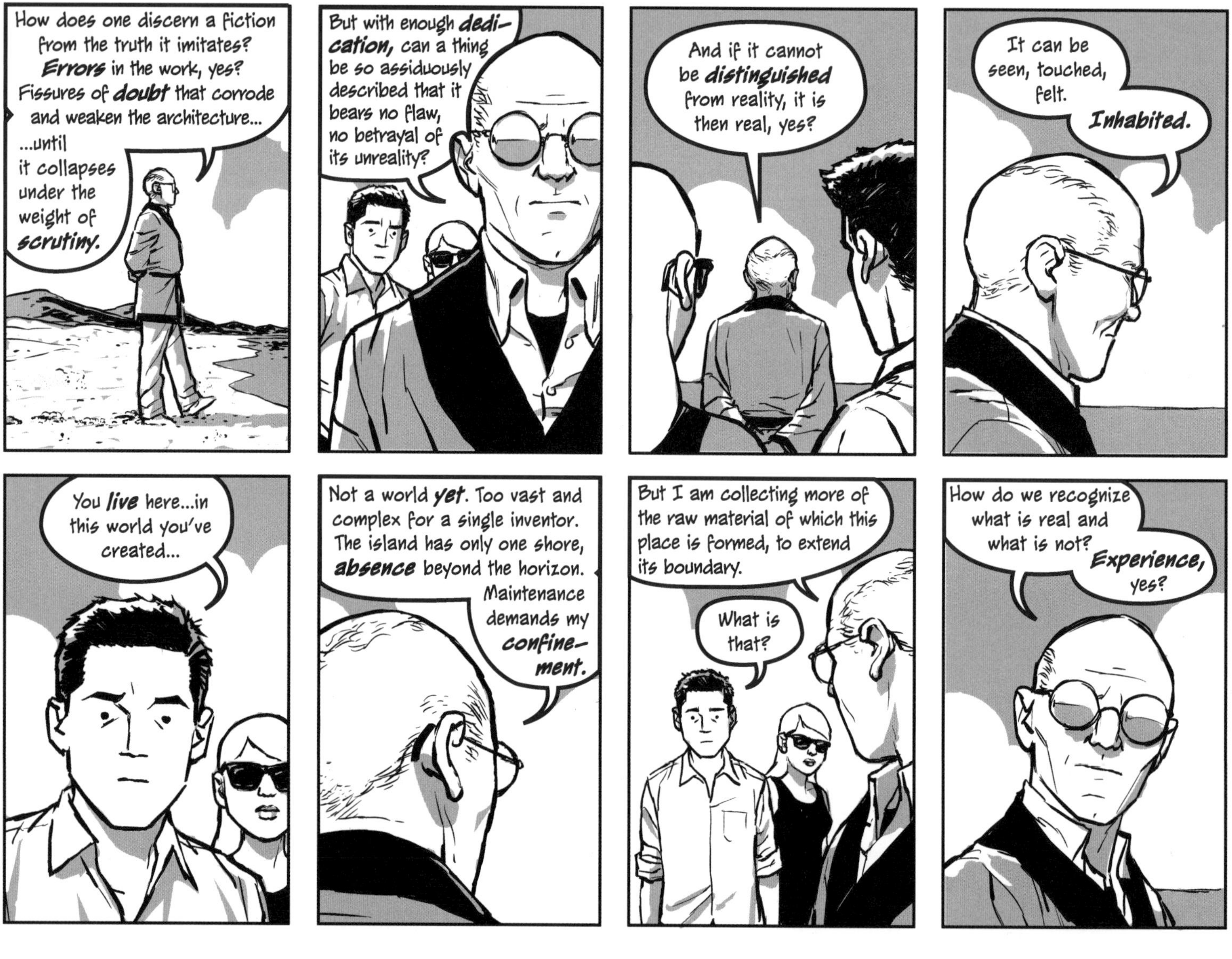

How does one discern a fiction from the truth it imitates? Errors in the work, yes? Fissures of doubt that corrode and weaken the architecture...
...until it collapses under the weight of scrutiny.
But with enough dedication, can a thing be so assiduously described that it bears no flaw, no betrayal of its unreality?
And if it cannot be distinguished from reality, it is then real, yes?
It can be seen, touched, felt.
Inhabited.
You live here...in this world you've created...
Not a world yet. Too vast and complex for a single inventor. The island has only one shore, absence beyond the horizon.
Maintenance demands my confinement.
But I am collecting more of the raw material of which this place is formed, to extend its boundary.
What is that?
How do we recognize what is real and what is not?
Experience, yes?

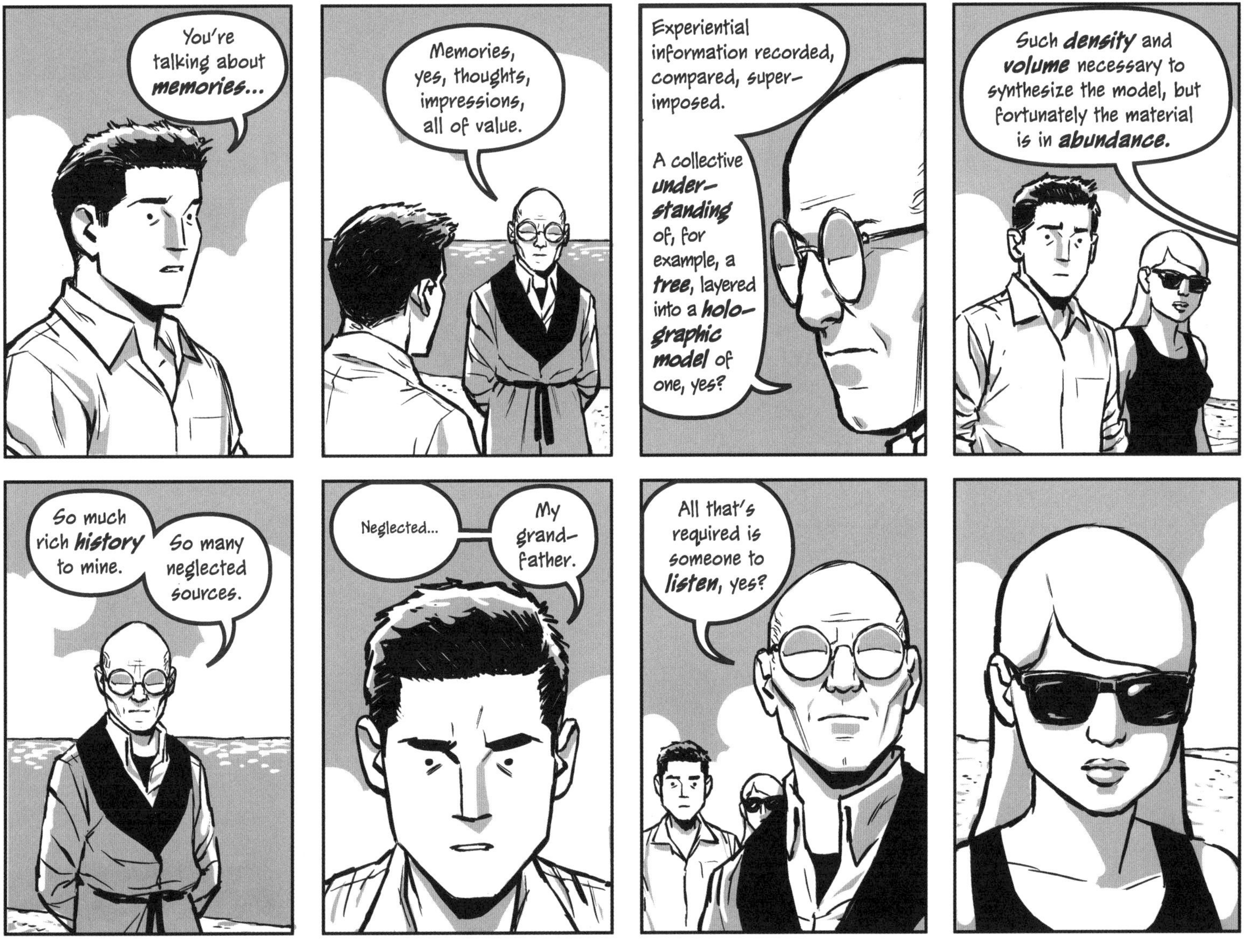
You're talking about **memories...**
Memories, yes, thoughts, impressions, all of value.
Experiential information recorded, compared, super-imposed.
A collective **under-standing** of, for example, a **tree**, layered into a **holo-graphic model** of one, yes?
Such **density** and **volume** necessary to synthesize the model, but fortunately the material is in **abundance.**
So much rich **history** to mine.
So many neglected sources.
Neglected...
My grand-father.
All that's required is someone to **listen**, yes?

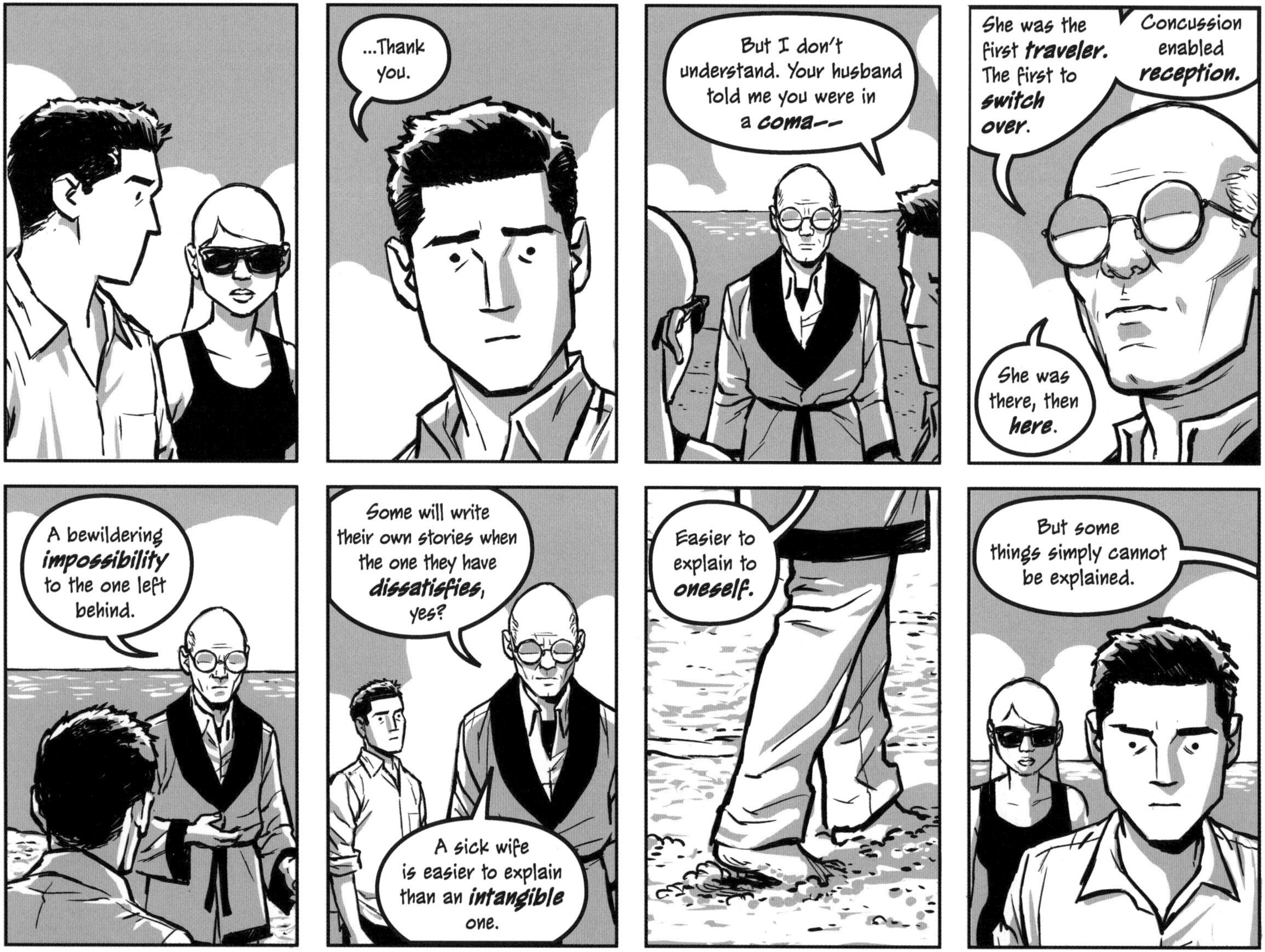
...Thank you.
But I don't understand. Your husband told me you were in a *coma--*
She was the first *traveler.* The first to *switch over.*
Concussion enabled *reception.*
She was there, then *here.*
A bewildering *impossibility* to the one left behind.
Some will write their own stories when the one they have *dissatisfies,* yes?
A sick wife is easier to explain than an *intangible* one.
Easier to explain to *oneself.*
But some things simply cannot be explained.

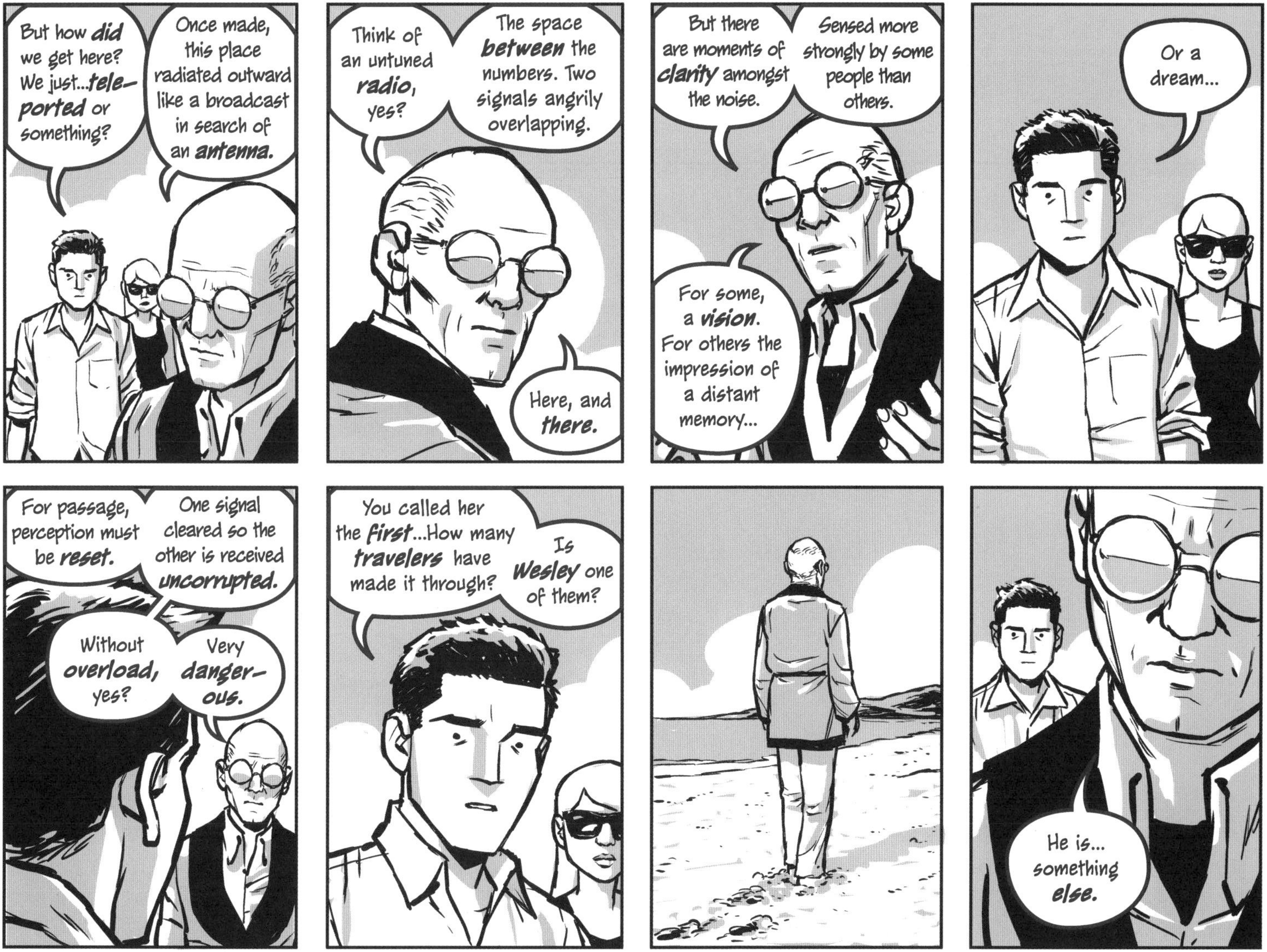
But how did we get here? We just...tele-ported or something?
Once made, this place radiated outward like a broadcast in search of an antenna.
Think of an untuned radio, yes?
The space between the numbers. Two signals angrily overlapping.
Here, and there.
But there are moments of clarity amongst the noise.
Sensed more strongly by some people than others.
For some, a vision. For others the impression of a distant memory...
Or a dream...
For passage, perception must be reset.
One signal cleared so the other is received uncorrupted.
Without overload, yes?
Very danger-ous.
You called her the first...How many travelers have made it through?
Is Wesley one of them?
He is... something else.

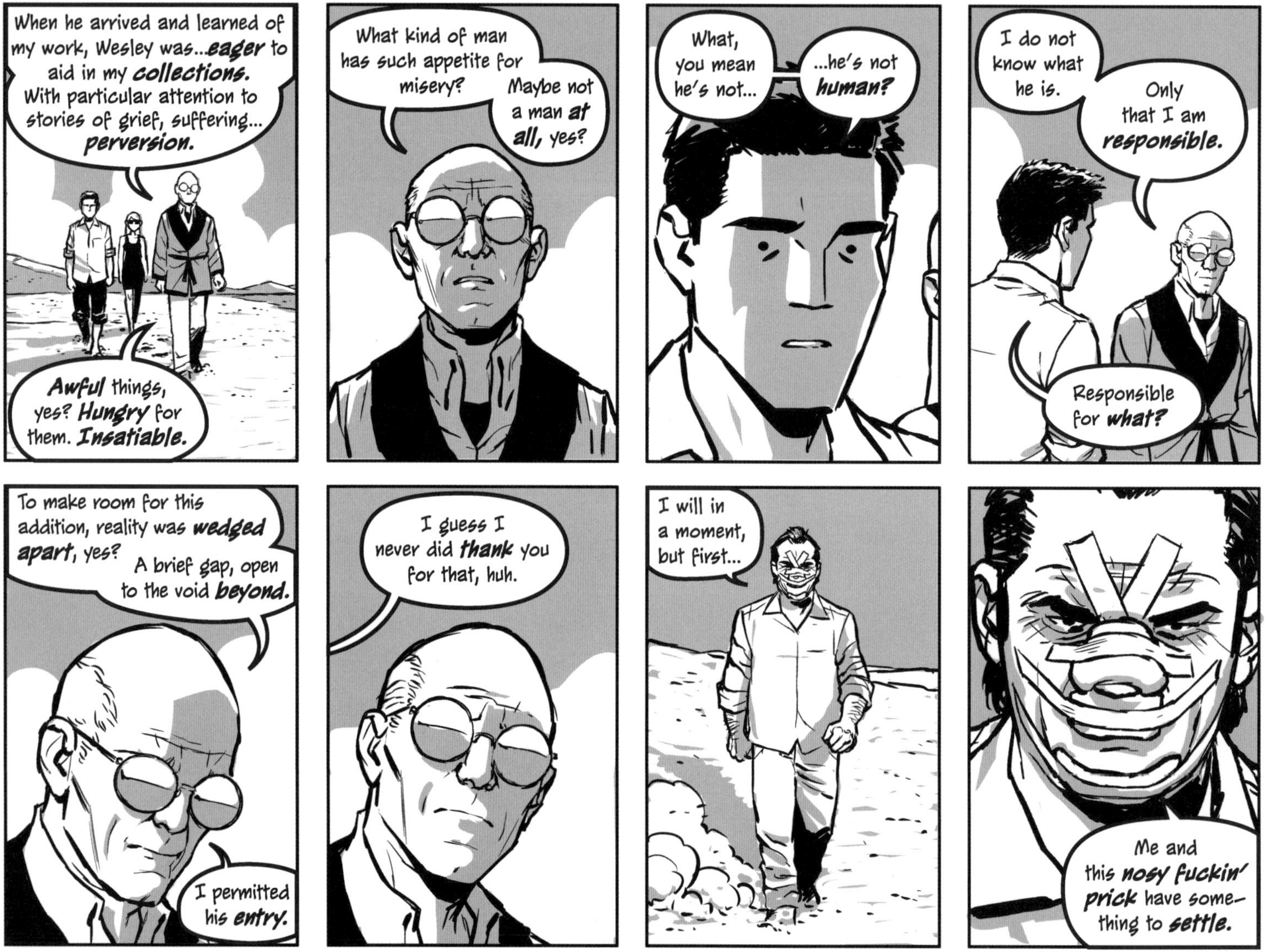
When he arrived and learned of my work, Wesley was...eager to aid in my collections. With particular attention to stories of grief, suffering... perversion.
Awful things, yes? Hungry for them. Insatiable.
What kind of man has such appetite for misery?
Maybe not a man at all, yes?
What, you mean he's not...
...he's not human?
I do not know what he is.
Only that I am responsible.
Responsible for what?
To make room for this addition, reality was wedged apart, yes?
A brief gap, open to the void beyond.
I permitted his entry.
I guess I never did thank you for that, huh.
I will in a moment, but first...
Me and this nosy fuckin' prick have some-thing to settle.

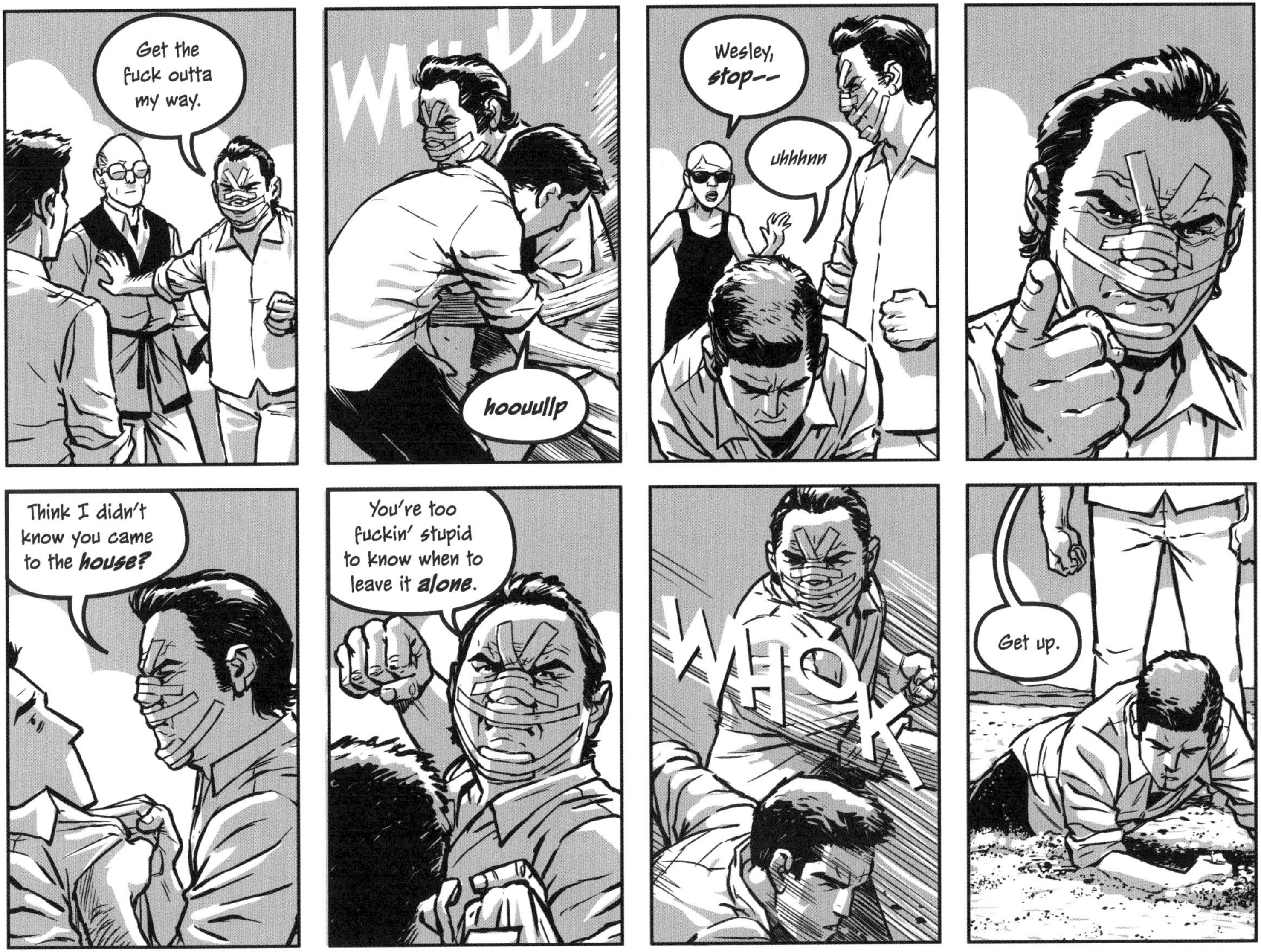
Get the fuck outta my way.
hoouullp
Wesley, stop--
uhhhnn
Think I didn't know you came to the house?
You're too fuckin' stupid to know when to leave it alone.
WHOK
Get up.

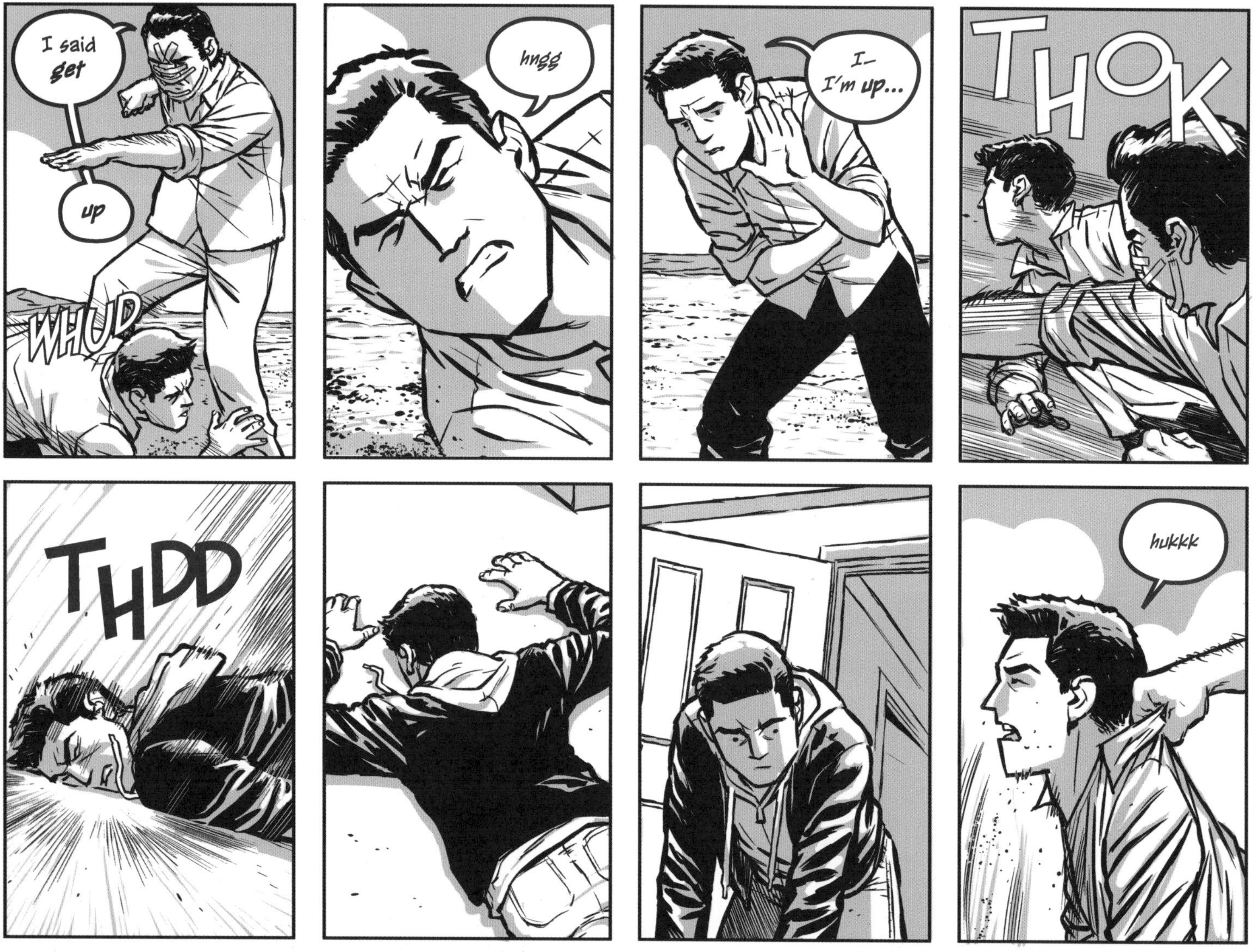
I said get
up
WHUD
hngg
I–
I'm up...
THOK
THDD
hukkk

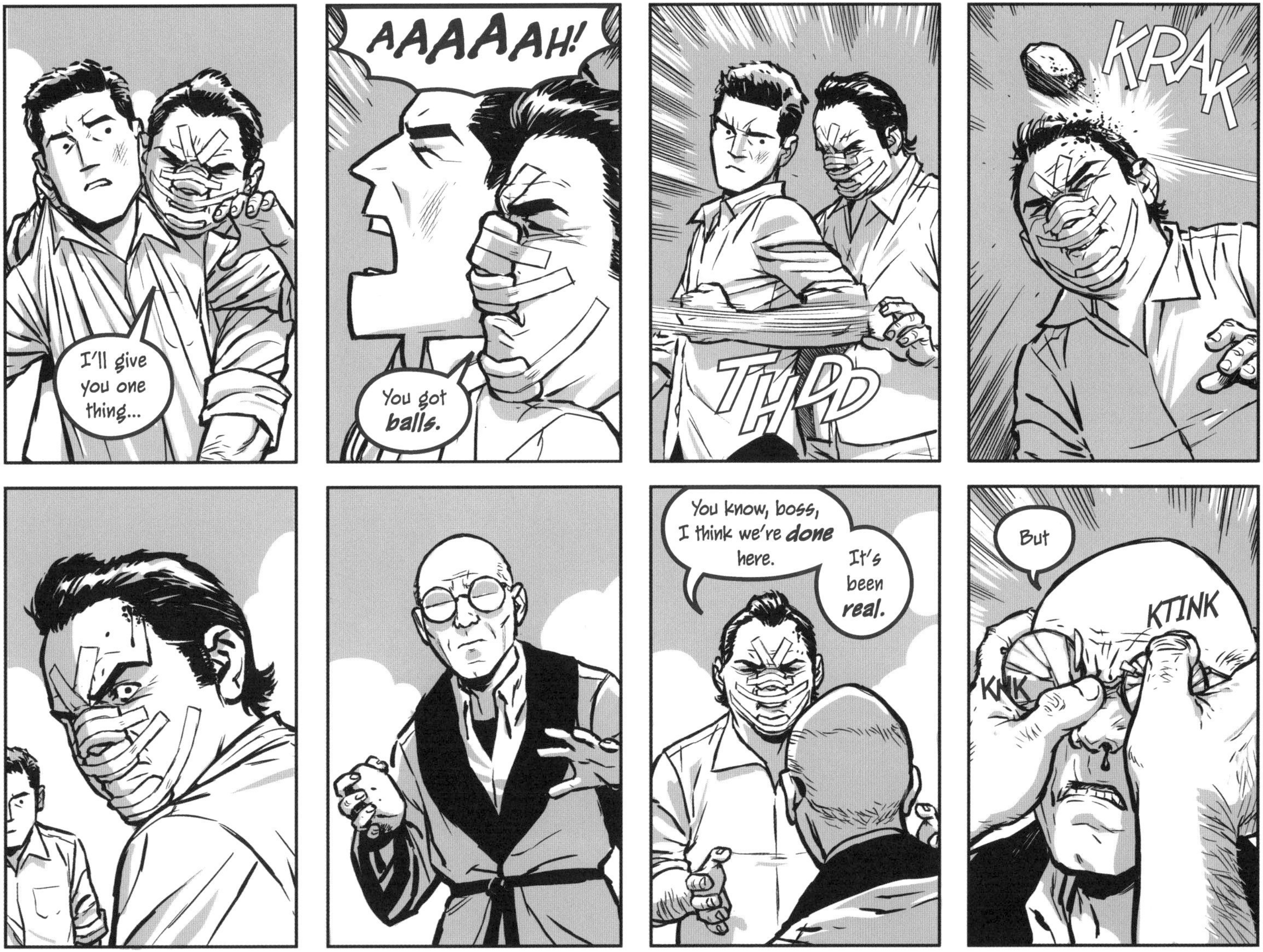
I'll give you one thing...
AAAAAH!
You got balls.
THDD
KRAK
You know, boss, I think we're done here.
It's been real.
But
KTINK
KNK

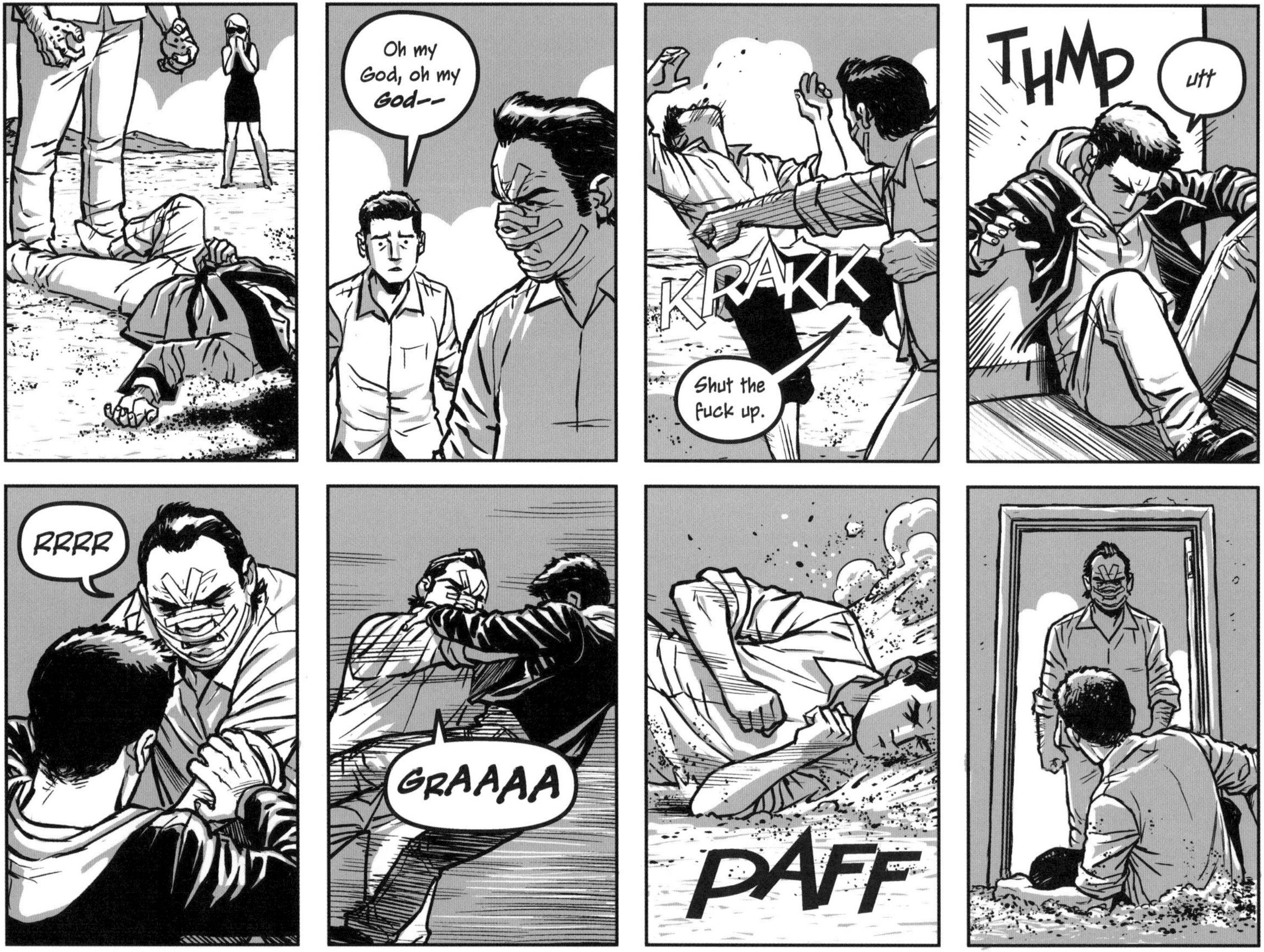
Oh my God, oh my God--
KRAKK
Shut the fuck up.
THMP
utt
RRRR
GRAAAA
PAFF

150

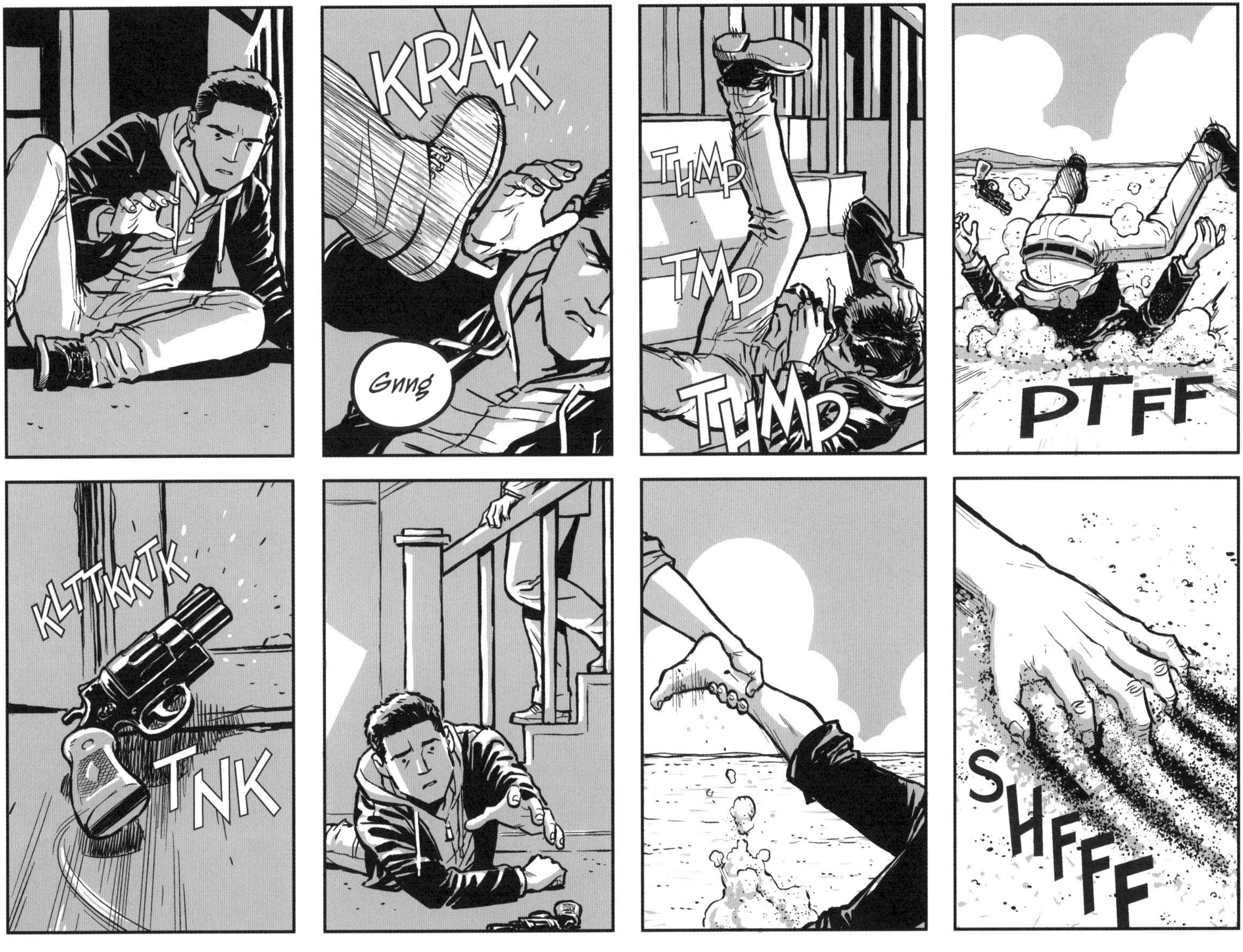
KRAK
Gnng
THMP
TMP
THMP
PTFF
KLTTKKTK
TNK
SHFFF

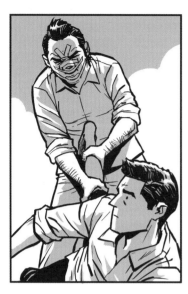

WHFF

GNAARR

Mother-FUCK!!

urff

KTUNK

KRRNK

SPLUSHH

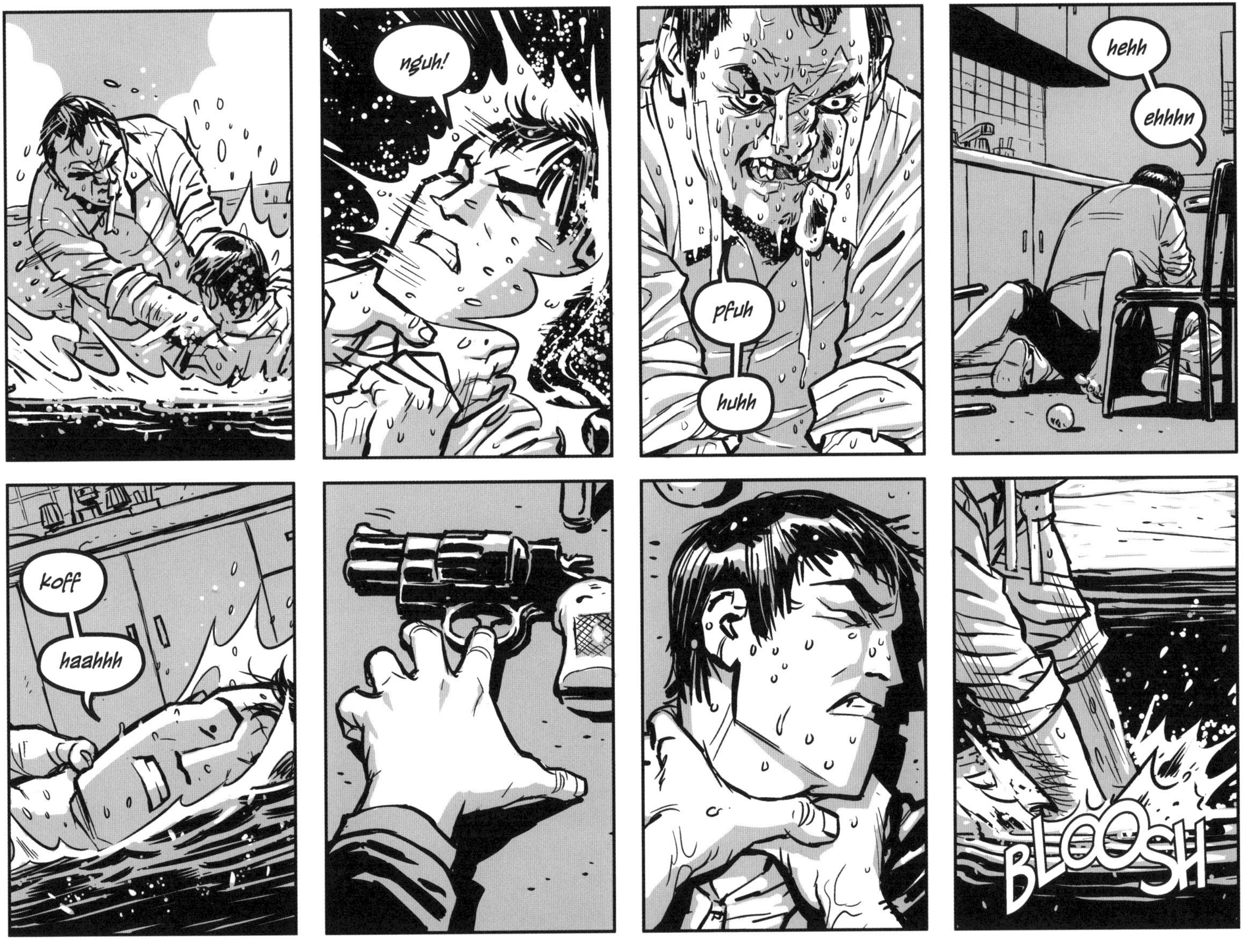

nguh!
pfuh
huhh
hehh
ehhhn
koff
haahhh
BLOOSH

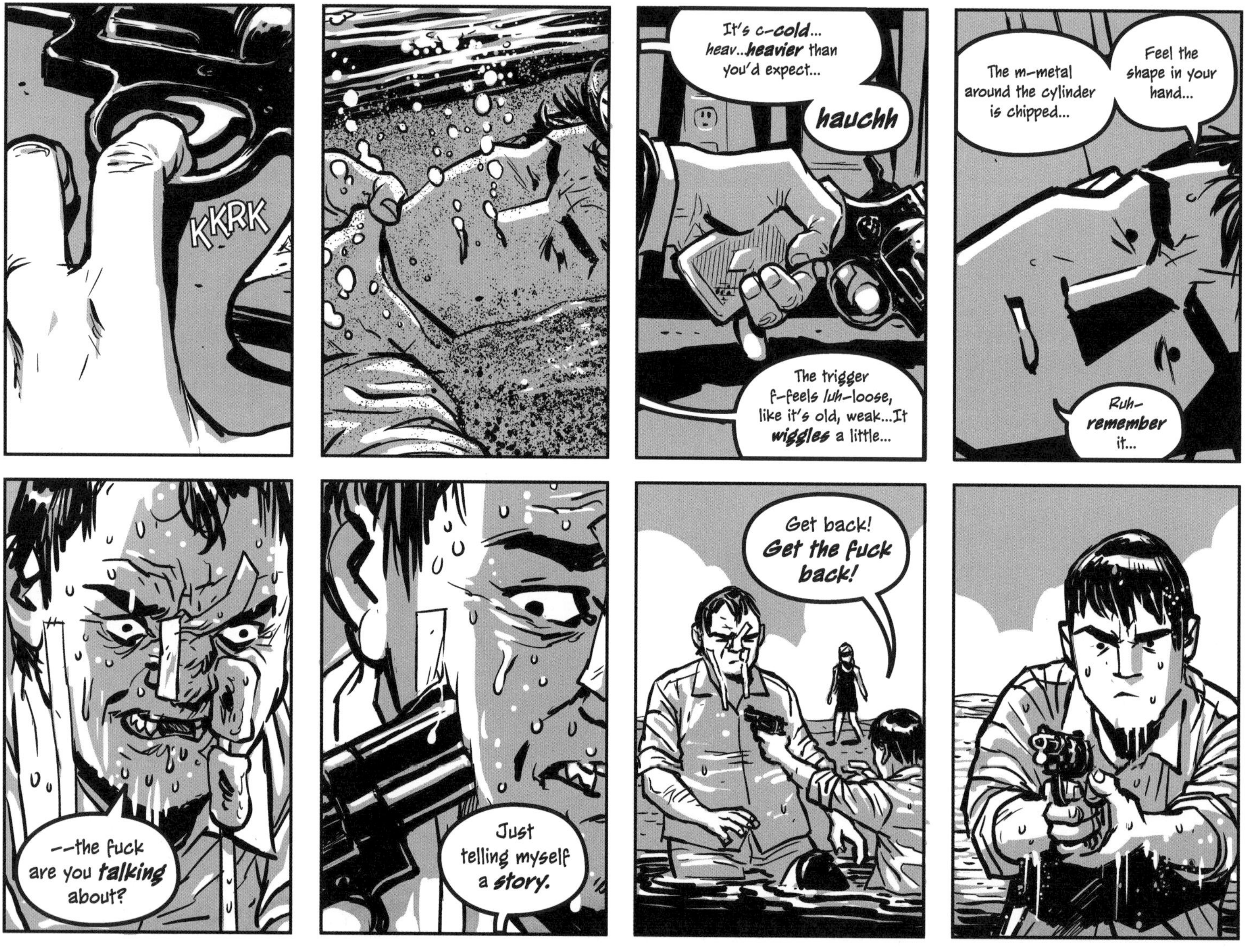
KKRK
It's c-cold... heav...heavier than you'd expect...
hauchh
The trigger f-feels luh-loose, like it's old, weak...It wiggles a little...
The m-metal around the cylinder is chipped...
Feel the shape in your hand...
Ruh-remember it...
--the fuck are you talking about?
Just telling myself a story.
Get back! Get the fuck back!

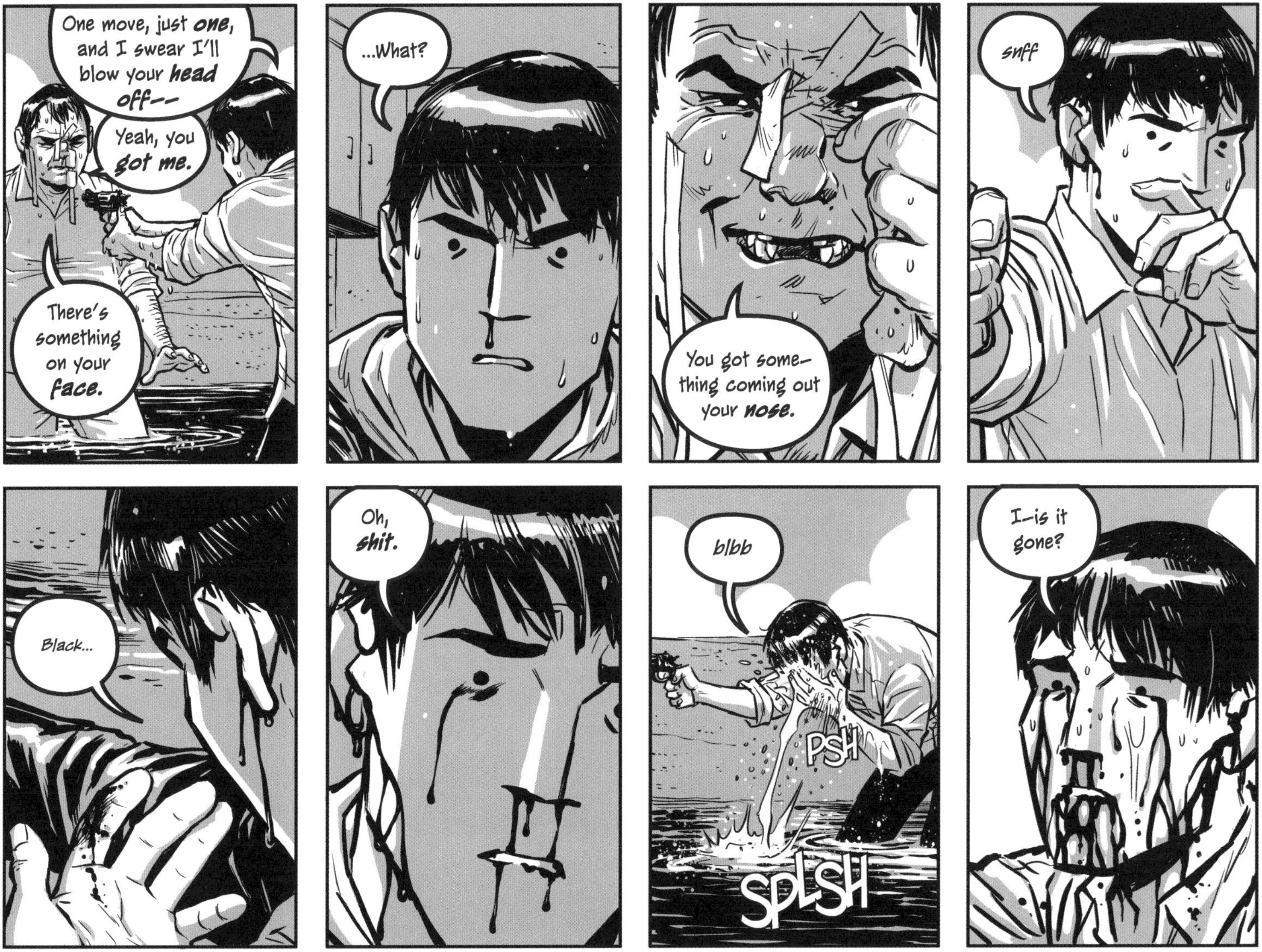

One move, just **one**, and I swear I'll blow your **head off--**
Yeah, you **got me.**
There's something on your **face.**
...What?
You got something coming out your **nose.**
snff
Black...
Oh, **shit.**
blbb
PSH
SPLSH
I-is it gone?

155

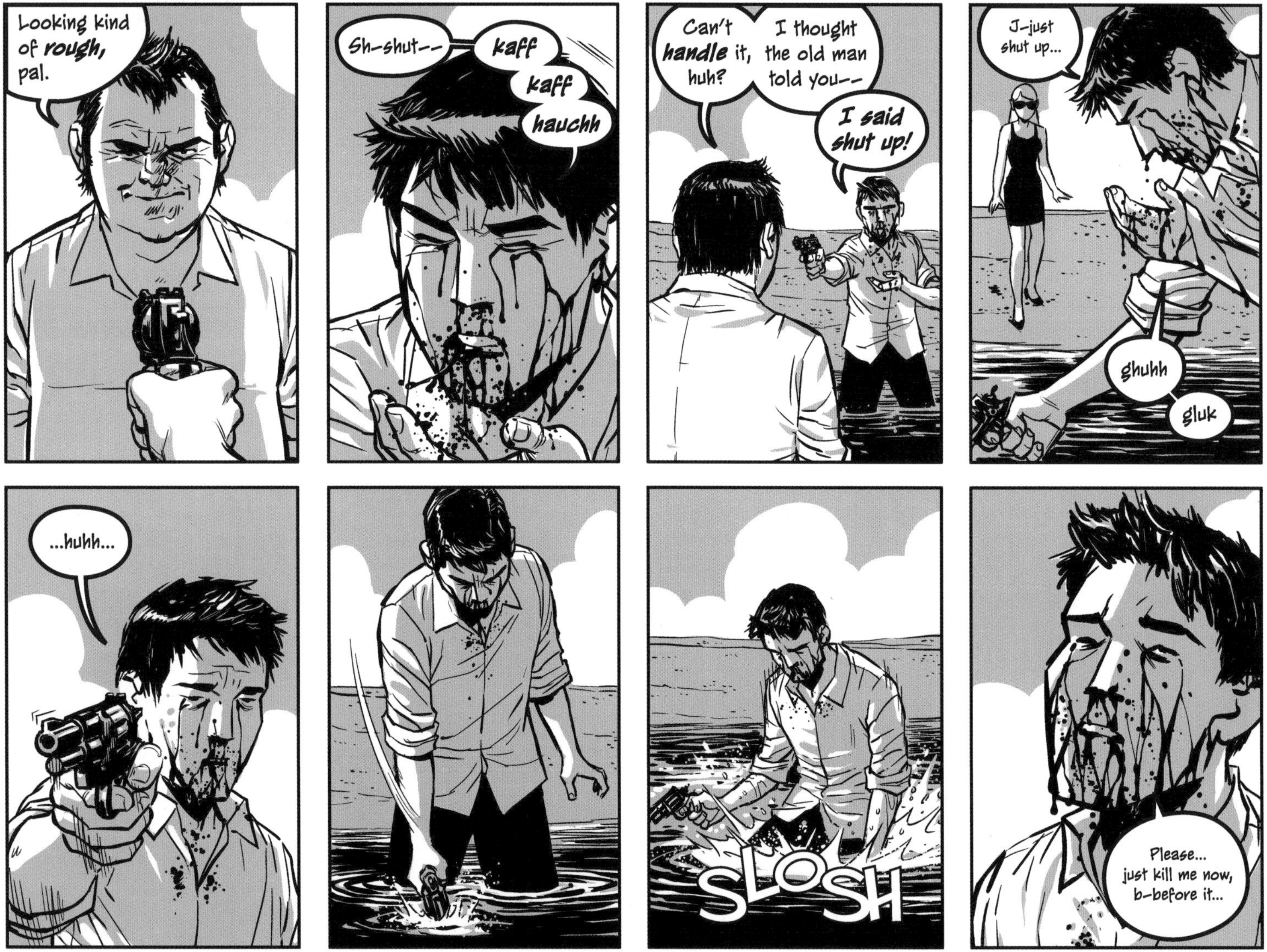
Looking kind of **rough**, pal.
Sh-shut--
kaff
kaff
hauchh
Can't **handle** it, huh?
I thought the old man told you--
I said shut up!
J-just shut up...
ghuhh
gluk
...huhh...
SLOSH
Please... just kill me now, b-before it...

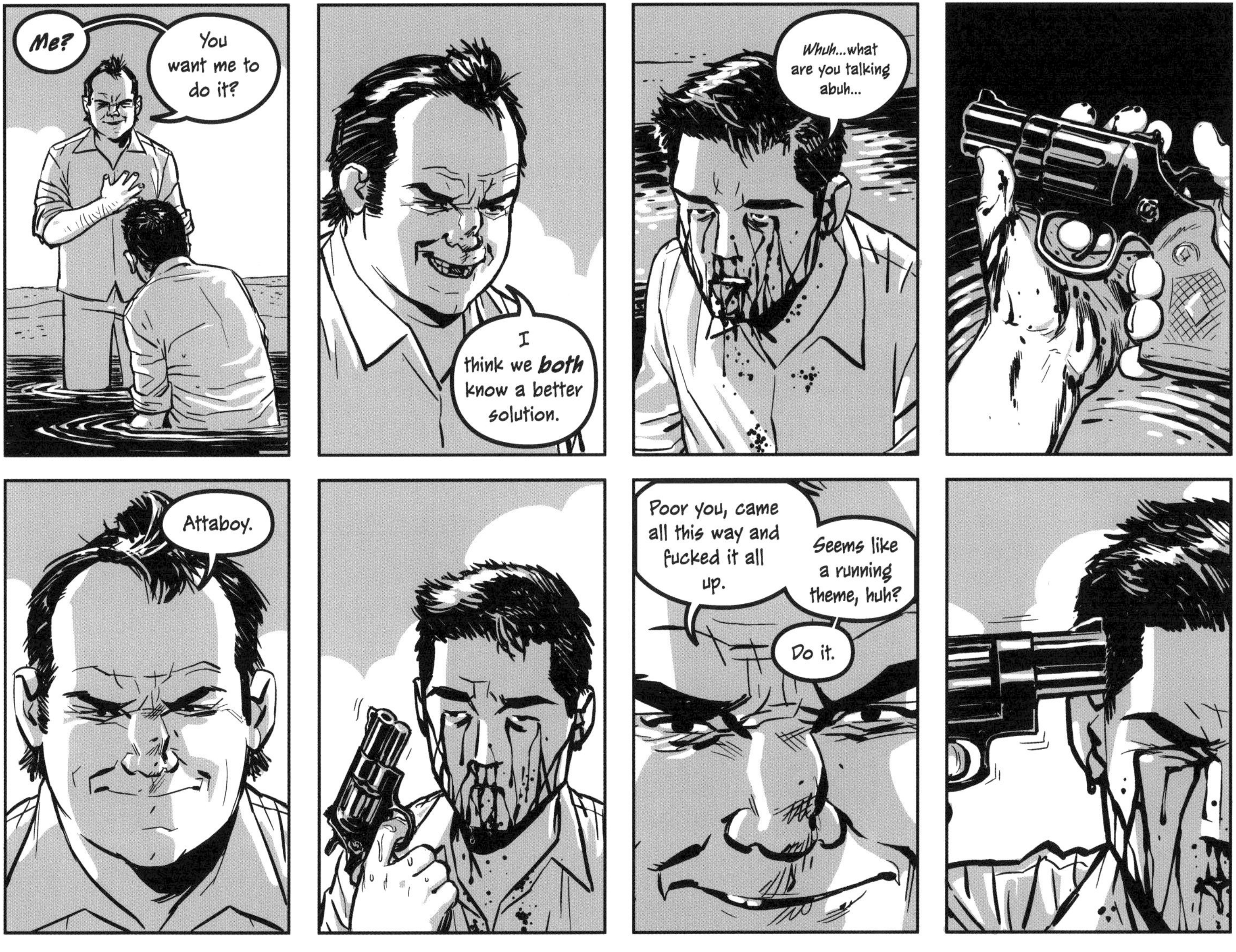
Me?
You want me to do it?
I think we *both* know a better solution.
Whuh...what are you talking abuh...
Attaboy.
Poor you, came all this way and fucked it all up.
Seems like a running theme, huh?
Do it.

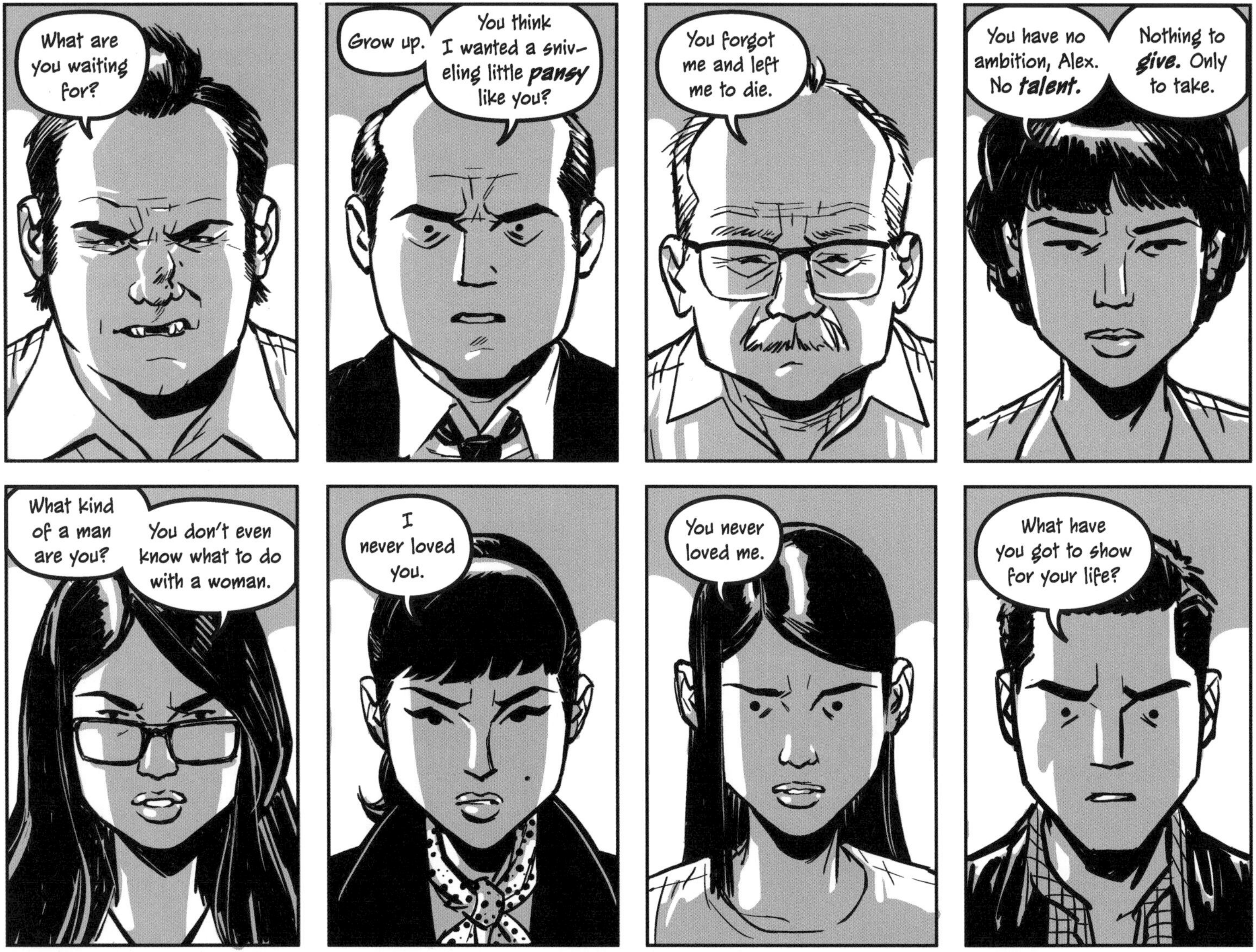
What are you waiting for?
Grow up.
You think I wanted a sniv-eling little *pansy* like you?
You forgot me and left me to die.
You have no ambition, Alex. No *talent.*
Nothing to *give.* Only to take.
What kind of a man are you?
You don't even know what to do with a woman.
I never loved you.
You never loved me.
What have you got to show for your life?

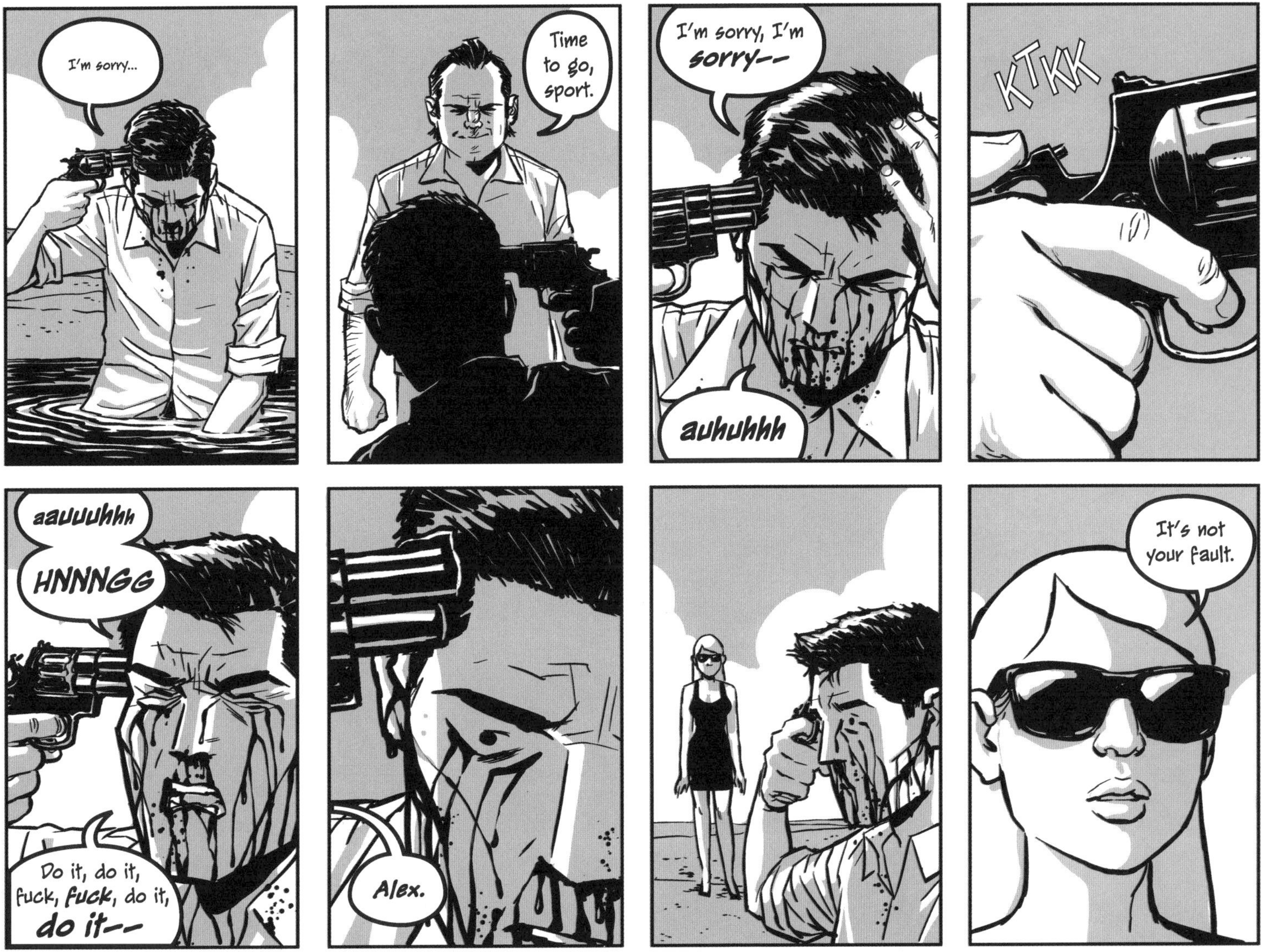
I'm sorry...
Time to go, sport.
I'm sorry, I'm sorry--
auhuhhh
KTKK
aauuuhhh
HNNNGG
Do it, do it, fuck, fuck, do it, do it--
Alex.
It's not your fault.

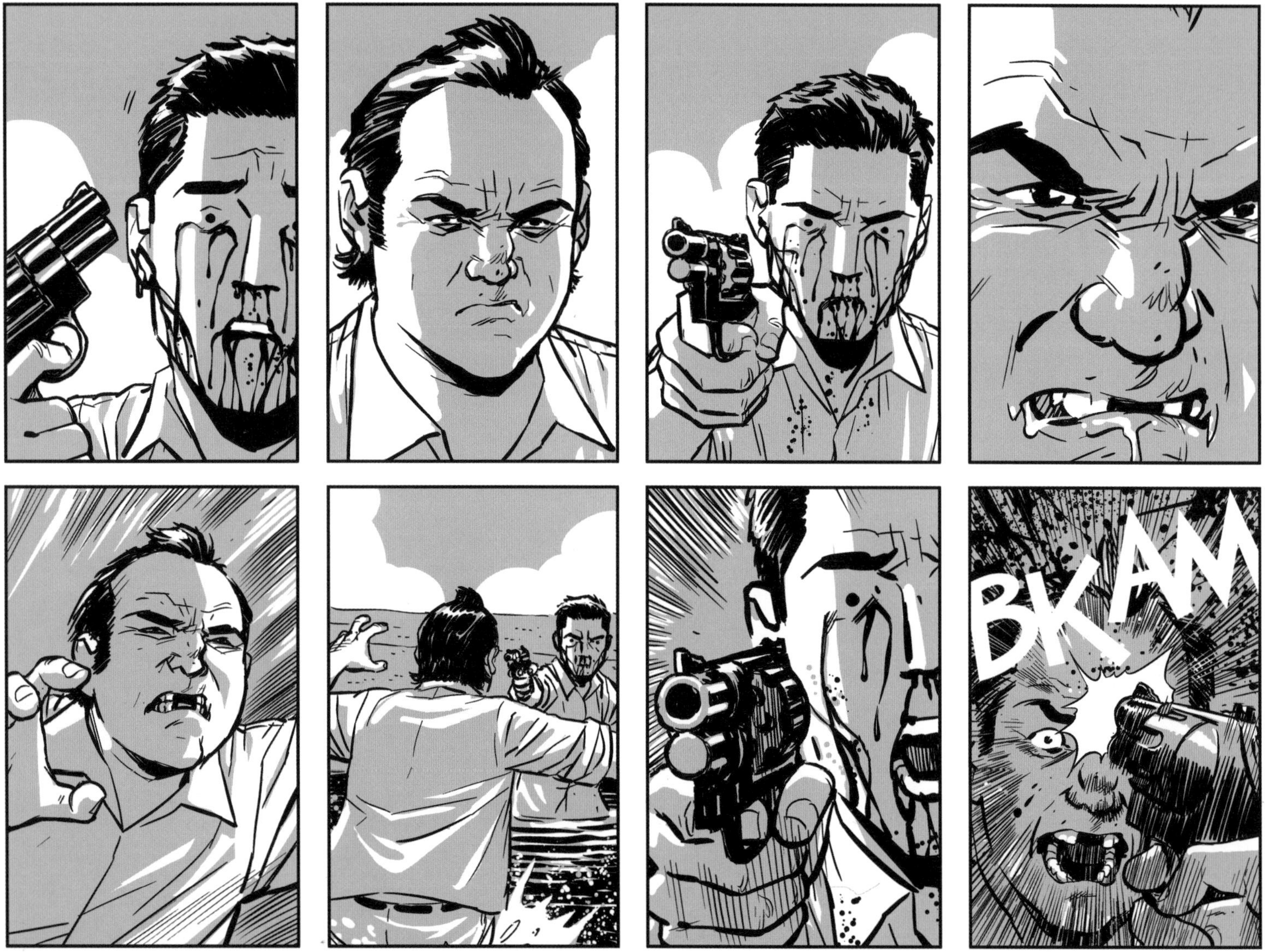
BKAM

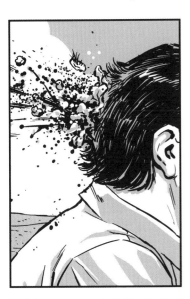

SPLOSH

BKAM

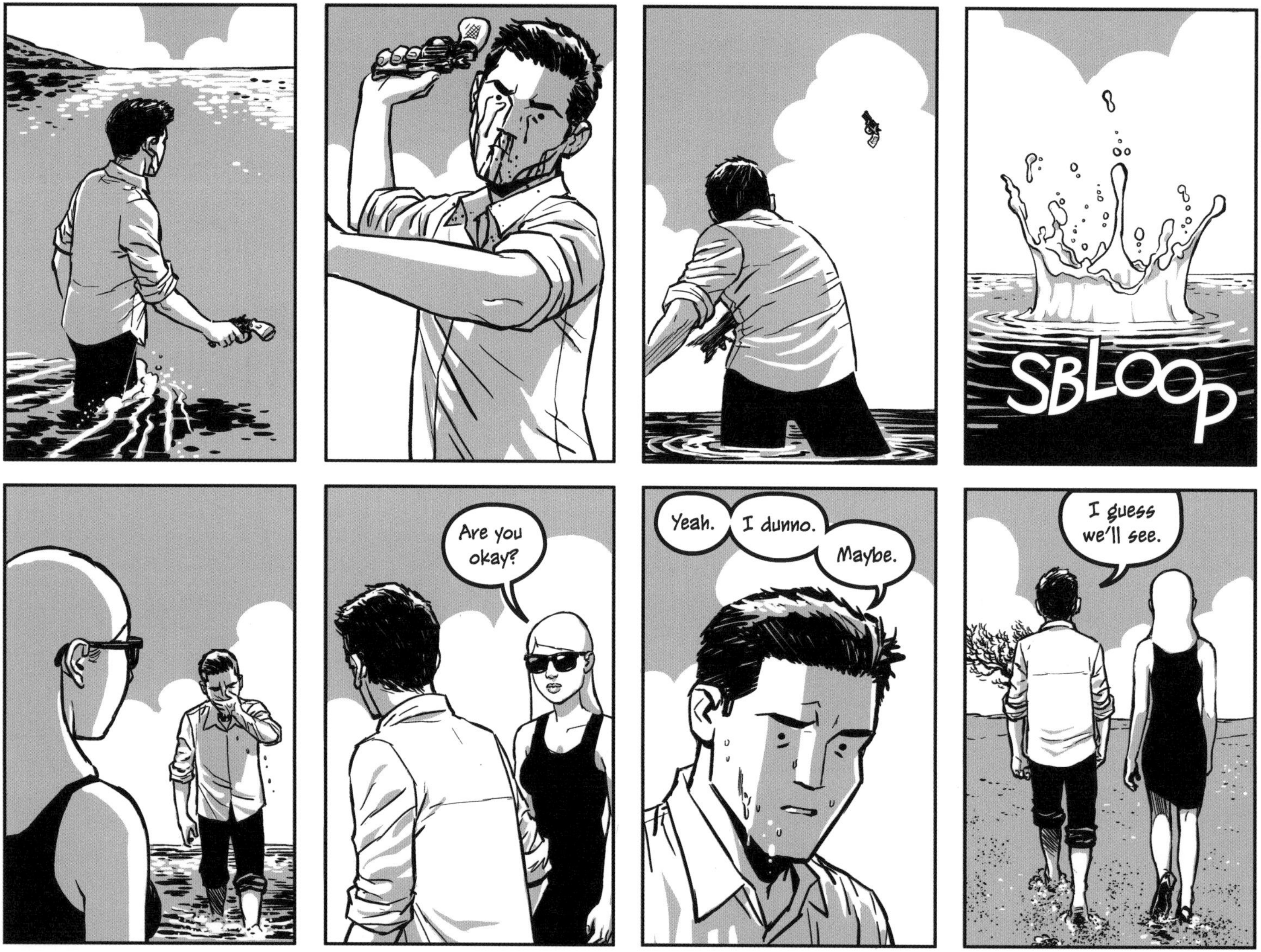
SBLOOP
Are you okay?
Yeah.
I dunno.
Maybe.
I guess we'll see.

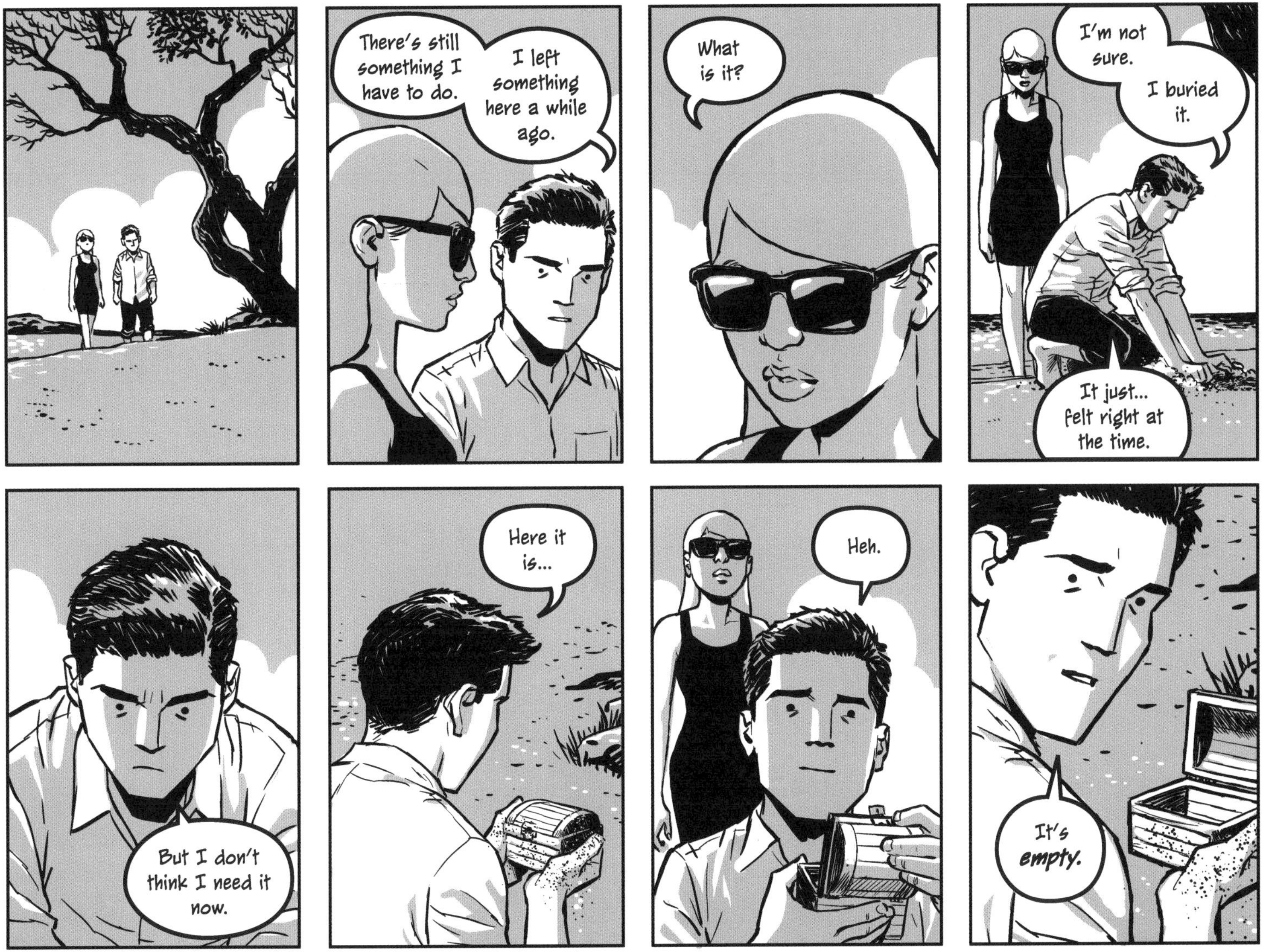

There's still something I have to do.
I left something here a while ago.
What is it?
I'm not sure.
I buried it.
It just... felt right at the time.
But I don't think I need it now.
Here it is...
Heh.
It's *empty*.

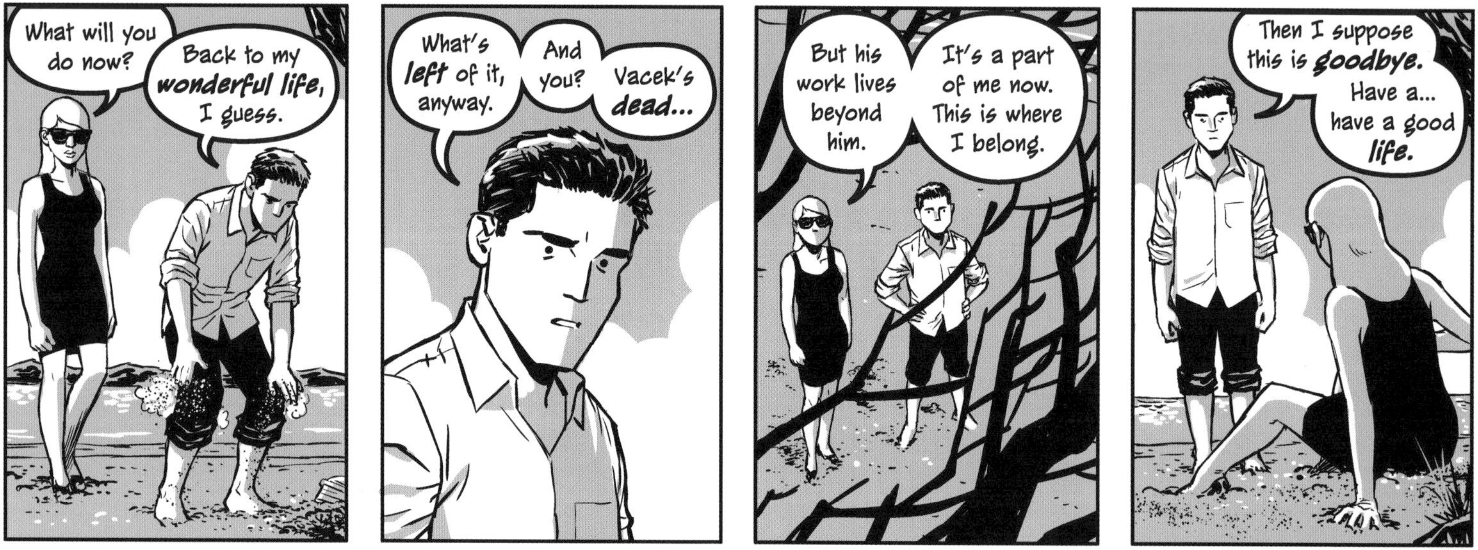

What will you do now?
Back to my **wonderful life**, I guess.
What's **left** of it, anyway.
And you?
Vacek's **dead...**
But his work lives beyond him.
It's a part of me now. This is where I belong.
Then I suppose this is **goodbye.**
Have a... have a good **life.**

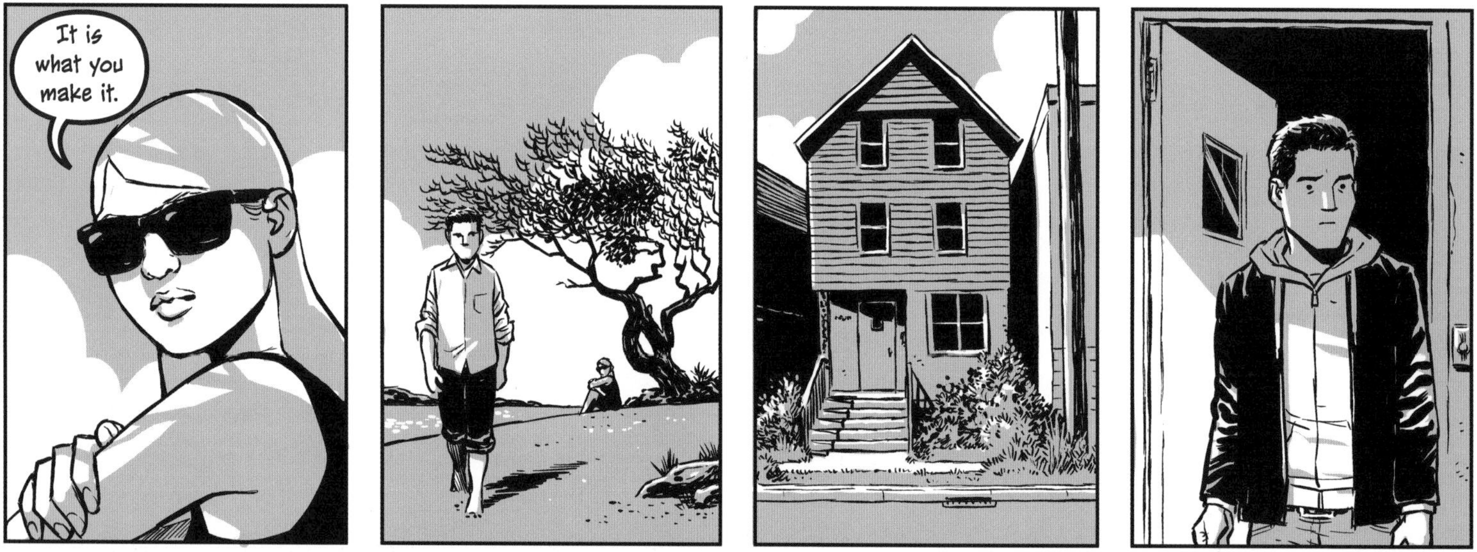

It is what you make it.

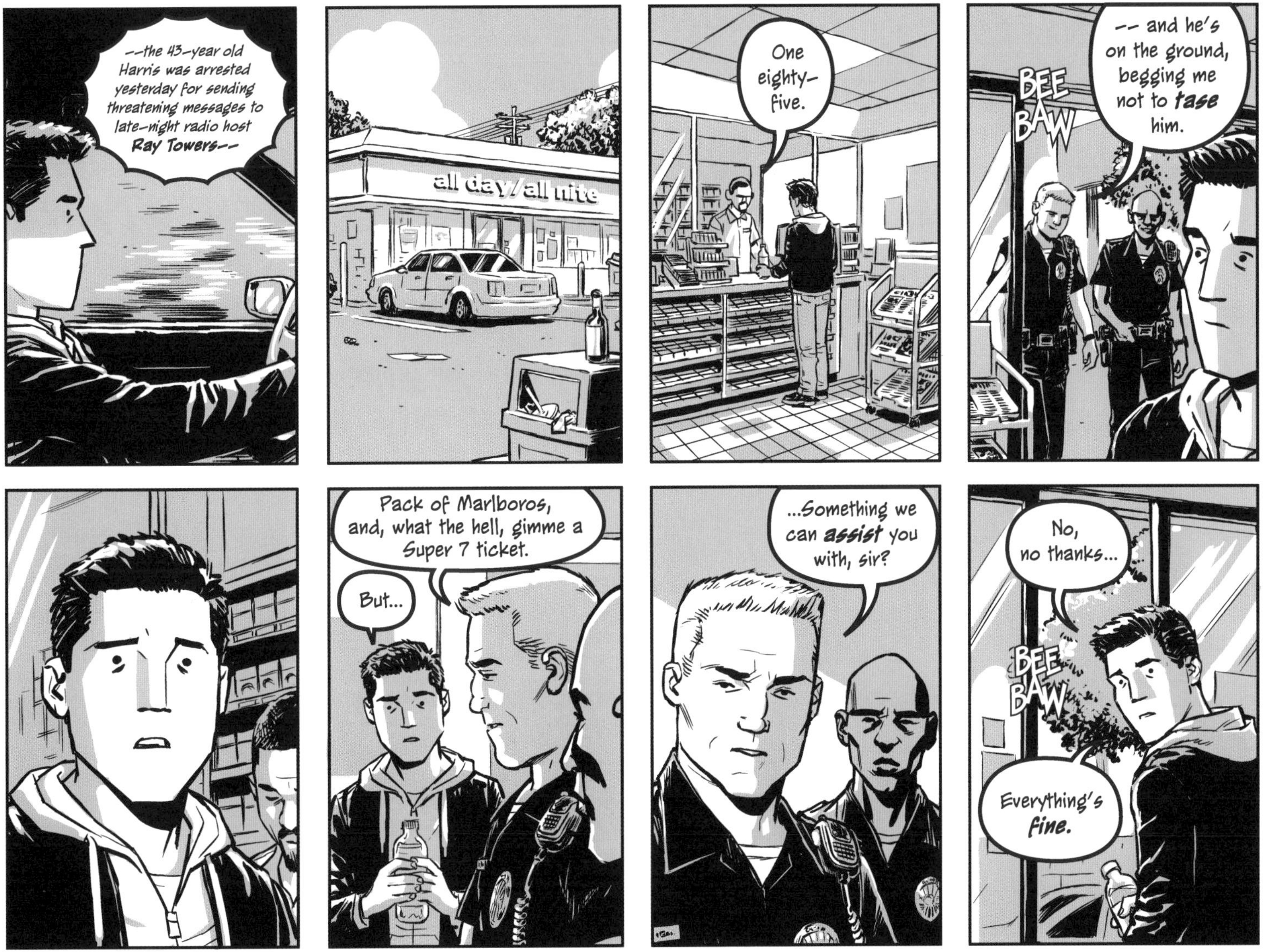
--the 43-year old Harris was arrested yesterday for sending threatening messages to late-night radio host **Ray Towers**--
all day/all nite
One eighty-five.
BEE BAW
-- and he's on the ground, begging me not to ***tase*** him.
Pack of Marlboros, and, what the hell, gimme a Super 7 ticket.
But...
...Something we can ***assist*** you with, sir?
No, no thanks...
BEE BAW
Everything's ***fine.***

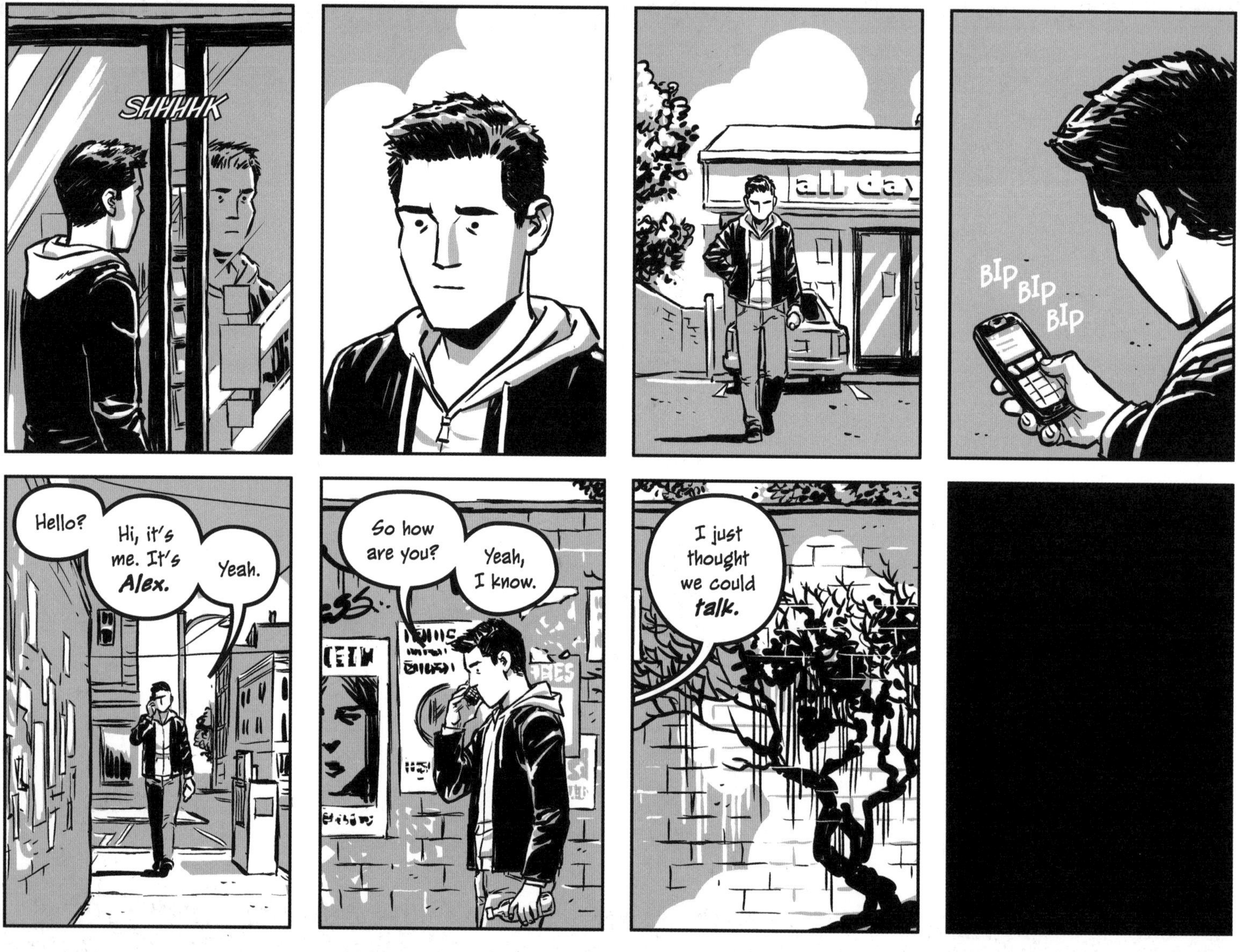
SHHHHK
BIP BIP BIP
all day
Hello?
Hi, it's me. It's Alex.
Yeah.
So how are you?
Yeah, I know.
I just thought we could talk.

FINDER

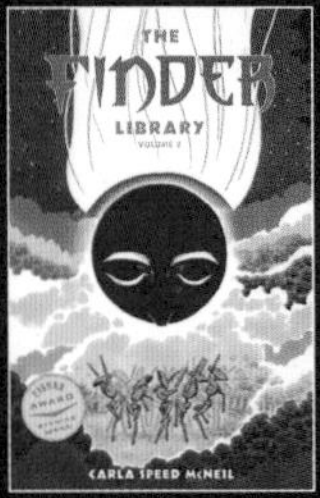
THE
FINDER
LIBRARY
CARLA SPEED McNEIL

Carla Speed McNeil

Since 1996, the Eisner Award–winning *Finder* has set the bar for science-fiction storytelling, with a lush, intricate world and compelling characters.

Finder: Voice TPB | ISBN 978-1-59582-651-0 | $19.99
Finder Library Volume 1 TPB | ISBN 978-1-59582-652-7 | $24.99
Finder Library Volume 2 TPB | ISBN 978-1-59582-653-4 | $24.99
Finder: Talisman HC | ISBN 978-1-61655-027-1 | $19.99

CITIZEN REX HC

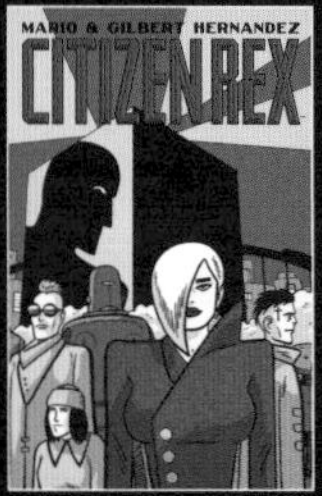
MARIO & GILBERT HERNANDEZ
CITIZEN REX

Mario Hernandez and Gilbert Hernandez

When gossip blogger Sergio Bauntin investigates the elusive robot celebrity CTZ-RX-1, he provokes the city's shady power players, who don't want the story to get out! It's a surreal sci-fi adventure as only Los Bros. Hernandez can do it! This collection includes an extensive sketchbook section from Mario, and a special pinup from third Hernandez brother Jaime (*Love & Rockets*)!

ISBN 978-1-59582-556-8 | $19.99

BLACKSAD HC

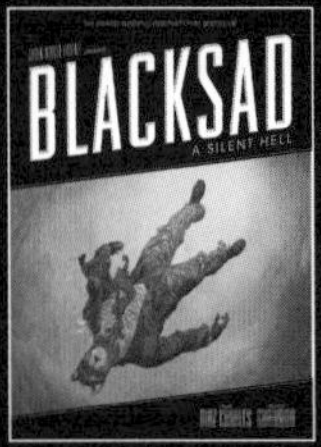
BLACKSAD
A SILENT HELL

Juan Díaz Canales and Juanjo Guarnido

Private investigator John Blacksad is up to his feline ears in mystery, digging into the backstories behind murders, child abductions, and nuclear secrets. Whether Blacksad is falling for dangerous women or getting beaten to within an inch of his life, his stories are, simply put, unforgettable.

Blacksad | ISBN 978-1-59582-393-9 | $29.99
Blacksad: A Silent Hell | ISBN 978-1-59582-931-3 | $19.99

CHANNEL ZERO TPB

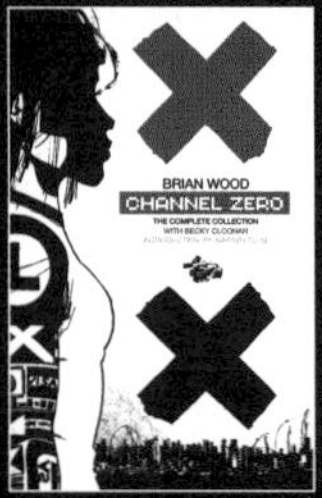
BRIAN WOOD
CHANNEL ZERO

Brian Wood and Becky Cloonan

A blistering take on media control in a repressive future America! *DMZ* and *The Massive* creator Brian Wood launched an all-out assault on the comics medium in 1997 with *Channel Zero*, an influential, forward-thinking series that combined art, politics, and graphic design in a unique way.

ISBN 978-1-59582-936-8 | $19.99

MOTEL ART IMPROVEMENT SERVICE HC

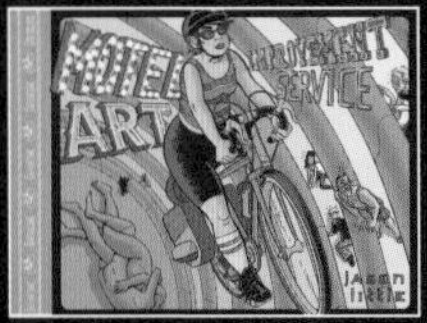
MOTEL ART
IMPROVEMENT SERVICE
Jason Little

Jason Little

Eighteen-year-old Bee has finally saved up enough to embark on her long-planned cross-country bicycle trip. However, she doesn't make it very far before disaster leaves her stranded at a motel. *Motel Art Improvement Service* explores crime, young love, and the purpose of art, in a story that's equal parts thrilling, funny, and sexy!

ISBN 978-1-59582-550-6 | $19.99

MIND MGMT VOLUME 1: THE MANAGER HC

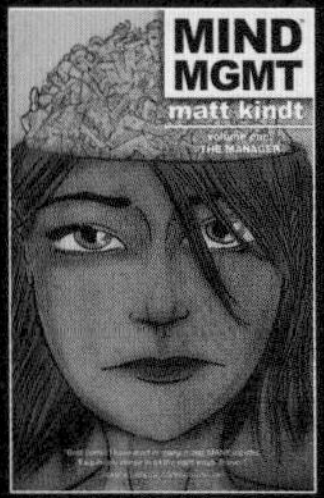
MIND
MGMT
matt kindt

Matt Kindt

Reporting on a commercial flight where everyone aboard lost their memories, a young journalist stumbles onto a much bigger story: the top-secret Mind Management program. Her ensuing journey involves weaponized psychics, hypnotic advertising, talking dolphins, and seemingly immortal pursuers, as she attempts to find the flight's missing passenger.

ISBN 978-1-59582-797-5 | $19.99

AVAILABLE AT YOUR LOCAL COMICS SHOP OR BOOKSTORE! • To find a comics shop in your area, call 1-888-266-4226.
For more information or to order direct visit DarkHorse.com or call 1-800-862-0052 Mon.–Fri. 9 AM to 5 PM Pacific Time. Prices and availability subject to change without notice.

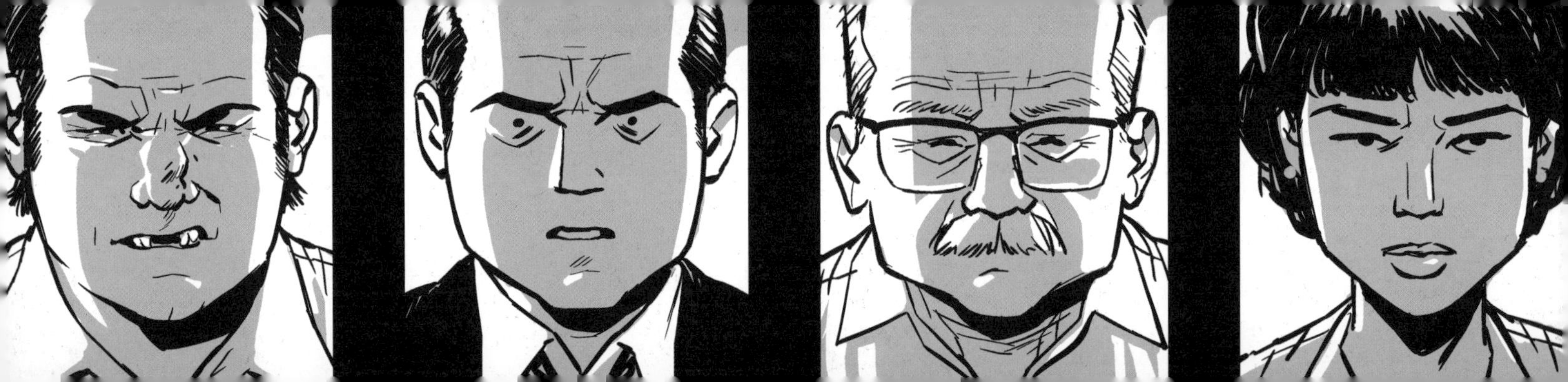